Steve —

Here's to what you
have done and will
do for our community —
(In the spirit of the
Pioneers of Israel)

Mel Alpu

March 15, 2005

PIONEERS OF ISRAEL

Printed in United States of America

The Blazer Group, 15060 Ventura Boulevard,
Sherman Oaks, CA 91403
818/786-4000   Fax: 818/380-9232
E-Mail: Blazergrp@aol.com
Website: www.worldjewishlife.com

PIONEERS OF ISRAEL

Modern Day Heroes
of the State of Israel

Phil Blazer, Author
Shelley Portnoy, Editor
HeNing, Artist

Blazer Communications
Sherman Oaks, California

Ilan Ramon
1954-2003
We dedicate this book in his honor

Imagine being the first pioneer in space for your country. Ilan Ramon, a fighter pilot, a devoted husband and father, a courageous and gentle man who believed that anything was possible, that even the furthest star was attainable—was the first astronaut proudly to represent Israel in exploring the heavens.

One night when we were having dinner in my home, I asked Ilan if as a child he looked up to the stars and dreamed about going into space. "I was lying on my back in the Sinai Desert, as a soldier, and saw so many stars in the heavens. It was then that I thought about the universe, but I never dreamed I could be an astronaut. Now it's true, it's a reality," he told me.

In 1997, Ilan received a call of congratulations. He had been selected as Israel's first astronaut. He and his wife, Rona, and their four children moved to Houston where Ilan would begin his astronaut training at the Johnson Space Center. Upon accepting this great honor, Ilan said: "As Israel's first astronaut I feel that I am not only representing the people of Israel, but the Jewish community throughout the world. We are one."

During his training, some months before the launch, Ilan and I were talking about the preparations for his trip into space. We discussed how he would be able to communicate with his family and the world from space, the scientific projects he would carry out, and the food they would have on board the space module. Would he have kosher food on the flight? Ilan asked NASA to make these arrangements, and his historic request was granted. Another first for space travel.

Ramon's story begins in the heart of Israel. Ilan's parents represent the strength and spirit of the heroes who built the modern State of Israel. His mother was a Holocaust survivor. His father fought in the 1948 War of Independence. Ilan confided in me during one of our television interviews that he "fulfilled their dream, one that they wouldn't have dared to dream."

A *sabra*, Ilan was born in Tel Aviv on June 20, 1954. After graduating high school in 1972, he entered military service and began flight training. He fought in the Yom Kippur War while continuing his studies and he received his college degree when he was thirty-three. That delay was fine with Ilan because he was flying. "I love to fly," Ilan often said in his quiet way. He flew nearly all the Israeli Air Force planes, including the A-4, the Mirage III-C, and the F-16.

In 1981, Ilan Ramon was one of the eight Israeli pilots who destroyed the nuclear reactor near Baghdad in a lightning raid that stunned the world. To accomplish the mission successfully, the planes flew over enemy Arab territory for hours without detection. It was a strategic milestone in Israeli aviation history. In 1994, Ramon was awarded the rank of colonel and he assumed command of Israel's Air Force Weapon Development and Acquisition Department.

On a clear day brilliantly lit by sunshine emanating from a sky as blue as a robin's egg, with hundreds of us watching at the United States Space Center in Florida and millions viewing on television, Ilan Ramon launched into space in the Colombia shuttle. The historic date was January 16, 2003. Six Americans and one Israeli enthralled and captivated the world with video messages from space, transmitting their excitement from millions of miles away. "I am going to conduct an Israeli experiment in space," Ilan reported. "It deals with dust aerosols in the atmosphere. The experiment is in cooperation with a research group of well known professors at the University of Tel Aviv."

The information from this successful experiment was transmitted from the Colombia space shuttle to Earth, and its results will have a major impact on the environment and also enable important breakthroughs in medical research. The experiment and its results remind us that Israel, a tiny piece of the world's total land mass and the only democracy in the Middle East, continues to astonish us with its extraordinary brainpower and enduring soul.

Ilan found these wonderful contributions, including Israel's role in saving lives around the world through its medical research, not surprising but rather typical of the nation in which he was born and which he served so heroically. He told me, "I believe that we Israelis grew up fighting for our lives. This made us ambitious and very curious. Our curiosity and ambitions and interests made us capable and produced remarkable scientists and technicians. I believe that this helped to make us who we are." Ilan Ramon was a pioneer of Israel and a pioneer in space. I am proud to have known him, humbled by his accomplishments, inspired by his life, and honored to call him my friend.

— Phil Blazer

TABLE OF CONTENTS

"Pioneering is Israel's life blood, as it is the life blood of all mankind. Going to the moon and coming to the desert to plant saplings are similar acts in my opinion. Man must reach for the stars, it is in his nature. We have seen that the Bible first defined this aspect of human existence. But the stars are only a symbol. There is much to do on earth. The Jews today have the opportunity missed by so many generations in exile. They can follow the prophets who demanded that Israel be two things: That it represent a covenant between all Jews so as to strengthen their cohesion as a people and that its mission also be to act as an example, 'a light unto the nations' for all mankind. For me, pioneering is setting the example and there can be no higher Jewish Ideal than creating from this bare, besieged little land a rich and enduring way of life that in its plentitude will never stop searching for new areas of endeavor but that will serve as a model to inspire humanity everywhere."

— from *Reflections* by David Ben-Gurion

David Ben-Gurion, My Grandfather

When I look at the life and times of my grandfather David Ben-Gurion, I see the struggles and dedication of the young pioneers who came from the four corners of the earth to build the new State of Israel. They endured hardships that today are difficult to comprehend. During the years between the First Aliyah in 1882 and the establishment of the State of Israel in 1948, these heroes exercised their ingenuity and fortitude to build and develop the new "land of milk and honey."

The folklore of our new state tells the wonderful and heartwarming stories of these pioneers. Over the years, and especially after his death in 1973, many people have shared anecdotes of how they met and came to know my grandfather. Through these stories, I gained a wealth of fascinating knowledge about David Ben-Gurion and his contemporaries that cannot be found in history books.

Alon Ben-Gurion with his grandfather

When we are children growing up, we take our parents and grandparents for granted. For me, David Ben-Gurion was simply my grandfather. He also happened to be the prime minister and founder of Israel.

I remember that he always kept a little book with him that contained the birthdays of his children and grandchildren, not unlike most other grandfathers. He would prepare for birthdays by coming over to me on the day before, and asking, "Alon, what would you like for your birthday?" It's not as if we expected to go to Toys-R-Us—in our family, it always had to be a book. And I would answer, "Grandfather, I would like such and such a book."

On the occasion of my twelfth birthday, I was interested in learning about the Roman Empire. I made my request to him, "Grandfather, I would like to get some books about the Roman Empire." He responded, "Which period of the Roman Empire?" I answered, "Hannibal the Great." When he sat down with me and asked me why I was interested in Hannibal the Great, I replied, "It's just a very fascinating part of history." His face lit up, he sat up tall, giving me his full attention, and began a lecture about why he thought Hannibal the Great was one of the best military leaders in history. This was my present! An hour and a half about Hannibal! I just looked at him and said to myself, "Where did this man come from?" His brilliance was astounding. It was a great experience to listen and learn from him. He did not speak to me as if I were a child, but treated me as an adult, somehow knowing intuitively that I would understand him.

David Ben-Gurion was not a man for small talk. He discussed a whole array of specific subjects with me. He would ask me how I was doing in school. What was my favorite subject? If I said biology, he would ask what I was learning in biology. Once I responded that I was learning about human beings. I remember that he talked to me about the meeting he once had with Albert Einstein. He told me that he had a discussion with him about the "human being." Listening as a child, I just looked at him in awe; I was proud that he spoke to me with so much respect.

In 1996, I gave a speech in Los Angeles for one of the Jewish organizations there. A gentleman whom I had never met came up to me and said, "I would like to give you a present." It was a large framed picture of David Ben-Gurion. It was the most humane, the most beautiful picture of my grandfather I had ever seen. This man's young son had taken the photograph. This was the type of esteem that my grandfather inspired—he was a man who was deeply loved and admired by many people.

David Ben-Gurion always liked to meet children from all over the world—Jewish or not Jewish. Once, I asked him why he enjoyed being with children so much and he said, "Alon, politicians are politicians. When you ask a politician something, he'll give you a political answer. Children are honest. If you want to know what is happening in the world, talk to children—they'll tell you exactly what's happening." History books do not share this human aspect of the pioneers of Israel, people like my grandfather. That is why I so much appreciate the book you are about to read—it offers us an opportunity to have some insight into the lives and personalities of these pioneering heroes.

Another important event in my life demonstrated my grandfather's humanity. He adored my mother. One of the reasons he admired her was that although she was born in England, she left her home and family and unselfishly made a great sacrifice to come to Israel when it was Palestine. At that time my father was fighting against the British. My grandfather always appreciated my mother for her courage in coming to Palestine and her dedication to raising a family in Israel. One day we went to visit him. When my mother and I walked into his house, he walked over to greet us and she bent down to give him a kiss. She called him "father" and she said, "Father, you didn't shave today." "Just a minute," he said. He ran into the bathroom, shaved, splashed on some aftershave, came back, gave her his cheek and said, "Now give me the kiss." This was the sweet, warm, compassionate part of David Ben-Gurion that most people never saw.

In Israel, a lot of people ask me what Ben-Gurion would say about politics in Israel today—and the politics in the world. Israel has changed. Israel is not like it was 60 years ago, or 80 years ago, when my grandfather and his fellow pioneers dreamed about creating the new Jewish state.

I believe my grandfather would say: "I am proud that Israel is so strong militarily and economically, and that the prophecy of *aliyah* is being realized as a new Israeli identity is emerging—an identity that has blurred much of the distinction between Ashkenazi and Sephardic Jews." That said, I am sure he would pause and say with great sadness, "Why are the Israelis and Palestinians not living in peace?"

If my grandfather were with us today, he would definitely lament the fact that most of the Arab states do not have diplomatic relations with Israel. He would have hoped that the two sides could reconcile their differences. He would never let go of that hope.

The early pioneers built the new nation with the dream of peace in the region. Many were escaping from countries where they were persecuted and oppressed—they came to Israel wanting only peace for their families and for people throughout the country. My grandfather understood that in the very fabric of his being—it was one of the things that drove him to work as hard as he did.

Once we asked him, when did he decide that he wanted to build the country? He responded, "It was not in order to be the prime minister." He didn't care about titles. He answered this way, "It's not that you or I get up in the morning and decide let's create a state. One day, when I had questions and nobody could give me an answer, I realized 'I've got to give the answers.' But building a new state is not something easy—you have to put all the systems in place. We have to remember that we are a nation with a very, very rich history. We are a nation that came after two thousand years in exile where there were no rules and regulations. You take 600,000 Jews—that's what we had when Israel was declared—and you say, 'well today we are a state!' It doesn't work that fast. There are a lot of things that we take for granted. We need the foresight and planning to establish a parliament, to create a democracy. All these kinds of systems were necessary to build the State of Israel. Our society had to change. Our people woke up and they were in the middle of the desert. They said,

David and Alon at Druze village

'What's this?' You answer, 'This is your new home, so start digging.' You know, this is the way that we did things in those days."

The last time I saw him was in October 1973. It was a Wednesday. I was a paratrooper serving in the army and I had a chance to leave the base for a couple of hours. I met my father for lunch in Tel Aviv, but before going back to the base I asked my father, "Where's grandfather?" My father responded that he was in Tel Aviv. "Do you mind if we visit him to say hello?" I asked. We stopped by his house. When we got there I asked where he was and was told that he was sleeping. I looked at him sleeping, then walked out, not wanting to wake him, and just thanked the secret service guys. That was the last time I saw him—the 4th of October 1973. Shortly afterward, the Yom Kippur War started and I was badly wounded. I spent a year in the hospital. Although my grandfather was in another hospital, I knew about his condition. My parents did not want to worry him, so they did not tell him that I had been injured. When he asked, "How is Alon?" they answered, "He's on the battlefield." Sadly, this conversation among family members happens time and again in Israel.

My grandfather believed in commitment to Jewish values, and was devoted to the spiritual basis of Judaism. He was always a fighter for justice and equality, and he would have been hopeful and optimistic that Israel would light the way to peace for all nations. The battle to survive, the same battle fought by the pioneers of Israel, is still going on in Israel today. We will endure. We will survive. We owe it to those who built the modern State of Israel—the *Pioneers of Israel*.

— Alon Ben-Gurion

CHAPTER ONE

Setting the Stage
For the Pioneers

INTRODUCTION:

Creating a Nation

For centuries, spiritual leaders, scholars, and Bible purists have been studying and teaching the intricacies of the Bible and the origins and history of the Land of Israel, *Eretz Yisrael*. Deeply embedded in this history and tradition is the building and creation of the new nation of Israel, born from the blood and resilience and invincible will of a few thousand early pioneers.

Pioneers of Israel reveals the stories of many of the well-known figures who assumed leadership in the development of the new nation. These few are meant to represent the thousands, later the tens of thousands of pioneers who participated in the building of the country—

Pioneers training at farm in Berditchef, Ukraine before leaving for Palestine (1919)

many of whom remain anonymous. Some of these unnamed pioneers are included in photographs throughout this book. They are the people who worked the soil, developed business and industry, educated young people, raised families, provided innovation in scientific research and technology, and brought culture and socialization to the fledgling nation. This book is dedicated also to these unheralded modern heroes.

Picking grapes at Carmel's Vineyards (1899)

Pioneers in *Eretz Yisrael* struggled and persevered to lay the foundation for their new country. The State of Israel has been reborn in the modern era to provide a refuge for millions of persecuted Jews determined to reclaim their homeland. In this fight for independence these pioneers gained the respect and awe of millions of people worldwide who witnessed their commitment to make available a safe and secure country in which Jews could cherish their freedom and their heritage.

The creation of the modern State of Israel has been achieved in a little more than 100 years, a mere blink of an eye in the vast millennia of time. Israel, a nation brought forth virtually without resources, was created with the hearts, souls, and willing hands of an inspired group of men, women, and children. These courageous and unyielding early pioneers relentlessly carried on in their quest to conquer the desolate and arid land. While they farmed and built communities, they also were forced to defend themselves from the many enemies surrounding them, enemies who were fanatically committed to their annihilation and who pledged to drive them into the sea.

First government of Israel (1949)

As you read *Pioneers of Israel* you will note the descriptive word for Israel is "state." Why not "nation" or "country" or no descriptive preface? Historical explanation for the use of "state" emanates from the first half of the twentieth century, when states were usually smaller nationalistic entities than nations. It simply became common practice to call the new Jewish homeland a state, since it does not meet the typical size and population parameters of a large country.

Tending to the harvest in the Jezreel Valley (1920).

In ancient times the lands that made up the Jewish Kingdoms of Israel and Judah were quite extensive. Geographically they included the modern State of Israel, the West Bank and Gaza Strip, as well as parts of the modern Kingdom of Jordan (Transjordan), southwestern Syria and southern Lebanon. This territory was known as the Land of Israel or, by its Hebrew translation, *Eretz Yisrael*. It is a description that has been used by Jews and Christians throughout history.

When the political and geographical entity known as Palestine was controlled by the Ottoman Empire and the British Mandate, the Jewish pioneers identified their new homeland by using the biblical term *Eretz Yisrael* or the translation "the Land of Israel." During the British Mandate, the name *Eretz Yisrael* was part of the official name of the territory whenever the name was written in Hebrew. Because of the realignment of the geographical territory while under British control, the modern usage of the term *Eretz Yisrael* altered and now usually denotes the land that is currently Israel, the West Bank, Gaza Strip and sometimes Transjordan.

Pioneer hikers on their way to Palestine stop in Vienna for Fourteenth Zionist Congress

In *Eretz Yisrael* the Jews found a place to come together again, to return from the exile of the Diaspora to their homeland. When the Jewish people were driven out of the Land of Israel, as the story is so beautifully and sorrowfully told in the Bible, that was said to mark the beginning of the Diaspora. The Jewish Diaspora refers to the dispersion of the Jewish people throughout the world. Diaspora is commonly accepted to have begun with the Babylonian captivity in 597 BCE. The Jews were scattered after being crushed by the Romans in the first century. They lost their state of Judea and many were sold into slavery throughout the Roman Empire. Subsequent numerous exiles and persecution as well as political and economic conditions affected the numbers and dynamics of Jewish Diaspora.

Constructing Kibbutz Masada (1937)

Pioneers of Israel traces many paths of the Diaspora Jews—from Eastern and Western Europe, United States, Canada, Middle East and North Africa, Ethiopia and South Africa. These heroes struggled against seemingly insurmountable odds to establish the State of Israel. Their biographies coalesce poignantly and dramatically into the historic saga of a developing nation. These stories, pieces of the modern history of the Jewish people and their inspired battle for independence, must be read and understood by today's generation and preserved for all generations to come. *Pioneers of Israel* reveals the courage, desperation, ingenuity, fortitude and indomitable will of more than fifty women and men who helped build the State of Israel from the mid-1800s through its declaration as a nation in 1948, and in the building and development of the country in the years that followed.

Building Kibbutz Shomer Hatzair near the Burma Road (1948)

Sir Moses Montefiore
1784 - 1885

Palestine must belong to the Jews, and Jerusalem is destined to become the seat of a Jewish Commonwealth.
— Sir Moses Montefiore

Sir Moses Montefiore probably was the most famous British Jew in the nineteenth century. Montefiore was a financier, stockbroker, philanthropist and a sheriff in London. He was born in Livorno, Italy in 1784, to an Italian-Jewish family that settled in England in the early eighteenth century. Brought up in London, he was taught Hebrew by his mother's brother. In later life, as an Orthodox Sephardic Jew and dedicated philanthropist, he was a zealous fighter for the rights of oppressed Jews all over the world. Success in attaining the Balfour Declaration in 1917 must be credited, at least in part, to this esteemed citizen who lived during the Victorian era.

In 1803, at the age of nineteen, Montefiore became one of the twelve Jewish brokers licensed by the city of London and was therefore able to have a seat on the London Stock Exchange. He quickly established an excellent reputation and partnered with his brother Abraham to form a company, "Montefiore Brothers." He had a close friendship with Nathan Rothschild, of the well-known banking family, and also served in the Surrey Militia.

He met and married Judith Cohen, the daughter of Levi Barenth Cohen, one of the wealthiest English Jews at this time. She also was the sister-in-law of Mayer Anschel Rothschild. Montefiore's firm acted as brokers for the Rothschilds, which financially was quite advantageous for him. His personal wealth enabled him to retire from the Exchange when he was only forty and devote himself to philanthropy and social interests.

Montefiore from an engraving by G. Richmond

Both Sir Moses and Lady Judith were strictly Orthodox in their Judaism. Their diaries contain frequent references to their daily prayer. They observed the holidays and abstained from work on the Sabbath. Their marriage was particularly happy and they lived together for fifty years with the closest intimacy and warmth.

Montefiore was extremely influential and held many prestigious positions during his lifetime. He was a fellow of the Royal Society, and was the first Jewish sheriff in London, elected in 1837. In the same year he was knighted by Queen Victoria. He received a baronetcy in 1846, in recognition of his humanitarian efforts on behalf of the Jews. For forty years, from

1834 to 1874, he served as president of the Board of Deputies of British Jews. His physical stature was impressive: he was six feet, three inches tall. The admiration and respect of Queen Victoria contributed to his esteemed reputation.

Montefiore was not a religious Jew in his youth. He took his first trip to *Eretz Yisrael* in 1827, and "fell in love" with the Holy Land. The experience moved him so deeply that he became a strictly observant Jew. He built and maintained his own synagogue on his estate, and traveled with his own *shohet* [a person charged with the ritual slaughter of animals in accordance with Jewish law]. He brought his own dishes and food to banquets so that he could eat kosher food.

Between 1827 and 1875, Montefiore visited the Land of Israel seven times. The first journey was one of the most memorable. After an arduous trip to Egypt sailing in convoy with four other boats, he and his wife reached the Egyptian shores. From there they boarded another ship that took them to Jaffa, then traveled on to Ramleh where they spent the night. On the next day, late in the afternoon, when they had their first sight of the city of Jerusalem, they stopped to recite special prayers in memory of the destruction of the Temple.

The Montefiores spent three days and four nights in the Holy City listening to the plight of the local Jewish population. They visited the Wailing Wall and the Tomb of Rachel, and they were received by the governor of Jerusalem. Sir Moses wrote in his diary about his trip, "I hope I shall ever live and die in the society of my brethren of Israel."

In *Eretz Yisrael*, Sir Moses Montefiore helped to establish hospitals and agricultural settlements, and he built synagogues, apartments and tombs. These actions represented the earliest form of his own personal Zionism. He purchased land for and founded the *Yemin Moshe* quarter adjacent to the Old City of Jerusalem. Meant to house both Ashkenazi and Sephardic Jews, the quarter had two long buildings containing sixteen small apartments, with an Ashkenazi synagogue at one end and a Sephardic synagogue at the other. There were baths, cooking ovens and a flourmill, which stands at the entrance to the quarter and which since has been converted into a museum. The windmill now is a prominent landmark near the center of modern Jerusalem.

Sir Moses initiated another important innovation. In 1839, Montefiore commissioned the first of five censuses of the Jewish population then living in *Eretz Yisrael*. These censuses were continued after his death. They revealed that in 1800 there were about 2,000 Jews living in Israel out of a population of 8,750.

Montefiore was an influential and respected philanthropist for both Jews and non-Jews. He was committed in his battle against oppression, employing diplomacy to accomplish this lifetime pursuit. Battling oppression was Montefiore's *cause celebre*. Sir Moses' philanthropic work on behalf of exploited Jewish communities brought him accolades and praise. The celebration of his 100th birthday was marked with great ceremony and outpourings of affection and admiration. His birthday was observed as a holiday in London and acknowledged by Jewish communities worldwide. He lived to be 101 years old.

The members of the *Hovevei Zion* [Lovers of Zion] movement held Montefiore in particularly high esteem. This Zionist movement, which began in Russia and Poland after the Russian pogroms of 1881, had as its goals the establishment of settlements in the Land of Israel, and the encouragement of immigration to build up the Jewish population. The movement struggled throughout the 1880s and 1890s with limited success. Eventually it was taken over by the rising tide of the political Zionists led by Theodor Herzl. On Sir Moses' 100th birthday, the *Hovevei Zion* group presented the centenarian with an historic album signed by all the leaders and dignitaries in the Jewish community. Clearly, Sir Moses helped to set the stage for Herzl and the rise of the Zionist movement.

In 1877, when Sir Moses was ninety-three years old, one of his relatives, Leonard Montefiore, visited him at his mansion in Ramsgate. During their conversation, Leonard asked Sir Moses what had inspired him to become a prominent defender of the Jews and to take a leading role in the development of the Jewish homeland. Sir Moses pointed to a ring he was wearing which had Hebrew writing inscribed on it. He said, "I have worn this signet for many years as a reminder of

Sir Moses Montefiore from an engraving by G. Richmond

the first wondrous event which led me to travel to the Land of Israel." He described an "awakening" he had experienced.

He explained to Leonard that he had had a dream in which he saw a venerated old man. The man "showed me a picture of Eliyahu with one hand while pointing in the direction of the Land of Israel with the other. He then whispered in my ear in Hebrew, 'possessor of everything.'" Sir Moses said he went back to sleep and the dream was repeated twice more. Leonard listened enthralled, as the Zionist continued, "This dream made such a deep impression on me, that I felt compelled to act on the promise I had just made Judith [to visit the Holy Land] much sooner than I had thought to. In fact, I immediately let all my other commitments fall to the side and prepared for the journey with my wife without delay. We wanted to see how our fellow Jews were faring in the Holy Land."

Montefiore once was asked how much he was worth. He answered, "I am worth 40,000 pounds." The questioner was taken aback, saying, "I thought you were worth millions." Montefiore smiled and said, "I do possess millions. But you asked me how much I am worth, and since 40,000 pounds is what I distributed during the last year to charitable institutions, I regard this sum as the barometer of my true worth. For it is not how much a person possesses, but how much he is willing to share with those less fortunate that determines his actual worth."

CHAPTER TWO

Early History —
Breaking New Ground

Baron Edmund de Rothschild
1845 - 1934

{It is} appropriate that a special Jewish unit...should be gathered for the overthrow {of the Nazis}.
— Baron Edmund de Rothschild

In 1882, a group of fifteen idealistic Jews sailed to Palestine with the intention of establishing their own agricultural settlement. They had heard about the struggling attempts at *Rosh Pinna* and *Petach Tikvah*, and they hoped to be more successful. The group of fifteen called themselves the BILU, an acronym for the Hebrew "House of Jacob, let us go up." They comprised, as far as we know, the first Jewish immigration to Palestine inspired by the political purpose of establishing a Jewish homeland. Consequently, they were called the First Aliyah [going up].

The BILU went to *Mikveh Israel* (now in the Tel Aviv suburb of Holon), an agricultural school, where they encountered terrible adversity. Nearby, they built an independent settlement called *Rishon Le Zion*, which nearly failed because of the scarcity of fresh water and the pioneers' struggles against malaria. In desperation, the BILU turned to Baron Edmund de Rothschild for help.

Edmund de Rothschild, a member of the Rothschild family banking empire, chose not to join the family banking business. Born in Paris in 1845, he found his niche in the world of art and culture, preferring to be a humanitarian and philanthropist. He responded to the threats facing the Jewish people in Europe by supporting massive land purchases and underwriting Jewish settlements in *Eretz Yisrael*. He described this work as the most fulfilling of his life's accomplishments.

As with many Jewish activists in the late nineteenth century, Rothschild became active in Jewish causes after witnessing the horror of the pogroms in Russia in the 1880s. Based in Paris, he financially sup-

Rothschild greets Tel Avivians from balcony (1925)

ported the first settlements in Palestine, *Rishon Le Zion* and *Zikhron Ya'akov*.

Rishon Le Zion was founded in 1882 by the fifteen Russian BILU pioneers when they managed to acquire 835 acres of land to start the village. In a short time, about one hundred other settlers joined them. Inexperienced in agricultural methods and plagued by an acute shortage of water, these original settlers faced a severe crisis. Responding quickly, Rothschild contributed money for a well, provided for the upkeep of the families, and sent experts to help with the agricultural challenges.

The inspiration for the founding of the community came from Rabbi Shmuel Mohliwer, one of the leaders of the early Zionist movement and one of the founders of religious Zionism. Following the pogroms of 1881 and 1882, it was Mohliwer who was influential in convincing Baron Edmund de Rothschild to support the establishment of Jewish agricultural communities in Palestine. Rothschild's only stipulations were that the people who founded these settlements must

Rothschild with Sir Herbert Samuel

themselves become farmers and that they come to Palestine at their own expense.

One of the reasons it was so difficult for most of these early pioneers was that they were students and intellectuals trying to become farmers. This was no easy task. Jews had been forbidden to own land in most of Europe for centuries and there hardly were any farmers among them.

Rothschild provided these first settlers with more than funds and agricultural experts; he also sent them French vines to create a wine industry. *Rishon Le Zion* later became well known for its prosperous vineyards, wine cellars and citrus groves. Carmel Wines evolved from these early enterprises.

The Baron's assistance proved crucial, but his participation in the internal affairs of the town often caused uneasiness among some people. Rothschild differed with Theodor Herzl and members of *Hovevei Zion* on the interpretation of political Zionism. To avoid internal disagreement, he formed a group of twelve settlements under the auspices of Rothschild's Jewish Colonization Association (ICA). The ICA's combined twelve settlements covered 62,500 acres of land in 1900, and continued to develop in the years that followed.

By 1914, Rothschild had visited the expanded settlements and also was growing closer to the Zionist Organization. Toward the end of World War I, Edmund's son James arrived in

Palestine with the British army and was among the recruiters for the Jewish battalions in the *yishuv* (farm settlements). James took over the leadership of the newly organized Palestine Jewish Colonization Association (PICA) in 1923. Its first settlement was *Binyamina*, a derivative of his father's Hebrew name.

The Rothschild name has become synonymous with settlement activity in pre-state Israel, including cultural, political and spiritual matters. Edmund's work was recognized and honored everywhere in the *yishuv* and in the Zionist Organization. Rothschild joined the political activity of the Zionists by aiding Chaim Weizmann and Nahum Sokolow in the early 1920s. He was made honorary president of the expanded Jewish Agency in 1929. He died in Paris in 1934, leaving a legacy that included the reclamation of nearly 125,000 acres of land and almost thirty settlements. In 1954 his remains and those of his wife were brought to *Zikhron Ya'akov* to rest in the land that he loved.

Rothschild on train to Jerusalem during visit to Palestine (1914)

General store in Moisesville, Argentina - a community sponsored by Rothschild (1924)

Arthur Ruppin
1876 - 1943

> *Zionism is not a national or chauvinistic caprice, but the last desperate stand of the Jews against annihilation.*
> — Arthur Ruppin

Zionist, economist, and sociologist Arthur Ruppin is acknowledged as the "father of Zionist settlement" and the "father of Jewish sociology." These convergent careers—one pragmatic, the other academic—reflect the extensive range of Ruppin's concerns. He was responsible for merging the principles of political Zionism with the practical elements of developing the land.

Born in Germany to an affluent family that encountered serious financial problems, Ruppin left school when he was fifteen to find work. His experiences as a young man strongly influenced his pragmatic thinking as an adult. Ruppin's background helped him to understand basic social changes in both Eastern and Western European Jewry, guiding his future course as a Zionist leader.

He worked hard as a teenager and young adult in the grain industry. Attending evening classes, he finally received his high school diploma in 1899 when he was twenty-three, and went on to study law and economics at university, earning a doctorate. From 1902 to 1907 he apprenticed in a law court, simultaneously launching his career in sociology. In 1904 Ruppin published *Die Juden der Gegenwart*, a descriptive sociology of the Jews. This decisive work, released in a number of editions and languages, was groundbreaking. It predicated the circumstances of the Jews on demographic and statistical analysis, instead of the rhetorical ideology that generally dominated such discussions.

Ruppin (left) at his 60th birthday in Deganyah (1936)

In 1907 he was sent by the Jewish Agency to Palestine to assess possibilities for Zionist settlement. A year later Ruppin settled in Jaffa, having been appointed director of the World Zionist Organization's (WZO) Palestine office by David Wolffsohn. Established in 1908, the office aimed to acquire land and establish Jewish settlements. While serving in this position, Ruppin conducted the first census of the city of Jerusalem since the time of Emperor Augustus.

Ruppin began executing his ambitious and comprehensive projects, paving the way for the practical work of the WZO. He maintained that the most important component in settlement work was the "settler." He insisted that the settler and the agency work together as equal partners in every enterprise. With this foundation Ruppin successfully created a framework for the pioneers' activities and channeled their enthusiasm into a driving force for settlement of the country.

This fundamental philosophy of working closely with the new immigrants generated innovative forms of settlements: the *kvutzah* [little community group], the *kibbutz* [agricultural farm], cooperatives, middle-class villages, and towns. Ruppin defended the pioneers against opponents of these "communal" structures. His mission was to support the Jewish settlements, and in his crusade to achieve this goal he was an advocate of "practical" or "pragmatic" Zionism. He felt that the most pressing need was to acquire land and, through the building of communities, settle the country and build the state.

Practical Zionism emphasized practical means of attaining Zionist goals, such as *aliyah* [immigration], rural settlement, and providing educational institutions. On the other hand, there was little attention paid to political conditions. First build the country, these Zionists maintained, then resolve the political concerns. The champions of this doctrine were the immigrants of the Second Aliyah, who had been arriving in Palestine in great numbers since 1905. Under the leadership of Ruppin, they intensified the development of rural settlements, some along cooperative principles. The built modern towns, and established the first industrial enterprises.

Ruppin's goal was to purchase land for agricultural settlement and the support of a self-governing population. He acquired large tracts of land in the Jezreel Valley on behalf of the Palestine Land Development Corporation (established in 1908) and for the Jewish National Fund. He asserted that solitary settlers or a small village could not survive in the face of the innumerable difficulties in Palestine. The soil, neglected and abused for centuries, could be

Ben-Gurion addressing Ruppin's 60th birthday in Deganyah (1936)

restored only in a communal and unselfish effort. Since he and others believed that an agricultural base was the most fundamental issue, he needed the pioneers to do the job.

His sociological and political background compelled Ruppin also to consider the problem of Arab-Jewish relationships and their consequences. In his Jerusalem home in November 1925, together with a small group of friends, he established *Brit Shalom* [Covenant of Peace], which he led until 1929. This independent association supported the concept of better understanding between Jews and Arabs. Their premise was a Jewish national homeland based on equality for Jews and Arabs in a bi-national state. Witnessing the Arab riots in 1929 and the early 1930s, Ruppin determined that the political merging of the two cultures in one country was unrealistic. Instead, it was necessary to strengthen the Jewish position in the country, economically and politically, in order to foster cooperation from both sides. He became insistent on the need for a Jewish state.

Arthur Ruppin (1920)

Ruppin's ambitious work projects can be divided into four periods:

•*1908-1914: laying the foundations for Jewish settlement in Palestine*

•*1914-18: saving the yishuv from failure*

•*1920-33: systematic expansion of settlement in the cities and rural areas emphasizing political and economic conditions*

•*1933-1942: assisting with absorption of tens of thousands of European immigrants of the Fifth Aliyah, using his expertise on the sociology of the Jews*

In 1925, Arthur Ruppin attended the dedication ceremony for Hebrew University in an amphitheater overlooking the Judean desert, along with 7,000 others. He joined the faculty of the university the following year and taught Sociology of the Jews. In the years that followed until his death in 1943, Arthur Ruppin combined his academic responsibilities and research with dynamic public works.

Pinchas Rutenberg
1860 - 1904

When the city's lights came on for the first time, pedestrians in Tel Aviv started dancing spontaneously.

— Jerusalem Post

Pinchas Rutenberg was a charismatic man of contradictions, a Russian Jewish émigré to Palestine, a businessman, a visionary, and according to some people, a "Bolshevik enforcer." His early life in Russia remains clad in mystery. His talent for business and his ability to charm world leaders into supporting his dreams converge to form an intriguing personality.

Rutenberg was born in 1879 in Romni, Russia. He studied engineering and was an active member of the Socialist Revolutionary movement. In 1905 when the revolution in Russia was suppressed, Rutenberg fled the country and found refuge in Italy, where he worked as an engineer.

He traveled to the United States, became interested in Zionism and vigorously supported the establishment of the Jewish Legion. Returning to Russia after the fall of the czarist regime in early 1917, he was appointed a minister in the local government in northern Russia. He lived in Moscow and Odessa, finally immigrating to Palestine in 1919, shortly after the communists seized the Ukraine and the local "White" government began to collapse.

During the 1920 Arab riots, Rutenberg joined Ze'ev Jabotinsky to create a defense force for Jerusalem—the Haganah (later the Israel Defense Forces). In Tel Aviv, Rutenberg served

Joining Rutenberg (far right) are (left to right) Menachem Ussishkin, Lord Rufus Reading and Chaim Arlozoroff

as head of the Haganah office, participating in the delineation of Palestine's northern border. Rutenberg was well-suited to military leadership. The *Jerusalem Post* explained: "The change of setting, from revolutionary Russia's frost and lawlessness to Palestine's heat and British veneer may have been sharp, but Rutenberg…remained the same gruff, no-nonsense revolutionary who had done time in a communist jail and was no stranger to violence…. It was only natural, then, that he helped pioneer the *yishuv*'s self-defense system."

Rutenberg's dream was to use Jordan River water to produce electricity and build a modern, industrialized country, at the

The Rutenberg Hydroelectric Power Station, Naharayim (1933)

same time protecting rural development. In 1921, he received the first concession from Great Britain regarding the development of an electric company. Stepping into this opening, Rutenberg founded the Palestine Electric Corporation in 1923 and launched what became one of the most important economic enterprises in *Eretz Yisrael*. The *Jerusalem Post* described the first time that Tel Aviv was "electrified. The astonishment and euphoria that accompanied all this was so fierce that when the city's lights came on for the first time, pedestrians in Tel Aviv started dancing spontaneously."

Reading power station made possible by Rutenberg

Most of Rutenberg's life was devoted to the Palestine Electric Corporation. The corporation initially consisted of a small diesel plant in Tel Aviv but soon expanded to serve the needs of neighboring Jaffa; two years later, two additional plants were established in Haifa and Tiberias.

In 1927, negotiations with Emir Abdullah of Transjordan resulted in an agreement allowing the Palestine Electric Corporation to use 6,000 dunams of land under Transjordanian control for a hydroelectric project. It went online in summer 1933, using the water from the Jordan and Yarmuk rivers, and provided power for the major part of Palestine.

Water flows from the Naharayim power station (1933)

In 1935 and 1938 two thermal power stations were built in Haifa and Tel Aviv, which served as the main suppliers of electricity for both Jews and Arabs until 1948. Unfortunately, in 1948 the Arab Legion destroyed them.

Rutenberg concentrated on economic rather than political affairs. He is considered a Zionist leader for his incisive vision in foreseeing the needs of the Jewish state and his ability to construct foundations to ensure future development. The Pinchas Rutenberg Institute for Youth Education was founded in Haifa, fulfilling one of his last requests; the donation of his home and his personal wealth for youth programs.

As his biographer Eli Shaltiel noted: "The real Pinchas Rutenberg was not necessarily the cloak-and-dagger adventurer some portrayed, nor was he a war monger; actually he was a meticulous planner, a visionary progressive, an imaginative entrepreneur, and in fact, a peace crusader."

Builders of the power station with Rutenberg at bottom center wearing glasses (1923)

Eliezer Ben-Yehuda
1858 - 1922

In every new event, every step, even the smallest in the path of progress, it is necessary that there be one pioneer who will lead the way.
— Eliezer Ben-Yehuda

While in conversation with each other, we do not often think about how our language began and what it would be like to be responsible for initiating a new language and bringing it to a new nation. This was the mission that Eliezer Ben-Yehuda took on as his life's work.

Eliezer Ben-Yehuda was born Eliezer Yitzhak Perelman in the Lithuanian village of Luzhky in 1858. As with virtually all Jewish children of that era, he learned Hebrew at a very young age as part of his religious upbringing. He was an excellent scholar and it was hoped that he would become a rabbi. Instead he became interested in the secular world and ultimately exchanged the *yeshiva* for a Russian gymnasium [high school], completing his studies in 1877.

Ben-Yehuda began focusing his interests on the problems of the Jewish people, a threatened minority in nineteenth-century Europe. The Russo-Turkish war and the nationalist struggles in the Balkans deeply influenced Ben-Yehuda. He came to the conclusion that the European concept of "national fulfillment" should also be applied to his people, the Jews. He felt deeply that if the Bulgarians (who were trying to regain their independence from the Turks) could demand and obtain a state of their own, then the Jews, the "People of the Book" and the "heirs of historic Jerusalem," deserved the same. He was convinced that the Jews must return to their land and begin once again to speak their own language. In this way, Ben-Yehuda was one of the first modern Zionists, and he began to advocate the establishment of a Jewish national homeland in *Eretz Yisrael*.

Ben-Yehuda and his family at the site of their house to be built in Talpiot, Jerusalem

He left Russia in 1878, first going to Paris to study medicine but leaving because of health problems associated with tuberculosis. He arrived in Palestine in 1881 with his revival plans for the Hebrew language intact. He pondered the revival question deeply and published several articles in Hebrew periodicals. These articles can be regarded as forerunners of modern political Zionism. They considered the basic elements pertinent to Jewish nationalism: settlement policy and revival of the Hebrew language, literature, and culture in the national homeland. His vision of a new Jewish homeland was not one to which masses of Jews would immigrate but, rather, one that would serve as a spiritual and linguistic center unifying and strengthening the Jews of the Diaspora. It would be, as it had been centuries ago, the unifying center of the Jewish people and their culture.

Ben-Yehuda soon recognized the inherent problem in trying to bring an ancient tongue to life. Hebrew was better suited to the world of the Bible than to that of the nineteenth century—it lacked the vocabulary necessary to describe modern life. Undaunted by the challenge, Ben-Yehuda began what would become his life's work: the re-creation of the Hebrew language into one that could describe life in the 1900s and into the future.

Just prior to arriving in Palestine, Ben-Yehuda had decided to speak only Hebrew with every Jew he met, proving to himself that this was possible. Ben-Yehuda soon settled in Jerusalem with his wife Deborah. When their first child, Ben-Zion Ben-Yehuda (known as Itamar Ben-Avi) was born in 1882, they agreed that they would raise their son as the first all-Hebrew speaking child in modern history. Consequently they would speak to the boy only in Hebrew.

This extraordinary experiment symbolized the intensity of the commitment that Ben-Yehuda took on, and underscored his dedication to the future of the revival. It meant that not only his parents and family, but also all visitors, friends, and acquaintances, would have to speak to Itamar on everyday topics solely in Hebrew.

Itamar Ben-Avi describes in his autobiography some of the drastic precautions that Ben-Yehuda took to ensure that his son only would hear, and therefore only speak, Hebrew. He wrote that his mother occasionally forgot about the language instruction, and one day, absent-mindedly, she began singing in Russian. Ben-Yehuda was quite angry when he overheard his wife, which startled Itamar. This was the moment that Itamar remembered that he spoke his first words—and they were in Hebrew.

The fact that there was a child in the house accentuated the need to find appropriate Hebrew words for things in everyday life; Ben-Yehuda coined new words for objects such as "doll," "ice cream," "jelly," "omelet," "handkerchief," "towel," "bicycle," and hundreds more. He invented new words to describe the social, political and technological subjects of the modern world, some of which he adapted from foreign languages while inventing others by modifying ancient Hebrew words and roots. His work was infused with the goal of transforming a language of liturgy into a simple language that could be spoken by adults and children, in everyday life.

Of all the steps Ben-Yehuda took to revive Hebrew, using Hebrew in the schools was the most important. He advocated that rabbis and teachers use Hebrew as the language of instruction in the Jewish schools in Palestine for all subjects, both religious and secular. Ben-Yehuda was convinced that the revival could succeed, especially if the younger generation would begin to speak Hebrew freely. Ben-Yehuda himself taught at the Jerusalem Alliance School where he was influential in initiating Hebrew as the language of instruction.

Ben-Yehuda also wanted to attract adults to his ideas. To this end, in 1884 he began publishing his own newspaper, *Hatzvi*, as an instrument for teaching adults, both through its content and language. Ben-Yehuda believed that if he published a low-priced newspaper, people would become confident in their ability to express in Hebrew everything they would want to say. He used the newspaper to introduce new words that were missing in the everyday world, and Palestinian Jews became avid readers.

Perhaps his most monumental task was the compilation of a Hebrew dictionary. Ben-Yehuda became a scientific lexicographer. The results of his arduous labors are remarkable, culminating in his 17-volume *A Complete Dictionary of Ancient and Modern Hebrew*. It was completed by his second wife, Hemda, and his son after Ben-Yehuda died. To this day it is unique in the annals of Hebrew lexicography.

Eliezer and Hemda Ben-Yehuda, leaders of the new Yeshuv in Jerusalem

What helped Ben-Yehuda most in his linguistic crusade was that the year 1881 also earmarked the beginning of the early immigration of waves of Jewish settlers into Palestine. They were young, idealistic and educated; they came from similar Eastern European Jewish socio-economic backgrounds, and they had decided to begin their lives in the land of their forefathers. They passed on Modern Hebrew to their children at home and in schools throughout the country. Within a generation, a core of young, fervent Hebrew language speakers was formed, with Hebrew as the symbol of their "linguistic nationalism." This fact was recognized and endorsed by the British mandate authorities by their decreeing "Hebrew as the official language of the Jews of Palestine" on November 29, 1922.

Although Theodor Herzl and other Zionist founders had not envisioned Hebrew as the language of the Jewish state, Israeli Jews and Arabs (Christians and Bedouin, as well as Palestinian) today all speak Ben-Yehuda's version of Modern Hebrew.

Ben-Yehuda wrote in his newspaper, *Hatzvi*, in 1908:

> *For everything there is needed only one wise, clever and active man, with the initiative to devote all his energies to it, and the matter will progress, all obstacles in the way notwithstanding.... In every new event, every step, even the smallest in the path of progress, it is necessary that there be one pioneer who will lead the way without leaving any possibility of turning back.*

For the enormous contribution made to the State of Israel—the revival of the Hebrew language—that pioneer was Eliezer Ben-Yehuda.

Yigal Allon
1918 - 1980

Zionism is the embodiment of a unique pioneering spirit, of the dignity of labor, and of enduring human values....
— Yigal Allon

As with many of the pioneers of Israel, Yigal Allon inherited his enthusiasm for Zionism from his parents. His father, Reuven Yosef Paicovitch, was a member of *Hovevei Zion* in his hometown of Grodno, Russia. His parents moved to Palestine in 1882 as part of the First Aliyah [BILU]. Allon was a *sabra*, a native-born Israeli, born in 1918 at *Kfar Tavor* in the Lower Galilee.

Yigal Allon never forgot the day that he was almost killed. When he was barely a teenager, he lived through an experience that would determine his destiny as a future military commander. He was just thirteen years old when his father called him to the grain shed, spoke with him about his recent *bar mitzvah*, and told him there was another way to proclaim his manhood. His father took his pistol from a metal can in the shed where it was buried, giving it to Yigal on the condition that he learn how to use it. "Tonight you will be on guard duty," he was told.

The young pioneer Israeli was excited to assume his role as a man participating in defending his home. Just after sunset, he found the place where he was to be stationed—under an oak tree beside a large rock formation. In the stillness of the dark night he listened to the sounds of the evening. Shortly after midnight Yigal heard an Arab caravan passing by him, and his instincts told him there was trouble.

He saw three men on horses dismount and begin to fill empty sacks with the harvest from the settlement. His father had instructed him to shout out a warning in Arabic if something like this occurred. If that failed, he was to fire his weapon into the air. He yelled the Arabic word, lowering the tone of his voice to try to sound older than his thirteen years. *"Andak!"* [be careful] he shout-

Palmach Commander Yigal Allon during liberation of Central Galilee (1948)

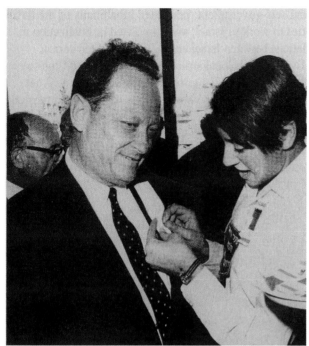

Yigal Allon campaigning for his "Unity of Labor" party (1968)

ed, and clicked his pistol. Surprisingly, the intruders were prepared to fight their way out. Suddenly, Yigal heard several rifle shots and screams in Arabic. The thieves fled, leaving the crops behind. His father had been hiding nearby. While Yigal was becoming a "man" as a settlement guard, his father had also been protecting his son. When Yigal Paicovitch later selected his Hebrew name, he chose "Allon," which means "oak tree."

In 1937, Yigal Allon graduated from the Kadoorie Agricultural School and became a founding member of *Kibbutz Ginnosar*. His activities in underground defense began during the Arab riots of 1936-1939, when he served under Yitzhak Sadeh in a special unit of the Haganah. He became adept at defense training and combat action, which prepared him for his long and distinguished military career. In 1941 Allon was one of the founders of the Palmach, the special commando unit of the Haganah. He led troops into Lebanon and Syria to fight alongside the Allies during World War II.

Yigal Allon became commander of the Palmach in 1945, responsible for planning the training program and operations. This included carrying on the fight for Jewish independence, defending Jews against Arab bandits, and continuing to oppose British policy and administration in Palestine. He was among the activists who demanded intensified opposition to the British. As Palmach commander he was also accountable for the implementation of *Aliyah Bet*. This was the "illegal" smuggling of refugees through British lines, a program that clandestinely brought by ships nearly 70,000 Holocaust survivors to Palestine.

During Israel's War of Independence, Allon directed decisive operations throughout the country, ranging from settlement security to full-scale battles with the enemy. Allon distin-

Allon addresses thousands of Israelis protesting return of Egyptian territory in 1957

guished himself as commander of the southern front by driving the invading Arab armies out of the Negev, including Eilat. He was acknowledged as the most experienced field commander in the Israel Defense Forces (IDF) and had great influence in the training of the Israeli officer corps.

Allon retired from the IDF after David Ben-Gurion disbanded the Palmach. He attended Hebrew University and Oxford University, concentrating on academic study for the decade from 1950 to 1960. He also entered politics and was elected to the Knesset in 1954.

From 1961 to 1968 Yigal Allon served in the cabinet as minister of labor. He assisted in improving the state employment service and increased work productivity. Having initiated legislation on labor relations, he helped to create laws dealing with strikes and lockouts.

Allon joins Minister of Defense Moshe Dayan as they survey fire damage to the al-Aqsa Mosque (1969)

Allon was appointed deputy prime minister and minister for immigrant absorption in 1968. He proposed the Allon Plan to resolve Israel's border problems following the Six Day War. The Allon Plan, which was adopted by the Labor government, sought to integrate into Israel the minimum amount of territory vital for security after the 1967 war. It called for Israel to retain the uninhabited Jordan Valley, which would be settled by Jews, while the populated Arab areas of Judea and Samaria would revert to Arab rule.

In 1969, while remaining in his post as deputy prime minister, he also was appointed minister of education and culture. Allon continued to serve the government of Israel with distinction in various positions: from 1974 to 1977, Allon was foreign minister and deputy premier; he served as a member of the Knesset on the Committee on Foreign Affairs and Security; he completed his career as a statesman as chairman of the World Zionist movement from 1978 until his death in 1980.

Yigal Allon is an excellent example of the magnificent pioneers who were born in Israel, inspired from an early age to dedicate themselves to building and defending their new country. He was one of the first *sabras* to serve in senior government positions, create military policy and strategy, and plan for the protection and defense of Israel. These accomplishments were especially significant in light of the challenges that would face the young nation as it moved into the future.

CHAPTER THREE

Young Patriots

Hannah Senesh
1921 - 1944

> *There are people whose brilliance continues to light the world though they are no longer among the living.*
> — Hannah Senesh

Hannah Senesh sacrificed her life for the cause of Jewish freedom. She was just twenty-three years old when she died. Born in Budapest in 1921 she grew up in a loving home filled with books, music, and plays. Her father, Bela Senesh, was a famous journalist and playwright, and it is from him that Hannah inherited her love of writing. She demonstrated her own literary talent at an early age, keeping a diary from age thirteen until shortly before her death.

Born into an assimilated family, she learned little about Judaism during her childhood. Her father died when she was only six years old and she felt his loss very deeply. Hannah was very close with her mother, Katherine, with whom she lived, along with her brother, George.

Despite the fact that Judaism was not emphasized in her home life, Hannah's diary entries show that she was very concerned about the rising anti-Semitism in Europe. She was a brilliant student, at the

Senesh relaxes at home in Palestine

top of her high school class. Because of discrimination against the Jews in Hungary, her family was forced to pay triple the tuition to her school in order for her to be admitted.

Official anti-Semitism grew and was openly institutionalized in Hungary, as when anti-Jewish legislation was passed by the Hungarian government. At seventeen, Hannah was elected president of the high school's literary society, but was informed that she could not take office since "a Jew could not serve as president." Hannah chronicled the events in her diary:

> *You have to be someone exceptional to fight anti-Semitism...only now am I beginning to see what it really means to be a Jew in a Christian society, but I don't mind at all. It is because we have to struggle, because it is more difficult for us to reach our goal that we develop outstanding qualities. Had I been born a Christian, every profession would be open to me.*

> *I've become a Zionist. This word stands for a tremendous number of things. To me it means, in short, that I now consciously and strongly feel I am a Jew, and am proud of it. My primary aim is to go to Palestine, to work for it.*

Rejecting conversion to Christianity, both Hannah and her brother became Zionists and immigrated to Israel in 1939. She began her studies in agriculture at *Kibbutz Nahalal* in the

Jewish parachutist training in the fields of the Jezreel Valley (1944)

Galilee. Two years later she moved to *Kibbutz Sedot Yam* where she wrote one of her most powerful poems, *Toward Caesarea*, or, as it is more commonly known, *My God, My God [Eli, Eli].*

Near the end of 1942, worried about her mother who was still in Hungary, she joined the British Army so she could enlist in the Haganah and volunteer to be parachuted into Europe. The Haganah organized an undercover unit of parachutists and Hannah was selected to train as part of this group. Their mission was to help the Allied efforts in Europe and establish contact with partisan fighters in an attempt to assist besieged Jewish communities and organize the resistance. She went through training in Egypt, along with one hundred and ten other young men and women. Only thirty-seven were actually dropped. Of those thirty-seven young Jewish fighters, twelve were captured and seven were executed by Germans.

On March 13, 1944, Hannah parachuted into Yugoslavia where she camped with Marshall Tito's troops. During this short stay she wrote her poem, *Blessed is the Match*, in which her idealism and commitment to her cause are joyously celebrated.

During the peak of Jewish deportation from Hungary, on June 7, 1944, she crossed the border and was met by an alleged guide who was actually a traitor. By this time, the Germans were occupying Hungary. Hannah was betrayed by the "guide," arrested by the Hungarian police and handed over to the Gestapo.

Senesh carried a radio transmitter and her captors wanted the code. Despite enduring five months of incarceration and extreme torture, she refused to reveal any information or the code. A comrade wrote about her: "Her behavior before members of the Gestapo and SS was quite remarkable. She always stood up to them, warning them plainly of the bitter fate they would suffer after their defeat. Curiously, these wild animals, in which every spark of humanity had been extinguished, felt awed in the presence of this refined, fearless young girl."

In a secret court proceeding, Hannah was convicted of treason against Hungary and on November 7, 1944, she was sentenced to execution by a firing squad. Hannah Senesh was one of seven young people from this group executed by Germans. At her execution she refused a blindfold, staring squarely at her executioners and her fate.

Hannah's last note to her mother, written in her prison cell just prior to her execution on November 8, was heart wrenching: "Dearest Mother, I don't know what to

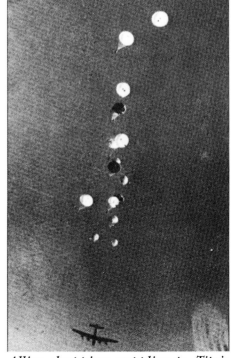
Allies dropping supplies to Tito's resistance forces (1944)

say—only this: a million thanks, and forgive me, if you can. You know well why words aren't necessary. With love forever. Your daughter, Hannah."

Her final courageous words to her imprisoned friends were: "Continue on the way, don't be deterred. Continue the struggle 'til the end, until the day of liberty comes, the day of victory for our people." In Israel and throughout Zionist circles her life became a symbol of strength, valor, and sacrifice, truly an inspiration to patriots everywhere.

In 1950, Hannah Senesh's remains and those of her six fellow paratroopers were sent to Israel. They were buried together in the military cemetery on Mount Herzl, Jerusalem. Senesh's diary and poems were published in Hebrew in 1945. They also have been translated and published in several other languages, including Hungarian.

In a fitting though bittersweet footnote, on November 5, 1993, Hannah Senesh's family in Israel received a copy of the Hungarian military court's verdict exonerating Senesh of the treason charges for which she was executed. Israel's Prime Minister Yitzhak Rabin, attending the Tel Aviv ceremony where the document was turned over to the family, noted solemnly that for Hannah "there is little use for the new verdict. Nor does it offer much comfort to her family. But historic *Justice* is also a value and the new verdict ... represents a measure of reason triumphing over evil."

Hannah Senesh's words of hope and inspiration are memorialized in many of her poems and songs, especially this beautiful prayer:

> *God—may there be no end*
> *To sea, to sand*
> *Water's splash*
> *Lightning's flash,*
> *The prayer of man.*

Jewish women begin training in the Auxilliary Territorial Service (1942)

NILI

The Strength of Israel will not lie....   I Samuel 15:29

The situation in Palestine in 1914 at the start of World War I presented a striking contrast between the groups living there. The Jews actively were supporting their passionate affinity for *Eretz Yisrael* by striving to develop the country while, conversely, the Arabs seemed unaware of Palestine as a political and geographical entity. To the young proponents of the Zionist dream, the meaning of Turkey's entry into the war on the side of Germany was clear from the outset. It was an historic opportunity to defeat the Turkish Empire and break its tyrannical hold on Palestine.

Jewish activists decided they must position themselves on the side of the British, against their mutual enemy—the Turkish regime—in their effort to restore the Jewish people to their homeland. The Jews had no sovereign power and no national base of operations. They were a collection of minority communities scattered throughout the world. Worldwide they were, in fact, fighting as citizens in the armies on both sides. Yet out of the carnage of World War I, there emerged a new phenomenon—an urgent hunger for Jewish independence and a willingness to sacrifice for *Eretz Yisrael*.

Aaron Aaronsohn, one of the Jewish leaders living in Palestine at this time, was responsible for a significant contribution to the conduct of the Allied campaign in Palestine. A brilliant and versatile man, by 1914 Aaronsohn had won worldwide fame as a scientist for his discovery of wild wheat. He also was chosen by the Turkish government to direct the campaign against the plague of locusts that ravaged the region during the first year of the war.

At this time, Jews in Palestine were being terrorized and deported under the Turkish regime, and it seemed impossible to fight this tyranny. The leaders of the modest Jewish community were frustrated by the futility of the circumstances and they struggled against feelings of resignation. Aaronsohn, convinced that a British victory was vital for the Jewish future, organized the NILI group—an intelligence service to support the British behind the Turkish lines.

NILI, a secret pro-British spying organization, operated in Syria and Palestine from 1915 to 1919 under the leadership of Aaron Aaronsohn, his sister Sarah Aaronsohn, and their friends, Avshalom

Zionist commission arrives in Palestine with Aaron Aaronsohn (leaning against rail on train)

Feinberg, Yosef Lishansky and Na'aman Belkind. The name "NILI" consists of the initial letters of the Hebrew verse *Nezah Yisrael Lo Yeshaker*, which translates to "the Strength of Israel will not lie." (I Samuel 15:29). The phrase also served as the group's password.

Angry about the Turks' treatment of the Jewish population and fearing a fate similar to that of the Turkish extermination of 2,000,000 Armenians, the young NILI pioneers concluded that the establishment of a new Jewish homeland depended on Palestine being taken over by Great Britain.

Aaronsohn's knowledge of the terrain in all its aspects—population, climate, water and transport problems—was unique. It positioned Aaronsohn successfully to direct NILI and also to serve as an essential advisor to British headquarters in preparation for the approaching invasion of Palestine, to be led by Commander-in-Chief General Edmund H. H. Allenby. Throughout that invasion and also the war, a stream of vital current military information came from NILI.

In January 1917, Feinberg and Lishansky, disguised as Bedouin tribesmen, attempted to reach Egypt to contact the British. They were attacked by the Bedouins and Feinberg was killed near the British front in Sinai. Lishansky was wounded but found his way to the British lines, where he joined Aaronsohn. A British boat took Lishansky to the Egyptian coast, and in February 1917 contact was established between the espionage center in Atlit (near Haifa) and British intelligence in Egypt. These connections were maintained by sea for several months and the British received crucial information collected by the group.

Sarah Aaronsohn and Yosef Lishansky

The price paid by Aaronsohn's group, however, was extremely high. Some months later, in September 1917, the Turks uncovered the NILI network by intercepting a carrier pigeon sent from Atlit to Egypt, which provided them with proof of espionage. Two of NILI's leaders, Na'aman Belkind and Yosef Lishansky, were hanged in Damascus; many of the others were imprisoned and tortured. Among them was Aaronsohn's sister Sarah, who had served as his deputy. During a respite from torture, she committed suicide.

Her brother, Aaron, had been sent by Chaim Weizmann on a political and public relations mission to the United States; it was there that Aaron learned of his sister's tragic death. He returned to Palestine in the spring of 1918 with the Zionist Commission. When he died in an air accident on May 15, 1919, NILI was disbanded.

Between 1915 and 1919, intelligence gathered and transmitted by NILI proved indispensable. British General Gribbon expressed the opinion that in the critical battle for Beersheba alone, the secret information saved 30,000 British lives. Even more explicit were Allenby's own words regarding Aaron Aaronsohn: "He was mainly responsible for the formation of my Field Intelligence Organization behind the Turkish lines."

It is not possible to express the incredible courage displayed by these young pioneers. They took risks that went beyond what anyone could have asked of them. They volunteered to fight for a nation that was not theirs, in an effort to redeem their country—the Land of Israel from a fanatic, oppressive Turkish regime.

They lived under the cover of darkness, many times in disguise, with the most basic primitive methods of warfare available to them, including the use of carrier pigeons for communication. They withstood torture; they were forced to watch as their friends and close relatives were being persecuted and killed. But they would not succumb. They stood tall, they fought with relentless conviction, and in the end, they made the ultimate sacrifice in defense of their countrymen—their brothers and sisters. Sarah Aaronsohn was twenty-seven and Na'aman Belkind, Avshalom Feinberg, and Yosef Lishansky were twenty-eight years old when they who had lived as pioneers died as heroes.

Aaron Aaronsohn
1876 - 1919

This land could be made to blossom like the rose by Jewish skill and industry.

— Aaron Aaronsohn

When he was only six Aaron Aaronsohn's parents took him to *Eretz Yisrael*—a trip that profoundly influenced both his and his sister Sarah's life. Though he was born in Bacau, Romania, he grew up in *Zikhron Ya'akov*, a community in Palestine that his father helped to establish. Aaron felt strongly about his Jewish foundation and his ties to the land.

He studied agriculture at Grignon College in France, where he received his degree in agronomy. When he returned to Palestine in 1895, he was employed as an agronomist by Baron Edmond de Rothschild at *Metulla*. Rothschild first became involved in Jewish affairs after the pogroms in Russia in the 1880s, when he became interested in the development work of the settlers in *Eretz Yisrael*. The early settlements were faced with financial ruin, and Rothschild was approached to provide aid. He lent his assistance to both *Rishon Le Zion* and *Zikhron Ya'akov*. Although Rothschild contributed greatly to the settlement efforts in *Zikhron Ya'akov*, he and Aaronsohn did not agree on some issues, and Aaronsohn left the employ of Rothschild.

The young scientist did extensive explorations in Palestine and neighboring countries, and started a bureau to do technical and agricultural surveys. In 1906, he discovered specimens of wild wheat at *Rosh Pinah*, in the Galilee. This innovation brought him worldwide acclaim among scientists and agriculturists.

Aaronsohn's discovery of wild wheat caused a sensation in the botanical world. This breakthrough and his articles in European journals gave him eminent status in the scientific community. In 1909, he visited the United States at the invitation of the American Ministry of Agriculture. With the support of American Jews, Aaronsohn founded an agricultural research station in Atlit, just south of Haifa. It was here that he built a rich library, collected geological and botanical samples, and inspected crops.

Aaron Aaronsohn is invited by the pasha to defend Palestine against a plague of locusts which descended on the settlements (1914)

As a result of his strong ties to the United States, in 1915 he was appointed as one of a three-member committee to allocate American financial aid being sent to *Eretz Yisrael*. The region at that time was controlled by the Turkish Ottoman Empire, which became part of the Axis with Germany in World War I.

In 1914, the local Turkish pasha appointed Aaronsohn to be chief inspector in an attempt to control a plague of locusts that had attacked Palestine and Syria. While serving in this position, Aaronsohn was exposed to the terrible corruption rampant among Turkish officials. He was a horrified observer of the massacre of masses of Armenians by the Turks. Compounding these atrocities, Turkish rulers persecuted Jewish settlers and actively opposed the Zionist movement, which was gaining momentum. The corruption he encountered during his work with the Ottoman authorities—the persecution of Jewish settlers and the Armenian massacre—convinced Aaronsohn that only liberation from the Turks would enable progress for the Jewish settlements and the entire *yishuv*.

Aaron Aaronsohn and Avshalom Feinberg, his assistant at the agricultural experiment station, organized a small group of activists, consisting mainly of family and friends. How ironic that this man, who was raised and trained as an agronomist, dedicated to soil management and crop production, found himself compelled to fight for the right of human beings to live in freedom with dignity.

The secret intelligence group they organized was known as "NILI." The group was established for the purpose of assisting the British forces under General Edmund H.H. Allenby to conquer Palestine, an action that ultimately would help in realizing Zionist objectives. NILI believed that the future of the Jews depended on Palestine being taken over by Britain; consequently, NILI members became involved in espionage as allies with the British against the Ottoman Empire. "NILI" is an acronym based on a phrase in the Hebrew Bible: "The Strength of Israel does not lie."

In February 1917, communication was well established between NILI and the British command in Egypt. The intelligence and strategic plans that NILI collected were vital to British command in their effort to defeat the Turkish army. Aaronsohn, with valuable information gained from NILI members, helped British headquarters in Cairo plan the campaign for the invasion of Palestine.

Inside the Aaronsohn home in Zikhron Ya'akov

During Passover in 1917, the Jewish population of Jaffa and Tel Aviv were expelled, and Aaronsohn tried to arouse public opinion worldwide. Chaim Weizmann sent Aaronsohn on a political campaign to generate support in the United States. It was there that Aaronsohn was informed that the NILI organization had

The Aaronsohn family at Zikhron Ya'akov (Aaron is standing in the top center, Sarah is sitting in the center)

been discovered by the Ottoman authorities. He was shocked and heartbroken to learn of the tragic death of his sister, Sarah, while she was imprisoned by the Turks.

In 1918, Aaronsohn worked in conjunction with the Zionist Commission in Palestine and, in 1919, he cooperated with the Zionist delegation to the Paris Peace Conference, dealing with the problem of the Palestine boundaries. On May 15, 1919, on a flight from London to Paris, he was killed in a plane crash over the English Channel. He was forty-three years old. Aaronsohn's research and his exploration diaries were published posthumously, ensuring his influence for years to come.

Letterhead of the agricultural experimental station near Haifa

Sarah Aaronsohn
1890 - 1917

Anyone who calls himself a man would be proud to belong to NILI.

— Sarah Aaronsohn

The Aaronsohns were a family of pioneers who emigrated to *Eretz Yisrael* from Romania in 1882. Sarah's father, Ephraim Fischel, was a talented farmer and one of the founders of the settlement *Zikhron Ya'akov*. Sarah had two brothers, Aaron and Alexander.

Sarah Aaronsohn was one of the leaders of the clandestine group, NILI. (Israelis often refer to Sarah as the "heroine of NILI.") She was born and died in *Zikhron Ya'akov* in Palestine, which was then part of the Ottoman Empire. She lived briefly in Constantinople (Istanbul), soon returning home to Palestine. In her travels she was shocked to witness genocidal acts by the Turks against the Armenians who were being massacred because they were not Muslims.

In sympathy with the enemies of the Ottoman Empire, Sarah, along with her brother Aaron and their friend Avshalom Feinberg, formed NILI, an organization that aimed to assist the

Rivka Aaronsohn (far left) next to her sister Sarah at the home of Dr. Navtali Weitz in Jerusalem (1911)

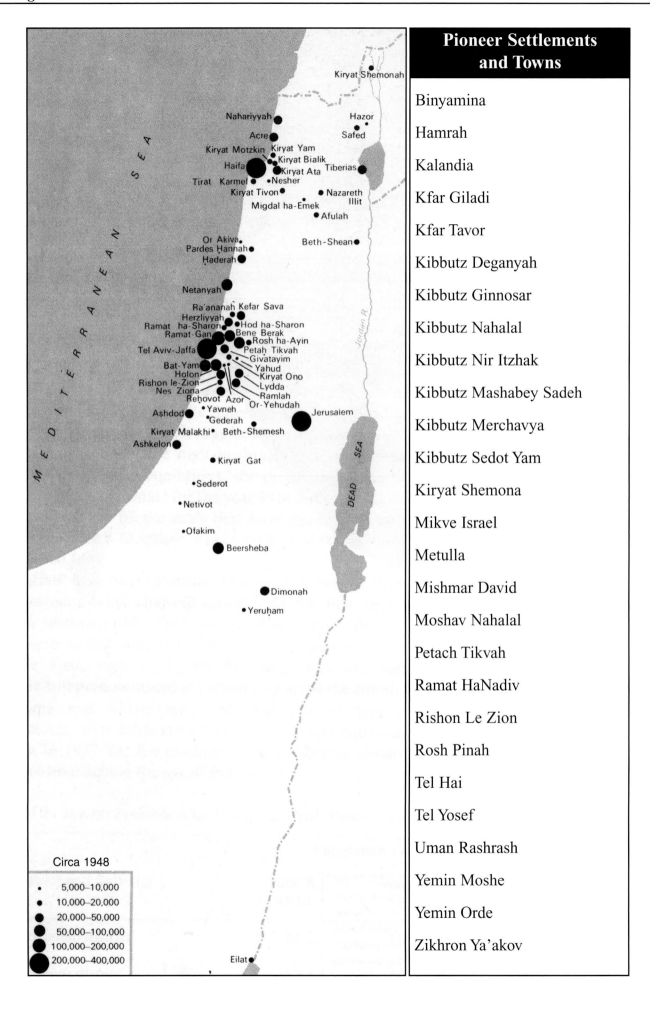

Pioneer Settlements and Towns

Binyamina

Hamrah

Kalandia

Kfar Giladi

Kfar Tavor

Kibbutz Deganyah

Kibbutz Ginnosar

Kibbutz Nahalal

Kibbutz Nir Itzhak

Kibbutz Mashabey Sadeh

Kibbutz Merchavya

Kibbutz Sedot Yam

Kiryat Shemona

Mikve Israel

Metulla

Mishmar David

Moshav Nahalal

Petach Tikvah

Ramat HaNadiv

Rishon Le Zion

Rosh Pinah

Tel Hai

Tel Yosef

Uman Rashrash

Yemin Moshe

Yemin Orde

Zikhron Ya'akov

British fight the Turks. These young pioneers were convinced that it was through this alliance with the British that the Jews could obtain their independence. Sarah was in charge of operations in *Zikhron Ya'akov*, passing their information to British agents.

The NILI group succeeded in collecting vital intelligence for the British. In the spring of 1917, while Sarah was on a secret mission to Egypt to visit Aaron and the British Command, her brother pleaded with her to remain in Egypt rather than endanger her life further. She refused, knowing she was needed at the settlement, and she returned to Palestine to continue leading NILI.

In the fall of 1917, the Turks discovered NILI's operations. In October they surrounded *Zikhron*

Sarah Aaronsohn pictured with her NILI colleague Yosef Lishansky in Zikhron Ya'akov (1917)

Ya'akov and captured and arrested Sarah in her home. In an effort to obtain information about the group, the Turks brutally tortured her for four days. She heroically endured this cruelty and disclosed no secrets. To escape further torture, she shot and killed herself. Other prisoners taken were incarcerated in Damascus, sentenced to death and hung. With the death of Sarah's brother, Aaron, in an airplane crash in May 1919, NILI was disbanded.

Within a month after Sarah's death, the British issued the Balfour Declaration, supporting the concept of a Jewish homeland. Less than two months later, Jerusalem was in British control. General Allenby, leader of the British forces, declared that NILI had played a crucial part in their victory over the Turks.

There have been many women in the history of Israel that have been heroes of the Jewish people, from the days of Ruth, Esther and Sarah in biblical times, to the many brave women who today fight alongside the men in the Israeli army. Sarah Aaronsohn, the coordinator of the pro-British underground organization, NILI, has become a symbol for the modern Hebrew-speaking woman, a patriot and Jewish heroine.

Na'aman Belkind
1889 - 1917

Jewish history through the ages has a rich record of martyrs who sacrificed their lives for the principles of right and justice, in defense of the Jewish people and the Jewish homeland. Many of these people played instrumental roles in laying the foundations for independence and the establishment of a Jewish state.

Acceptance of these goals brought with it the duties and responsibilities of a mature

Building the road to Ein Harod (1920)

nation. Those fighting for the cause of a Jewish state knew that their task was to free the land from foreign domination and rescue Jews from besieged war-torn Europe. Representative of those active during World War I were Na'aman Belkind, his cousin, Avshalom Feinberg, and their friend, Yosef Lishansky, all members of NILI, the pro-British intelligence service aimed at ejecting the Turks from Palestine.

Avshalom Feinberg was one of the few early pioneers of Israel actually born in the Holy Land, in the village of *Gederah* in 1889. He went to school in *Rishon Le Zion* and later worked in the local wine cellars. Feinberg belonged to a family of pioneer settlers that included his brothers, Yosef and Israel.

Feinberg, like many of the early pioneers, traveled outside of Palestine for international experience, and completed his education in Paris. Leaving Europe, Feinberg returned to work at the agricultural settlement in Atlit, *Zikhron Ya'akov*, which had been established by Aaron

Farmers in Zikhron Ya'akov (1900)

Avshalom Feinberg
1889 - 1917

Avshalom Feinberg (seated, right) as a youngster at his home in Hadera in the 1890s

Aaronsohn. Feinberg and Aaronsohn formed the intelligence network NILI to support the British, and ultimately to assist in the creation of a Jewish state.

Na'aman Belkind was the nephew of BILU founder Israel Belkind, and the son of BILU pioneer Shimshon Belkind. Na'aman was born in *Eretz Yisrael*, grew up in the BILU community of *Gederah*, and, like his cousin Avshalom Feinberg, also worked in the wine cellars of *Rishon Le Zion*. Na'aman joined his cousin, Avshalom, and his brother, Eytan, in working with NILI.

Building a kibbutz shelter for protection(1937)

Yosef Lishansky
1890 - 1917

In 1915, Feinberg reached Egypt on an American ship where he made contact with British naval intelligence. The British surreptitiously returned him to Palestine to enable him to continue his work. Throughout 1916 and 1917, he and other members of NILI transmitted important intelligence information to the British.

Yosef Lishansky, one of the key agents for NILI, was at the settlement *Zikhron Ya'akov* in October 1917 when the Turks surrounded the community. Lishansky managed to escape and sought refuge with the *Hashomer*, the watchman organization charged with guarding the Jewish colonies. Members of the *Hashomer* disapproved of his political ideas and felt he placed the settlement in danger. Before they could turn him over to the Turkish authorities in an attempt to save the settlement, Lishansky escaped.

In 1917, after working in NILI for several years, Feinberg and his friend Lishansky, disguised as Bedouin, traveled back to Egypt on foot. Bedouin raiders found them near the British front lines in the Sinai in El Arish in 1917 and handed them over to the Turkish military. They were then transferred to Damascus and publicly hung. On hearing the news of their deaths, Belkind traveled to Egypt to look into the circumstances of the hanging. He also was captured by the Bedouin in the Sinai, brought by the Turks to Damascus, convicted of spying, and then hanged. Lishansky and Belkind were buried beside each other in *Rishon Le Zion* in October 1919. Sixty years later, in 1979, the remains of Lishansky were reinterred in Jerusalem on Mt. Herzl.

Feinberg's remains were found in the Sinai desert following the Six Day War and also reburied in Mt. Herzl Cemetery in Jerusalem. It was known that he was carrying date seeds with him on his trip to Egypt when he was ambushed. Those who located him planted some of those seeds over his remains, and a palm tree now grows there, a symbol of Feinberg's heroism.

Avshalom Feinberg, Na'aman Belkind, and Yosef Lishansky, became martyrs in the Zionist mission to establish a homeland for the Jewish people. Their letters and memoirs offer an insight into the mindset of the first generation born to the Jewish settlement pioneers. These brave and courageous heroes were among the many young people who fought and sacrificed their lives for the creation of the State of Israel.

Bringing wine barrels to winery at Zikhron Ya'akov (1910)

Chaim Arlozoroff
1899 - 1933

We need all the power we can muster in order to survive, to keep our identity, our culture, our being and our future.
— Chaim Arlozoroff

Arlozoroff seated fifth from the left, to the right of Weizmann at Arab-Jewish rapprochement in Jerusalem (1933)

Chaim Arlozoroff was a man of vision and action, a shrewd observer of sociological and economic process. He was an analytical writer and thinker, and composed poetry as a hobby. His short life ended in one of the most heartrending stories of the pioneers in the developing history of Israel.

Arlozoroff was born in the Ukraine in Russia, the grandson of Rabbi Eliezer Arlozoroff, the Rabbi of Romni of the Ukraine, author of numerous books on Jewish law. Arlozoroff's father was a wealthy merchant. In an effort to escape anti-Semitism and the pogroms of 1905, when Chaim was a child the family moved to Germany, where Chaim received his education. He studied at the University of Berlin, receiving a doctorate in economics. His early life in Germany gave him insight into and an understanding of the German mentality that had a vital impact in the years ahead.

In 1918, Arlozoroff joined *Hapoel*, a key Zionist movement, as its newspaper editor. He was the youngest member elected to the organization's executive board. He immigrated to Palestine in 1923. Three years later, when he was only twenty-seven years old, he joined the group representing Zionists at the League of Nations. In 1929, he was elected secretary of the political party now known as *Histadrut*.

In 1930, Arlozoroff brought together two large Zionist groups, creating the *Mapai* political party. He served as the editor of its journal, and was elected to the *Mapai* executive board. Arlozoroff's political astuteness led to his appointment as leader of the Jewish Agency. At thirty-two, he was universally acknowledged as a "foreign minister" of state in the making. He envisioned the return of the Jewish people to "Zion"—to their soil. There, and only there, he felt, could Jews prosper and grow. Like other Zionists of that time, his dream was a thriv-

Arlozoroff with Colonial Secretary Philip Lister (to his left) and Sir Arthur Wycoff (1933)

ing Jewish culture that would replace other unorganized groups in *Eretz Yisrael*.

Arlozoroff was a pioneer confident in his beliefs and flexible in his political philosophy if the circumstances warranted it. In his early years in Palestine he became a good friend of

Front page newspaper report of Arlozoroff murder, June 18, 1933

Chaim Weizmann. They fundamentally were in agreement in their political ideology, both supporting cooperation with the British. They believed that the British, if successful in defeating the Turks, would assist the Jews in their quest for independence. They also concluded that it was necessary to understand the Arabs' position in the region. However, as time progressed, the situation in Palestine became more hostile from both the British and the Arab camps, compelling Arlozoroff to reverse his thinking on both these issues.

In 1933, facing the grim rise of Hitler, Arlozoroff negotiated an agreement with the German government to enable some Jews to leave Germany with much of their property. This program was called *Ha'avara* [Transfer Agreement] and operated using a formula that would allow the German Jews to transfer some of their assets to Palestine, critically important as the Jews rushed to flee Germany. The Germans agreed to the program in a frantic effort to end a worldwide Jewish boycott of

Arlozoroff and his family (1931)

German products. The Jewish leaders reluctantly agreed to negotiate with the "enemy" in a desperate attempt to help as many Jews as possible escape Germany and enter Palestine.

Tragically, the promise of this brilliant and accomplished young man was not to come to fruition. Chaim Arlozoroff's life ended in a violent murder as he walked with his wife on the seashore of Tel Aviv. The killers were never found, and the case remains a mystery. Many theories were suggested, many accusations made; some purported the assailants to be fanatic revisionists, others said they were local Arab assassins. The murder caused serious internal friction among the Jewish settlers and in particular among the different political factions.

The murder of Arlozoroff robbed the Jewish people of one of their most gifted and exciting Zionist leaders. Much can be learned about his contribution to the pioneer spirit from his writings. As a result of his influence, the Jewish Agency flourished. Many of the early ideas in the Jewish state regarding government land ownership and inherent social structures were initiated through his inspired action. He was one of the most popular personalities in the *Mapai* political party and was considered one of the bright young men who might someday be prime minister. His loss was felt deeply by the people of Israel. Chaim Arlozoroff wrote poignantly of his vision of peace:

> *The Arabs, too, will have to understand that they have no other way except the politics of peace, that the determination of the Hebrew nation to build its national home in Eretz Yisrael is irrevocable. They should know that the more this land is soaked with Jewish blood, the more obstinate will be our will to strike roots in it.*

CHAPTER FOUR

Zionism — From the Beginning

Theodor Herzl
1860 - 1904

If you will it, it is not a dream.

— Theodor Herzl

Herzl, at his home in Vienna, preparing for First Zionist Congress (1897)

Writer and statesman, founder of national Zionism and the World Zionist Organization, Theodor Herzl is considered to be the "father of Zionism." His lifework centered on the political resurrection of the Jewish people. Through his efforts, the "Jewish problem" was elevated into an international political issue, an injustice requiring resolution.

Herzl was born in Budapest, Hungary in 1860 and educated in the spirit of the German-Jewish teachings of the time, which included an appreciation for secular culture. Although he had virtually no Jewish identity growing up, ironically his personality and charisma catapulted him into serving as one of the great Jewish leaders of modern history. He looked the part—tall, handsome, with a full but perfectly trimmed beard, a worldly aura about him. Theodor Herzl exuded confidence and leadership.

Though raised in the Hungarian capital, Herzl closely identified with the cosmopolitan cultural city of Vienna, where his family moved in 1878. His father gained and lost most of his fortune, convincing young Herzl to avoid business and instead to pursue a literary career. His mother, a dedicated German culturalist, contributed to his worldly manner and intellectual confidence.

Urged by his parents, Herzl studied law at the University of Vienna, in 1884 earning a doctorate of law. At the university he adapted his personal philosophy to the world around him. He became aware of anti-Semitism in student life on campus and felt repulsed by Jewish students who ignored or rejected their background. This confrontation with anti-Semitism altered his life and transformed the destiny of the Jews in the twentieth century.

Despite his law degree, the legal profession did not appeal to Herzl. With his father's financial support he turned to journalism and writing. Working as a correspondent for the influential liberal Vienna newspaper *Neue Freie Presse* in Paris, he again encountered the ugliness of anti-Semitism.

Herzl covered the notoriously anti-Semitic trial and court martial of Alfred Dreyfus, a Jewish French army officer, who was divested of his rank in a humiliating public ceremony in January 1895. Dreyfus was accused unjustly of treason. Herzl watched in shock as the French mob shouted "death to the Jews." This experience infuriated him and was a turning point in his life. His dream of a Jewish homeland was born. Herzl wrote, "what made me into a Zionist was the Dreyfus case."

He regarded the "Jewish problem" as a social issue and wrote a drama, *The Ghetto*, in 1894, in which assimilation and conversion were not acceptable solutions. His hope was that *The Ghetto* would stimulate debate and resolution, based on mutual tolerance and respect between Jews and Christians. He believed that because anti-Semitism was a "stable and immutable factor in human society," assimilation would not resolve the issue.

Herzl mulled over the idea of Jewish sovereignty and, despite derision from Jewish leaders, published *Der Judenstaat* [*The Jewish State*] in 1896. The pamphlet was translated into

The city walls of Jerusalem, including the citadel of King David (1898)

Herzl and his companions (wearing white helmets) with Jewish family next to their home on Mamillah Road in Jerusalem (October 28, 1898)

a dozen languages and became the "bible" for Zionism. Herzl wrote in this masterpiece: "The world will be freer by our liberty, richer by our wealth, greater by our greatness." Within months of the original printing of five hundred copies, the article received worldwide attention.

Herzl's position was that the essence of the "Jewish problem" was not individual but national, and that Jews could gain worldwide acceptance only if they were seen as "one people." He believed that the problem would be transformed positively by establishing a Jewish state. He recognized that this would require the sanction of the community of international powers. Originally he wrote that it did not matter where Jews went, but ultimately he realized that a national home in Palestine was the answer.

In *The Jewish State* Herzl wrote:

> *No human being is wealthy or powerful enough to transplant a people from one place of residence to another. Only an idea can achieve that. The State idea surely has that power. The Jews have dreamed this princely dream throughout the long night of their history. "Next year in Jerusalem" is our age-old motto. It is now a matter of showing that the vague dream can be transformed into a clear and glowing idea.*

Herzl entered a new era in his life—persuading others and organizing what became the World Zionist Organization (WZO). Using his impressive writing skills he convinced wealthy and influential Jews to support his ideas. A loosely confederated organization called *Hovevei Zion* already existed in the Eastern European countries. This organization was preparing young Jews to settle the Land of Israel as agriculturists, and at the time it had the support of many wealthy Jews.

Temporarily ambivalent about which country or territory was given to the Jews, Herzl's greater interest was that the Jews settle in a region operating under their own authority. In this way, they would eliminate the egregious phenomenon of anti-Semitism. Herzl's genius for persuasion slowly began to bear fruit. Gradually the initial opposition to established Zionist organizations began to erode while Herzl's popularity increased among the masses. Many people admired his ideas on organization and financial planning that would fund the Jewish settlements. He proposed generating capital through a company owned by stockholders, whose purpose was to implement the goals of Zionism.

With financial support and the backing of Zionist groups and the masses, Herzl convened the First Zionist Congress in Basel, Switzerland on August 29, 1897, just three years after the Dreyfus trial. He rented the Basel Municipal Hall and asked his assistant David Wolffsohn to display a welcoming banner to greet the delegates. Wolffsohn used the blue and white colors from the traditional prayer shawl and included the Star of David, thus creating a preliminary early version of the national flag of Israel.

To instill a sense of the magnitude of the occasion, Herzl requested that the delegates dress in formal attire for the opening session. Two representatives from New York and one from Baltimore traveled by sea and train to arrive in Basel in time for the historic event. There were two hundred and eight delegates in attendance along with twenty-six correspondents and many non-Jewish Swiss supporters.

On the day before the opening of the Congress, in a considerate gesture to the Orthodox delegates, Herzl attended the Basel synagogue at the invitation of the city's first rabbi, Arthur Cohn. Herzl was called to the Torah, and having memorized the blessing, he performed without out error. Herzl wrote in his diary "reciting the Hebrew words of the blessing caused me more anxiety than my welcoming and closing address [to the Congress]."

Herzl and his Zionist delegation in Jerusalem before meeting the kaiser on November 2, 1898

On Sunday morning August 29,1897, Theodor Herzl walked to the podium. Some delegates reached out to kiss his hand; others wept. Successive waves of applause prevented him from speaking. The cheering lasted for over fifteen minutes. For three days various factions argued their platforms, and finally the Basel Plan was approved. At this moment modern Zionism found its voice.

The Basel program declared: "Zionism seeks to establish a

home for the Jewish people in Palestine secured under public law." At the Congress, the World Zionist Organization (WZO) was established as the political arm of the Jewish people, and Herzl was elected its first president.

Six Zionist Congresses were convened by Herzl between 1897 and 1902. It was at these meetings that the preliminary tools for Zionist activism were forged: the Jewish National Fund and the movement's newspaper *Die Welt*. After the First Congress, an international Zionist Congress was held nearly every year, and in 1936 the WZO, the center of Zionism, was transferred to Jerusalem.

Herzl worked diligently to find a territory for the Jews. The Sinai Desert and Cyprus were two territories under consideration. Then in 1903, the British offered Herzl Uganda.

(Bottom right) final photograph montage of Herzl and the kaiser. Photograph at left and top right make up the elements of the final photograph (1898)

At the time pogroms and oppression in Russia had reached a new high, a region was desperately needed, and Herzl felt that agreeing to Uganda was justified. He submitted the Uganda Plan to the Sixth Zionist Congress. The proposal aroused strong opposition and resentment. The Eastern European Jews regarded it as a betrayal of their dream to settle in the Land of Israel. So strong and hostile was the opposition that Herzl felt compelled to write his personal commitment to abandon the plan.

At the turn of the century, Palestine was a sleepy backwater of the Ottoman Empire. The region had been ruled from Constantinople (Istanbul) by the Turkish sultans for nearly five hundred years and was populated largely by Arab peasant farmers who never had heard of Zionism. Herzl and his followers paid little attention to the Arab population, and at first the Arabs knew little of Herzl's plans.

Some early communities of Jewish immigrants had been established in Palestine, and it was the intention of the Zionist leaders to build from this foundation. Meanwhile, thousands of additional Jewish immigrants were arriving in the primitive and desolate land, fleeing a new wave of anti-Semitic pogroms in Russia, Ukraine and Poland. These immigrants urgently were needed for developing the new country, and the refugees were eager to settle in a land they felt was their birthright.

In an effort at diplomacy, in 1898 Herzl visited Turkish-controlled Palestine, stopping en route in Constantinople to meet with the sultan of the Ottoman Empire. He timed his trip to Palestine to coincide with Germany's Kaiser Wilhelm. He made overtures to both leaders, speaking eloquently about a homeland for the Jewish people. The purpose of the trip was to reinforce credibility for the Zionist movement— Herzl meeting with major heads of state.

Herzl was accompanied on this trip by several of his supporters, including David Wolffsohn. Herzl needed a photo of himself with the kaiser to highlight the importance of the movement, and Wolffsohn was the "trip photographer." While taking the requisite photo of Herzl and Kaiser Wilhelm, Wolffsohn was so excited that he cut Herzl out of the frame. Understandably upset, Herzl had his picture taken the following day and attached it to the kaiser's photo, creating a "montage" and thus effectively capturing the historic moment in a photograph that was used for decades.

A sapling planted by Herzl in 1898 in Motza outside of Jerusalem which initiated the tree planting tradition of the Jewish National Fund (JNF)

During this trip, Herzl initiated another important custom in Jewish history. He stopped in Motza, on the western edge of Jerusalem, to plant a cedar tree with his own hands. The Jewish National Fund continued this tradition of planting trees in Israel to this day, inspiring people everywhere to form a connection to the Jewish soil.

With political and organizational development progressing, Herzl continued writing, affecting people with the passion and vision of his thoughts. Although *The Jewish State* and his address to the First Congress lacked any religious reference, his famous remark that "the return to Zion would be preceded by a return to Judaism" added spiritual inspiration to the movement.

Herzl's literary work, *Altneuland* [*Old New Land*, 1902], is devoted to Zionism. In it he describes the future Jewish state as a "socialist utopia." A new society would rise in the Land of Israel on a cooperative basis using science and technology to develop the land. The key themes of the story are the love for Zion and the changes in life to be achieved by embracing the best efforts and ideals of every race and nation. Included were details about his ideas for the future state's political structure, immigration, social laws, diplomatic relations, fundraising efforts, and relations between religion and state. He was prophetic about a cultured modern Jewish city (Tel Aviv). This book made a deep impression on Jews at the time, impeccable in its detailed and comprehensive representation of the Zionist vision for the Land of Israel.

Herzl quickly realized that his faith in "princes" had been misplaced. The "Great Powers," the Turks, the anti-Semites and even most wealthy Jews were apparently not going to play their assigned roles in the drama for Jewish independence. But those from whom he expected the least, the Jews of Eastern Europe, gave him the most. They supported him passionately and completely; they corrected him when he veered away from the path to *Eretz Yisrael*. Herzl organized them for international political action, saying, "I gradually hounded them into the mood for a state."

Overwhelmed by the Russian Jews' loyalty to *Eretz Yisrael*, Herzl communicated this passion and dedication to the British. Prime Minister Arthur James Balfour never forgot the Uganda incident. Nor did David Lloyd George, the politically active solicitor who prepared articles for the Uganda project. He was the wartime British prime minister who authorized Lord Balfour to issue the Balfour Declaration in 1917, supporting the establishment of a Jewish homeland in Palestine. Herzl did not live to see the British government's conferral of a charter in 1917. It was Chaim Weizmann, previously a heated opponent of Herzl's political ideas, who persuaded Balfour to issue the Declaration. It originated as a letter to the chairman of the British Zionists—Lord Rothschild, cousin of Baron Edmond.

The fierce struggles that Herzl had with the executive of the Zionist organizations ultimately proved too much for his health. He suffered from a heart ailment and, at only forty-four years old, died while seeking treatment. Although Herzl never lived to see his dreams fulfilled, his organizational skills moved the existing Zionist organizations from small ineffective groups to institutions supported worldwide.

When he died in 1904, Herzl's body was respectfully taken through Vienna, draped with a Zionist flag. A procession of 10,000 Jews followed his funeral carriage to the gravesite. Throughout Europe, from Vienna to Vilna, London to Odessa, streets and highways were packed with Jewish mourners. In 1949 Herzl's remains were reinterred in Jerusalem where they were buried on a hill, now called Mount Herzl.

More than any other thinker and politician, Herzl was directly responsible for the emergence of the State of Israel and is universally acknowledged as the state's true founder. One of his most prophetic statements was entered in his diary a few days after the close of the First Zionist Congress. On September 3, 1897, he wrote, "were I to sum up the Basel Congress in a word it would be this: in Basel I founded the Jewish State. If I said this out loud today, I would be answered by universal laughter. Perhaps in five years, and certainly in fifty, everyone will know it." On November 29, 1947, precisely fifty years after Herzl's prophecy, the United Nations' vote was announced, and the State of Israel became a reality.

Simple black gravestone of Theodor Herzl in Jerusalem

David Wolffsohn
1856 - 1914

We have a flag, and it is blue and white; {like} the tallit (prayer shawl) with which we wrap ourselves when we pray – that is our symbol.
— David Wolffsohn

David Wolffsohn was an eminent Zionist pioneer, known for many selfless contributions during his life but perhaps remembered most poignantly for designing the flag for the new State of Israel. His commitment to Zionism was strongly influenced by his close association with Theodor Herzl.

Born in 1856 in the Russian region of Lithuania, he received a traditional Jewish religious education. In order to avoid the barbaric custom of forced conscription of Jews into the czar's army, his parents reluctantly sent him out of the region to live with his brother. He studied at a Talmud Torah with one of the leading Zionist rabbis of the period and became a central figure in the *Hibbat Zion* movement.

As an adult, Wolffsohn moved from place to place. He found his vocation in the timber business, at first working for others, and then independently. His timber trade grew rapidly, making him financially prosperous. He was eager to support Zionism, and in 1893 he established the Cologne Association for the Development of Agriculture in the Land of Israel.

David Wolffsohn posing for picture (1908)

Wolffsohn's colleagues at the Zionist Congress (1903)

A man of great humility, Wolffsohn felt somewhat insecure among his contemporaries, believing that most of them had received a more formal and complete education than he had. Wolffsohn was strongly affected by Herzl's compelling and historic pamphlet, *The Jewish State*, which presented Herzl's plan for the creation of a Jewish homeland. He traveled to Vienna in 1896 to meet Herzl, and

Zionist friends join Wolffsohn for social outing

was captivated by this vibrant and energetic man, immediately pledging his total commitment to the goals of Zionism.

Wolffsohn's loyalty and acknowledgement of Herzl is well documented; what is not as well known is the caring and sensitive education that Herzl received from Wolffsohn about Jewish life and religious customs. On the occasion of the First Zionist Congress, Wolffsohn gave Herzl, the delegates, and the Jewish world two dramatic and lasting symbols—the blue and white flag of the Jewish nation, lovingly chosen from the colors of the *tallit*, and the ancient term "shekel," which was introduced to assess members' dues.

When Herzl went on an important journey to Constantinople and Palestine to meet Kaiser Wilhelm II and the Turkish sultan, Wolffsohn accompanied him. He was the official photographer for the trip and took the famous picture of Herzl and the kaiser. While taking the photo, he inadvertently omitted Herzl from the frame. Realizing the error, a single shot of Herzl was later photographed, and the two photos were metamorphosed into one, with the resulting montage of the two leaders released for Zionist public exposure.

Another of Wolffsohn's accomplishments was his role in establishing the Jewish Colonial Trust; later, he was elected the bank's first president. In this capacity he experienced some differences with Herzl, who attempted to include himself in the administration of the bank, despite his lack of financial experience. The Jewish Colonial Trust was the bank that Zionists used to

Wolffsohn (in the bow) with Herzl on excursion to Constantinople (1898)

mange their investments in Palestine. (The Jewish Colonial Trust was the official corporate name for Bank Leumi.)

When Herzl died in 1904, a huge vacuum existed in the Zionist organization. Max Nordau refused to take the reins, and although David Wolffsohn was next in line, he also declined. Ultimately, three men were chosen to lead the next Zionist Congress: Wolffsohn, Nordau and Otto Warburg. Eventually, Wolffsohn assumed the position of the second and sole president of the World Zionist Organization, strengthening the political and diplomatic priorities of his predecessor.

David Wolffsohn was a popular and respected leader, successfully positioning himself as a moderate among the many factions of Zionism. He wisely selected opponents as well as supporters to fill various positions and was able to bridge the gap between political and practical Zionists. He believed that this would have been Herzl's wish.

As with many great men, it was only after his death that David Wolffsohn's efforts and leadership were fully appreciated. He was called a "man of the people" who had come up through the ranks after many years of hard work. He had a special ability to persuade opposing factions to reach agreement by finding workable compromises and reaching middle ground. His life represented a successful synthesis of the Jewish cultures of both Eastern and Western Europe. David Wolffsohn died in Hamburg, Germany in 1914. In 1952 his remains were reinterred in Jerusalem next to his friend, Theodor Herzl.

Wolffsohn with Herzl at Jewish school in Smyrna (1898)

Zionist delegation in front of the Acropolis in Athens with David Wolffsohn sitting, far right (1898)

Max Nordau
1849 - 1923

Judaism is Zionism and Zionism is Judaism.

— Max Nordau

Max Nordau was a man truly ahead of his time. In his will in 1920 he wrote that Palestine should be settled by millions of Jews because of the danger inherent in Poland, Ukraine, Austria-Hungary, Germany and other European countries—that the Jewish population was destined to be eradicated if they had no homeland. As strikingly prophetic as his words were, early in the twentieth century there were virtually no Jews who took Nordau's warnings seriously.

Born in Budapest (the birthplace of Theodor Herzl), Nordau was the son of an Orthodox rabbi of Sephardic origin, and he received a traditional Jewish education. At age fourteen he published his first poem. Two years later he began writing as a theater critic. He remained an observant Jew until he was eighteen, and then became ambivalent about his religion.

He worked as a journalist, writing for many prominent newspapers from Vienna to Buenos Aires, but soon decided to change direction and study medicine. In 1875, Nordau received his university degree as a physician, settling in Paris in 1880. He practiced medicine, but it was in the literary field that his name ultimately would become well known. He was a perceptive thinker and social critic of society, religion, government, art and literature. Among his most famous publications are *The Conventional Lies of Our Civilization*, *Paradoxes*, and *Degeneration*.

Nordau first met Theodor Herzl in 1892. As Paris correspondents for German language newspapers, both witnessed anti-Semitism even more horrifying than the Dreyfus affair. In 1895, Herzl confided in Nordau his concept of a Jewish state. Nordau's enthusiastic endorse-

Nordau sits with Austrian Zionists at Seventh Zionist Congress in Basel (1905)

ment reinforced the credibility of Herzl's Zionist movement. With great eagerness Nordau promoted the idea of "political" Zionism and the immigration of large numbers of Diaspora Jews to *Eretz Yisrael*.

Nordau assisted Herzl in planning and organizing the First Zionist Congress in 1897 in Basel, Switzerland. He was Herzl's main lieutenant, and at the early Zionist Congresses his assessments and orations on world Jewish affairs became classics in Zionist literature. His writing was comprehensive and clear in its analysis.

Conscientiously, Nordau studied the Jewish situation in the world, both in the eastern and western regions. He described the physical and material difficulties

Nordau reviewing his speech for Congress

of the Jews in Eastern Europe, and compared them with the issues of those in the west. He wrote about the challenges of the assimilated Jews in Western Europe facing political and social anti-Semitism.

In an attempt to synthesize the needs of both cultures, Nordau created the Basel Program, presenting the premise of Zionism—the establishment of a Jewish nation. This document successfully managed to assuage the concerns of both groups, and delegates passed the Basel plan at the Congress. Nordau's service as vice president for the first six congresses and as president at the next four illustrated how highly people respected his leadership.

Addressing the First Zionist Congress on August 29, 1897, Nordau directed his words to people worldwide:

> *To Jewish distress no one can remain indifferent, neither Christian nor Jew. It is a great sin to let a race to whom even their worst enemies do not deny ability, degenerate in intellectual and physical distress. It is a sin against them and against the work of civilization, in the interest of which Jews have not been useless co-workers.*

At the Zionist Congress in 1911, with stunning accuracy he warned about the possibility of six million Jews vanishing because of the political situation in Europe. Nordau was convinced that only political Zionism could avert the tragedy. He was prophetic when he spoke in Berlin in 1899: "A day will come when Zionism will be needed by you proud Germans, as much as by those wretched East European Jews…. A day will come when you will beg for asylum in the land you now scorn."

Following Herzl's death, Nordau was offered but declined the position of president of the World Zionist Organization, preferring instead to serve as advisor to David Wolffsohn. He opposed the growing trend towards practical Zionism, instead remaining faithful to Herzl's political program.

Nordau remained true to Zionist ideals, although he detached himself from the Zionist organization, attending his last Zionist Congress in 1911. While living in Spain during World War I he endeavored to maintain contact with the movement. Chaim Weizmann attempted to bring him back into the organization, but Nordau remained outside the formal structure. In 1920 he had raised the idea of evacuating half a million Jews from Europe to Palestine, but no one took the idea seriously. His wish at the end of his life was to emigrate to *Eretz Yisrael*; unfortunately, his health was too fragile. He returned to Paris where he died in 1923. At his request he was reinterred in Tel Aviv in 1926.

Building the road to the Nordau neighborhood in Tel Aviv (1935)

Henrietta Szold
1860 - 1945

If not Zionism then nothing. I am more than ever convinced that our only salvation lies that way.

— Henrietta Szold

Henrietta Szold is acknowledged and honored as the founder of the women's Zionist organization, Hadassah. She struggled as a "grassroots" Jewish activist in search of spiritual and personal fulfillment as a woman, a Jew and an American. Szold symbolized a new identity for American Jewish women as community leaders in support of *Eretz Yisrael*. A role model, Szold seemed determined to achieve the ideal of a modern Jewish American woman, despite the restrictions and lack of opportunities available to women of her generation.

Henrietta Szold was born in Baltimore, Maryland in 1860. Shortly after her parents arrived in the United States, her father was appointed rabbi of Congregation *Oheb Shalom*. Szold was highly educated, growing up in a vibrant cultural environment that combined European, Jewish and American traditions. The eldest of five sisters, she became her father's most gifted student. She learned Hebrew, German, English, Judaism, and secular studies at a private school, conducted in the basement of the synagogue. She also learned more traditional skills from her mother—cooking, sewing, and gardening.

In 1877, she graduated from Western Female High School. For the next fifteen years, she taught French, German, botany and mathematics at the Misses Adam's School, a respected female academy in Baltimore. In the meantime, she attended public lectures at Johns Hopkins University and began publishing articles as the Baltimore correspondent for New York's *Jewish Messenger*.

Aware that Russian Jewish refugees were arriving in great numbers in Baltimore, in 1881 she started a night school for immigrants, attracting both Jews and non-Jews. Szold found this experience so gratifying that she remained as teacher and superintendent for twelve years. She learned many lessons from her work with immigrants—most importantly, she absorbed the nationalist hopes of those in the Russian intellectual community who believed that the creation of a Jewish community in Palestine would help to preserve Judaism as a meaningful way of life in the Diaspora.

She became an eager Zionist and joined the newly formed *Hebras Zion* in Baltimore. Writing about Zionism, Szold said it is "an ideal that can be embraced by all, no matter what their attitude may be to other Jewish questions." She became secretary of the editorial board of the Jewish Publication Society, and in 1899 she produced the first *American Jewish Year Book*. She also collaborated in the publishing of the *Jewish Encyclopedia*.

In 1902, Szold moved to New York and became the first female student to attend the Jewish Theological Seminary. A passionate and accom-

Szold with the first graduates of the Hadassah Nursing School, Jerusalem (1921)

plished student of Judaism, she was given permission to study Jewish texts at the then male-only Jewish Theological Seminary. The one caveat was that she "never agitates to be granted rabbinic ordination."

An event of considerable significance in Szold's life occurred in 1909, when she and her mother traveled to Palestine. She was impressed with the beauty of the Holy Land, albeit disturbed about the social, economic and medical conditions facing the new pioneers. Szold and her seventy-year-old mother visited struggling agricultural settlements in the Galilee. The poverty and disease rampant among Muslim, Christian, and Jewish inhabitants in the settlements was appalling.

Szold once was asked, "What was your inspiration for creating Hadassah?" She responded by quoting her mother's suggestion, as she viewed the terrible conditions in the Holy Land. Referring to her daughter's New York Zionist study circle, her mother recommended: "This is what your group ought to do…you should do practical work in Palestine." Szold visited Palestine the next year with many ideas for innovation and also accepted a position as secretary of the Federation of American Zionists.

Two years later an invitation was extended to a "meeting of interested women" prepared to support Jewish institutions in Palestine. On February 24, 1912, the [Hadassah Chapter of] Daughters of Zion was formed by the thirty-eight women who attended that historic gathering. The meeting took place at Temple Emanu-El in New York City. In 1914, the name of the group was changed to Hadassah, the Hebrew name of Queen Esther, in recognition of the fact that their first meeting was held during the holiday season of Purim. The group expressed its purpose: to foster ideals through education in the United States, and to begin public health

Szold during visit to the United States

At 75th birthday celebration which included Ben-Gurion, Ben-Zvi and Freier (1935)

programs in Palestine. Henrietta Szold was elected the group's first president.

By 1916, Hadassah's membership had grown to over 4,000. They took on the task of organizing the American Zionist Medical Unit, which consisted of doctors, nurses, administrators, vehicles and medical supplies. That same year, American Zionist groups were merged into a single body, the Zionist Organization of America (ZOA), with Szold heading its education department. She moved to *Eretz Yisrael* in 1920, one of the few American Jewish Zionist leaders to have a home in Jerusalem.

It was soon apparent that Szold was needed to direct a new institution, the Nurses' Training School in Jerusalem. At the end of 1922, the school was in dire financial straits. Fortunately, a donation by philanthropist Nathan Strauss not only saved it, but also enabled it to expand into the Hadassah Medical Organization. Szold managed the Hadassah Medical Organization for the next three years. Among the many achievements she instituted were programs for hygiene, the rehabilitation of juvenile delinquents, and the establishment of vocational schools.

During the 1930s, Szold involved Hadassah in a project to rescue Jewish youth from Germany and cities of persecution throughout Europe. Recha Freier, a Zionist living in Berlin, contacted her in 1932. Freier was working frantically on a daring plan to remove children from the Nazi threat. Coordinating closely together, Szold and Freier orchestrated a plan to send German Jewish children to Palestine for schooling—as a way to save their lives. To activate this, Szold initiated and directed a new department, Youth Aliyah, set up by the Jewish Agency. She and Freier coordinated their efforts, blazing through the red tape and bureaucracy that endangered the urgently needed program.

By 1948, over 30,000 children had come to Israel under this life-saving movement. They came not only from Germany, but also from France, Yemen, Turkey and Sweden, as well as many other countries. Although childless herself, Szold was "mother" to the thousands of

Attending the Sixteenth Zionist Congress in Zurich (1929)

young refugees from Nazi Germany who were saved from the Holocaust by the Youth Aliyah program.

For the next decade, until her death, Henrietta Szold continued in her mission to aid children, the sick, and those in need. She was extremely proud of her Hadassah "sisterhood" and what they had accomplished. Generations of American Jewish women were enlisted by Szold to assist in the practical work of supporting Jewish settlements in Palestine and later, in Israel.

In many respects, Szold was a forerunner of Jewish women's liberation. When her mother died in 1916, a close male friend, Haym Peretz, volunteered to say the Mourner's Kaddish, a Hebrew prayer recited when someone dies. Szold graciously declined the offer. "I believe" she wrote him, "that the elimination of women from such duties was never intended by our law and custom—women were freed from positive duties when they could not perform them [because of family responsibilities] but not when they could. It was never intended that, if they could perform them, their performance of them should not be considered as valuable and valid as when one of the male sex performed them."

As an essayist, translator, and editor, Szold became one of the few women to play a pivotal role in developing a significant Jewish culture in America. She triumphed despite being constrained by the limited opportunities that the Jewish world offered a woman of her brilliance, organizational abilities, and vision in that era.

Szold tried to deflect those who praised her special leadership or inspirational qualities. She claimed her talent was simply being a "hard worker." In an interview conducted when she was seventy-five years old, she

Aerial view of Hadassah Medical Center (1970)

noted that her greatest assets were "a strong constitution, a devotion to duty and a big conscience," together with "a flair for organization" and "a pretty big capacity for righteous indignation."

In her life and career, Szold posed questions and faced issues that today Jewish women in North America and around the world continue to explore. There was no need to speak of the "liberation" of women. Szold followed what she thought of as her "duty," and allowed her actions prove the power of women's activism. Seeing the futility of working within male-dominated organizations, she founded an organization of her own. Since Hadassah was established, members who have followed Szold have taken on the challenges raised by her, demonstrating through dedication and perseverance that women can powerfully transform the Jewish world.

Rabbi Judah L. Magnes, speaking in Jerusalem in 1945, eloquently paid tribute to Szold:

> *If you wish to know what is meant by the ethics of Judaism, search within the conscience of Henrietta Szold. If you wish to gain insight into the Jewish conscience, listen to her voice—a voice inspired by the lightnings of Sinai and the Prophets of Israel, and by the still, small voice of the traditionally compassionate woman in Israel, who, throughout the generations, hearkens to the weeping of mothers and children.*

Szold is praised as one of the genuine heroes in American-Jewish history—a scholarly woman, a passionately committed Jew, and a remarkable person credited with saving many thousands of lives.

20th meeting of the Executive with Szold as sole female member (1925)

Recha Freier
1892 - 1984

Our dream is to save at least 10,000 children.
— Recha Freier

Freier receiving Israel Prize from Begin (1981)

Without the vision of Recha Freier and the beginning of Youth Aliyah, it is difficult to imagine who would have undertaken responsibility for relocation and protection of so many children of the Holocaust—the youngest survivors. Who would have provided homes for so many Jewish children from Eastern Europe, Ethiopia and the Arab countries? Who was this woman whose determination and perseverance helped to save thousands of Jewish young people?

Recha Freier was born in 1892 in Norden, Germany, and grew up in a little town in Silesia. Because she honored the Orthodox restriction against writing on the Sabbath, she constantly was humiliated at school and tormented by her teachers, including by one who asked whether she "could even tie the ribbon of her pinafore" on Saturday. Gifted in music and poetry, she studied languages at the University of Breslau and after completing her studies worked as a teacher and pianist.

She married Rabbi Moritz Freier in 1919 and they moved to Bulgaria where they lived for seven years. Her husband was then called to Berlin as chief rabbi. Recha Freier kept herself busy researching children's tales, refusing to be defined solely through her husband's profession.

In 1931, a group of teenage boys in Berlin had been fired from their jobs because they were Jewish. Upset by their predicament and despondent over the economic and social conditions in Germany at the time, the boys approached Recha Freier. At first, it seemed there was little she could do. Unlike the Jewish employment office, she did not see the incident as an economic and social problem, but rather as a case of anti-Semitism. Freier went to the Jewish Labor Exchange where the harried director told her that the teenagers would get jobs when the economy improved.

Dissatisfied with this answer, Freier was determined to find another possibility—and soon thought of a solution. She recommended that the boys go to Palestine, work on an agricultural settlement and help build the new state. Thus, emerging from the pressing problem of caring for children in pre-war Germany, an idea began to germinate and the Youth Aliyah movement was born. Eagerly Freier presented her idea to the German Zionist leadership; they were distracted and indifferent. Freier would not be deterred.

The persistent Berliner already had found another way to deal with *aliyah*. In June 1932 she sent a few of the children from Germany to the *Ben Sheman* Children's Village. One of Freier's close friends pawned her jewelry as a financial guarantee for the children's support. Several boys finally departed Berlin on October 12, 1932 bound for *Eretz Yisrael*.

Grateful for this small victory, Freier still faced bureaucratic barriers and political uncertainty. She became even more stubborn in her quest to send the children to *Eretz Yisrael*. Speaking to a group of young people at a Zionist school filled with immigrants from Eastern Europe, she received overwhelming positive response to her ideas. Approached once again, the German Zionist leaders agreed to reconsider her proposal—with a condition. Freier needed to obtain a commitment from the Jewish National Assembly in Palestine to arrange for settlement and secure financial assistance. She was directed to Henrietta Szold, director of the Social Service Bureau in Jerusalem.

Freier sent a letter to Szold with her proposal, which at first surprised the Jerusalemite. Szold, who did not have children, envisioned youngsters coming to a strange land without their parents as harsh and upsetting. Szold initially rejected the idea from the German *rebbitzin*, but gradually came to see the necessity of providing these children with a safe place to live.

Freier soliciting support

Meanwhile, Freier continued to encounter resistance from all sides: from Zionist organizations, because "only top level professionals" were supposedly needed in Palestine and from parents and Jewish communities because they believed that the situation was "not that bad." Despite all of the apathy and opposition, on January 30, 1933 (ironically, the day of Hitler's ascent to power), Recha Freier registered the "Support Committee for Jewish Youth" at a lawyer's office. She was subjected to a daily onslaught of crises, agitation, and intrigues. Money and documents for trips to Palestine were needed. The young people had to be selected and prepared for life in an agricultural setting.

Freier's methods were somewhat controversial and she often worked in a legal "gray" area. For example, she reserved passages with shipping companies, stipulating that she had the necessary documents for immigration. Meanwhile, when speaking with the Palestine office, she used the ship tickets as leverage and demanded the required travel documents, warning of a scandal if they did not comply.

Henrietta Szold coordinated closely with Freier, and began directing the implementation of the program for Youth Aliyah in

Recha Freier with her daughter (1939)

Palestine. The connection between Youth Aliyah and Hadassah became official in 1935, when the two organizations agreed that Hadassah would be the agency for Youth Aliyah in the United States. In Great Britain and in Europe, organizations of Zionist women also became active in the Youth Aliyah cause. Women's mobilization provided an enormous resource for the ongoing rescue and absorption of European children.

In villages such as *Ben Shemen*, the young immigrants were taught the principles of agriculture, as well as Hebrew and other subjects. In her memoirs, *Let the Children Come*, Recha Freier described their efforts to organize Jewish children living in Germany for emigration to Palestine. She set up agriculture training sessions and worked closely with other agencies to adequately prepare these children and young adults for their move to a new country and life on their own.

It was from this modest beginning, a challenge undertaken by a determined Recha Freier, that the first chapter in the effort to save children from the Holocaust—and from worldwide oppression—was written. Freier persisted in her attempts to rescue the children from Nazi persecution and succeeded in relocating nearly 10,000 young Jews to Palestine between 1939 and 1941. She fled Germany in 1941, moved to Palestine, and founded the Agricultural Training Center for Children, which assisted underprivileged children in *kibbutz* boarding schools. Freier's Youth Aliyah, the immigration movement for orphaned children and children in need, continues its work today, assisting young people from all over the world.

In 1954 Albert Einstein recommended Recha Freier for the Nobel Peace Prize, in acknowledgement of her work. Although she did not receive the prize, she was honored by the gesture, moved by the outpouring of love, respect, and appreciation. She lived a long life committed to her work for the children of Israel. Members of the Youth Aliyah German Committee expressed their gratitude to Freier posthumously, in a ceremony in 2003:

> *We feel deeply honored that the great idea of Youth Aliyah was born in Germany. It was the vision of Recha Freier that not only enabled the rescue of so many children during the Holocaust – the darkest hour of mankind – but also created a unique network for the problems confronting Jewish children during the following decades.*

Rebecca Sieff
1890 - 1966

> *Take your work seriously, ladies, but never take yourselves seriously.*
>
> — Rebecca Sieff

By no means did women remain in the background as Zionism developed in Manchester England in the early twentieth century. As far back as 1900, there had been a counterpart to *B'nai Zion* called the *B'noth Zion* [Daughters of Zion]. It was this group of young women that introduced Rebecca Sieff to Zionism. She went on to become one of the most important and influential women in the history of modern Zionism.

Sieff, the eldest daughter of Michael Marks (founder of the department store Marks and Spencer), was born in Leeds in 1890 and educated in Manchester. She studied mathematics and literature, growing up in a wealthy and cultured environment.

When she was twenty years old, Rebecca Sieff attended a public meeting addressed by Chaim Weizmann. She was fascinated by his description of Zionist ideals, and was motivated into action. In 1910 she joined her first Zionist group, the Daughters of Zion, and by the summer of 1913 she had become an enthusiastic activist.

Sieff began to speak publicly in support of Zionism, becoming a recognized leader in the Jewish community. In 1916, Rebecca presided at a public meeting held in Maccabean Hall that advocated more active support for the Zionist cause from local women. Responding to her encouragement, these women passed a resolution to contact Britain's prime minister and to request his help in establishing a legally secure home in Palestine.

She instinctively was pulled into Zionism by her strong sense of tradition and historic continuity, both through her family and colleagues. Her husband, Baron Israel Sieff, and her

Sieff addresses meeting of prominent Zionists in the UK

WIZO nurses taking care of children at refugee camp near Tel Aviv (1948)

brother, Simon Marks, were close friends of Chaim Weizmann. Weizmann and his wife Vera often visited the Sieff's home. One evening at dinner, while Weizmann and their male friends were chatting about Zionism, Rebecca dressed up as a maid to eavesdrop on the men's conversation—and to make a statement. Her statement became a maxim—Jewish *women* would lead the way along the path to a new Jewish homeland.

Sieff's influence continued to grow, and in 1918 she founded and chaired the South Manchester Women's Zionist Society. This was an extremely significant development in that the new organization was the first in England to focus its activities *exclusively* on the welfare of women and children in Palestine.

The South Manchester Women's Zionist Society was one of twelve women's organizations affiliated under the umbrella of the Ladies' Committee to the English Zionist Federation (EZF). Their representatives met in London the same year and formed the Federation of Women Zionists. Sieff was the first president of the Federation of Women Zionists of Great Britain and Ireland. Other prominent members included Vera Weizmann, Miriam Sacher, Miriam Marks, and Marie Nahum. Just as the men banded together and formed their male Zionist organizations, the wives' institutional Zionism also was very much a "clan" effort.

Rebecca's husband traveled with Chaim Weizmann as part of the 1918 Zionist Commission to Palestine. Their assignment was to survey the situation and make recommendations as to how the Balfour Declaration could be implemented. In his memoirs, Israel Sieff recalls how his wife was upset "not so much because I was going away for a few months, but because she was not allowed to go herself. She had developed into an intrepid, independent-minded woman, believed in sexual equality, was a devoted Zionist, and saw no reason why she should not accompany us, rightly insisting that she could do my job better than I could."

She and her family moved to London where she immediately began working with the British Palestine Committee preparing for the Balfour Declaration. On a fact-finding mission in Palestine with Chaim Weizmann's wife, Dr. Vera Weizmann, and Edith Eder, the three women spent six months investigating the *yishuv*'s social and economic conditions, especially in Jerusalem's dilapidated Old City. The poverty and squalor they witnessed convinced Sieff that Jewish women must unite to remedy the situation.

Returning to England in July 1920, Romana Goodman and Henrietta Irwell joined her in establishing the Women's International Zionist Organization (WIZO), the chief vehicle through which women's Zionist activities would be promoted and channeled. In 1924, she was elected the first president of WIZO. She remained in this position for nearly forty-three years, until her death in 1966.

In 1933 Daniel Sieff, the son of Rebecca and Israel Sieff, and a promising young scientist, died tragically when he was only eighteen. Chaim Weizmann had confided to the Seiffs his intention to establish an institute for advanced scientific research in Palestine. As a tribute to their son, Israel and Rebecca offered to underwrite the cost of the new institute, asking only that the enterprise be named in memory of their son. The Daniel Sieff Research Institute was dedicated on April 3, 1934.

Rebecca Sieff was a powerful speaker with a brilliant mind. It was not unusual for her to bring audiences to their feet several times during her speeches. She traveled extensively for WIZO, opening new branches and passing the torch of Zionism to young women in dozens of countries. In 1938, she helped establish the Israel Philharmonic Orchestra, as well as many other social and cultural institutions in the new State of Israel.

Sieff leads Women's Zionist meeting

During and after World War II, her attention turned to the Holocaust and its survivors. Sieff was one of the first people to visit the Displaced Persons (DP) camps in Europe. The camps were strictly off-limits to civilians, so the British Foreign Office temporarily made her a lieutenant colonel. She made a dramatic plea to the United Nations to secure better conditions for the survivors.

At a session of the WIZO World Executive in 1966, Rebecca Sieff resigned the presidency due to poor health, but was unanimously acclaimed Honorary Life President of WIZO. She was the dominant figure of the movement throughout her life and guided it through years of trials and outstanding successes.

WIZO flourished under Rebecca Sieff's leadership, continuing to expand, and eventually enlisting over a quarter of a million women in fifty countries. Today it is responsible for over 500 institutions and programs in Israel—an extraordinary accomplishment and distinguished tribute to a remarkable pioneer.

Nahum Sokolow
1859 - 1936

> *. . . It was thought that the {Balfour} Declaration should contain two principles, (1) the recognition of Palestine as the national home of the Jewish people, (2) the recognition of the Zionist Organization.*
>
> — Nahum Sokolow

Nahum Sokolow was one of the prominent Zionist leaders who persuaded Great Britain to support a Jewish homeland in Palestine. This successful effort resulted in the Balfour Declaration of 1917. Sokolow was an articulate and versatile essayist, publicist, editor and writer. He wrote so much and on so many topics that the Hebrew poet Chaim Nachman Bialik once remarked, "It would take 300 camels to bring all his writings together in one place."

Born in 1859 in Wyszogrod, Russian-Poland to a family that had produced many rabbis as well as Polish public notables, Sokolow received both a religious and secular education. He mastered many languages while studying literature, including German, French, Spanish, and Italian as well as English, Yiddish, Hebrew, Polish, and Russian. A voracious reader of non-Jewish literature, his writing reflected a different perspective from many of his Zionist contemporaries.

Sokolow married at seventeen and moved into his father-in-law's house, where he began writing commentaries on Jewish themes, poetry, plays, and stories as well as scientific articles. Sokolow wrote for various Hebrew newspapers and in 1876 became a regular science columnist for the newspaper *Ha-Zefirah*; this experience was the impetus for his first book, which was about science.

In 1880, when he was just twenty-one, Sokolow moved to Warsaw and began writing about current affairs. Almost overnight his commentaries became extremely popular, transforming *Ha-Zefirah* into a dynamic publication. In 1886, he became one of the editors of the newspaper.

Sokolow was the first writer in the history of Hebrew press and literature to generate a vast reading public, appealing to both secular and religious Jews. One of his books was a best seller in America, a textbook of the English language for Yiddish-speaking people. The book was

Sokolow (second from left) in Palestine with Zionist leaders including Chaim Weizmann, Lord Balfour and Meir Dizengoff (1925)

Nahum Sokolow, respected Hebrew writer and Zionist leader

enthusiastically received and read by the masses of immigrants entering the United States.

From 1885 to 1894, he published six volumes of books filled with a variety of important literature, which he had translated into Hebrew. The broad scope of this project was unprecedented in Hebrew language publishing, and changed the landscape of Hebrew literature.

Life changed dramatically for Nahum Sokolow when he attended the First Zionist Congress in Basel in 1897 as a correspondent, and met Theodor Herzl. He became one of Herzl's greatest admirers and a loyal supporter. As evidence of his support, his newspaper became virtually a Hebrew publication for the Zionist movement.

Sokolow translated Herzl's *Altneuland* into Hebrew and gave it the title "Tel Aviv." When the citizens of that yet unnamed town were deciding what to call their community, their inspiration came from the title that Nahum Sokolow had given his Hebrew translation of Herzl's utopian romance. Sokolow thought of *"tel,"* a heap of ancient ruins as corresponding to *"alt,"* "old," and of "spring" as conveying the idea of rebirth suggested in *neu* "new." Thus the name, "Tel Aviv."

In 1906, two years after Herzl's death, *Ha-Zefirah* had ceased publication, and Sokolow accepted David Wolffsohn's invitation to serve as secretary general of the World Zionist Organization (WZO). Initially, Sokolow was not a member of the *Hovevei Zion* movement, even though his *Ha-Zefirah* was Zionist in persuasion. When Herzl's *The Jewish State* was published, Sokolow rejected the *Eretz Yisrael* option as infeasible. Sokolow, however, reversed his position and rallied to the Zionist organization. David Wolffsohn, Herzl's successor, asked Sokolow to replace him as leader of the WZO. Sokolow accepted and held this position from 1907 to 1909 but differences over the political nature of Wolffsohn's Zionism led to a rift between the two men.

In 1911, under a new WZO administration, Sokolow assumed responsibility for the political portfolio and worked to generate support for the Zionist idea, particularly in the United States and Great Britain. At the start of World War I he moved to England, working closely with Chaim Weizmann. His new political position allowed him to maintain contact with the Diaspora. On his first visit to the United States and Canada, he gathered tremendous support for the Zionist cause from both Jews and non-Jews.

Sokolow chaired the committee that proposed the language for the Balfour Declaration. He was a key figure in the negotiations, meeting with French officials and obtaining a pro-Zionist statement from them in May 1917. The Balfour Declaration originally was simply a letter from British Foreign Secretary Arthur James Balfour to Lionel Walter Rothschild, a leader in British Jewry. The letter later became an official document. The agreement, which had taken years to write, was finalized on November 2, 1917.

The Declaration was the British Government's attempt to gain support from the Jews and to influence America into joining the war effort. It was created through the combined efforts of Chaim Weizmann and Nahum Sokolow, both of whom were among the most prominent of the Zionist leaders. The gist of the agreement read as follows:

> *His Majesty's Government view with favour the establishment in Palestine of a national home for the Jewish people, and will use their best endeavours to facilitate the achievement of this object, it being clearly understood that nothing shall be done which may prejudice the civil and religious rights of existing non-Jewish communities in Palestine, or the rights and political status enjoyed by Jews in any other country.*

As he conscientiously worked on the Balfour project, Sokolow also began to write one of his most prodigious works, *The History of Zionism (1600-1918).* It was released in two volumes in 1919, with a shorter German version published a few years later. This new book powerfully connected world Jewry to the Jewish homeland, and also offered a persuasive expression of why non-Jews should support such a concept.

Sokolow was held in high esteem as a result of his efforts regarding the Balfour Declaration. He was invited to head the Jewish special delegation to the Paris Peace Plan Conference, where he delivered a most impressive speech. Chaim Weizmann said, "Without being sentimental, it was as if two thousand years of Jewish suffering rested on his shoulders." From that time on, Sokolow attended and addressed nearly every major Zionist and Jewish assembly, traveling the world to speak about his dream, the new State of Israel.

Nahum Sokolow was given the honor of chairing the Twelfth Zionist Congress in 1921 (the first after World War I), functioning in this role at every subsequent Congress until he died. Continuing the tradition begun by Max Nordau, he spoke at each Congress about the situation of Jews in the Diaspora. He closed each event saying, "It was a difficult Congress, but a good one."

Commemorative postcard of the Balfour Declaration (1917)

In 1929 he became chairman of the Jewish Agency. His leadership guided the Zionist movement through funding issues caused by the financial crisis in the United States, and the rise of Nazism in Germany and Europe. Sokolow assumed the position of president of the World Zionist Organization in 1931, following Weizmann's departure. When in 1935 Weizmann returned to the presidency, Sokolow was elected Honorary President and assumed responsibilities in the newly formed Cultural Department. He served with distinction as he had in all of his public service, until his death in 1936. His remains were reinterred at Mt. Herzl, Jerusalem in 1956.

CHAPTER FIVE

Artists, Poets, Writers

Ze'ev Dubnow
1858 - 1940

> *The Jews will yet arise and, arms in hand {if need be}, I declare that they are the masters of their homeland.*
>
> — Ze'ev Dubnow

Russian Jews were viciously persecuted under the czar's regime during the 1880s, rousing Russian Jewish youth to establish strong Zionist movements as their way to fight against this smothering oppression. Ze'ev Dubnow was one of these young patriots.

Not all of the early pioneers were able to endure the hardships of *Eretz Yisrael*. Dubnow went to Palestine, worked there and faced the challenges of bringing life into the desert. Afterward he returned home to his birthplace to instill and nurture the precepts and principles of Zionism in the Diaspora. He was a well-known historian, articulate and clear in his self-expression. An enthusiastic proponent of artists and their influence on developing the culture, he was instrumental in starting the first artisans' association in Palestine.

Born in White Russia, Belorussia, he was the older brother of Simon Dubnow, also a famous historian. Ze'ev learned a great deal from his brother Simon in their quest for a homeland for the Jewish people. Simon Dubnow is considered to be one of the greatest Jewish historians of the twentieth century. Known for his ten-volume *History of the Jews in Poland and Russia*, the book details the history of the Jews of Eastern Europe from early Greek times until 1910. This background guided him as one the founders of "autonomism," the movement that advocated Jewish national autonomy in the Diaspora. His brother Ze'ev embraced this philosophy and put it into action in a very different way. As with many Jewish activists, Ze'ev found his way to Zionism through a backdoor, under the banner of Russian revolutionary causes.

After the pogroms of 1881, Ze'ev Dubnow fled Russia, and in 1882 he arrived in Palestine with the First BILU [an acronym based on a verse from Isaiah: "House of Jacob, come ye and let us go"]. The group's founders believed that the time had come for Jews not only to *live* in *Eretz Yisrael*, but to be able to make their living there as well. They believed this could be accomplished by developing agricultural settlements. Dubnow emphasized that the ultimate aim of the Russian pioneers was to return *Eretz Yisrael* to the Jewish people, enabling them to regain their political and cultural independence.

Portrait of Ze'ev Dubnow

The entrance to the Mikve Yisrael agricultural school, founded in 1870 (1970)

Dubnow worked at the agricultural settlement *Mikve Israel* [Israel's Hope], which now is an historical site located in the Tel Aviv suburb of Holon. The young Russians founded and developed the settlement in 1870. This small commune became the prototype for what would become the *"kibbutz"* movement. Dubnow played an active part in this transition, which began as an experimental farming experience and evolved into the model for Israel's future agricultural, social and economic institution, the *kibbutz*. Although the *Bilu'im* did not accomplish all that they had envisioned, their dream of Jews living and supporting themselves in their own homeland is regarded as one of the important predecessors of the international Zionist movement that Theodor Herzl organized fifteen years later.

Along with several friends, Dubnow moved from *Mikve Israel* to Jerusalem. It was in the "golden city" that he and his comrades established SHAHU, a group whose name comes from the Hebrew initials for "return of the craftsmen and the smiths." SHAHU became what would be called today an association of artisans, and it gave creative opportunity to thousands of immigrants who were coming to the Holy Land. The organization provided an avenue for those artists whose talent was in their hands, helping them to perform their trade and earn money to sustain themselves. In years to come, this early organization that supported the arts would provide a foundation for financing the arts, important to the economic and cultural development of the State of Israel.

In Palestine, these first courageous pioneers, the *Bilu'im*, discovered that living in the country was extremely difficult. Conditions were stark, the land was unforgiving, and water was scarce. They constantly were being attacked by bands of Arabs intent on driving them off the land. Many of these early settlers also faced starvation. In 1885, Dubnow returned to Belorussia, frustrated by the hurdles that were obstacles to his dreams. Despite all of the hardships and the challenges, however, he remained an avid Zionist. He and his brother carried on the crusade for the development of the Land of Israel from the Diaspora—from outside the borders of *Eretz Yisrael*.

Simon Dubnow passionately expressed their dream:

The aim of our journey is rich in plans. We want to return our homeland to the Jews because of political independence, which was stolen from them two thousand years ago. And if you will it; it is not a dream. We must establish agricultural settlements, factories and industry. We must develop industry and put it into Jewish hands. And above all we must give young people military training and provide them with weapons [to defend themselves]. Then the Jews will declare that they are the masters of their ancient homeland.

Ze'ev Dubnow, pioneer and fighter for Zionism, represents the many activists from those early days through to the present who love Israel and sustain the country from abroad, from different parts of the world, all united in one common goal—supporting the development and strengthening of the State of Israel.

Dubnow with his literary colleagues Ben-Yehuda and Ya'acov Shertok

Ahad Ha'am
1856 - 1927

> *Palestine (Israel) will become our spiritual center only when the Jews are a majority of the population and own most of the land.*
> — Ahad Ha'am

A very early Zionist, and a prolific and respected writer, Asher Ginsberg, who became known as Ahad Ha'am, had roots deeply nourished in Judaism. He felt that a Jewish homeland had to be established not simply to save the Jews, but also to save Judaism.

Asher Hirsch Ginsberg was born into a Hasidic family in 1856 in the Kiev Province of Russia. He studied Talmud, medieval Jewish philosophy, and numerous languages, though he never received a formal education.

At a very young age, Ginsberg demonstrated the intelligence and independence that defined his life. When he developed a smoking habit at the age of eleven, a renowned physician convinced him it would kill him. Taking the warning seriously, the mature young Ginsberg turned instead to another distraction—learning. In his father's library he found an eighteenth century Hebrew book containing the basics of algebra and geometry; the child smoker gave up tobacco and substituted instead the study of Hebrew and Judaism.

Ahad Ha'am on visit to Palestine (1911)

Ginsberg settled in Odessa in 1884 and became involved in the *Hovevei Zion* [Sons of Moses]. He wrote his first important article, *This Is Not the Way*, in 1889 under the pen name Ahad Ha'am [One of the People] and wrote from then on under that name. In the article, Ahad Ha'am criticized the Zionists for focusing simply on going to the Land of Israel. In his opinion, "creating a nationalist Jewish state wasn't enough. Having Jewish farmers wasn't enough. Speaking Hebrew as a nationalist language wasn't enough." The Jewish nation needed to encompass a whole new value system of "equality, egalitarianism, and utopianism." The Jewish spirit had to "shine" in a Jewish state. Its residents had to be imbued with Jewish values and the Jewish tradition. The Jewish state had to be a "light" to other nations. To accomplish this new society, Ahad Ha'am felt that Jews had to know Jewish tradition. They had to purify themselves and live the values espoused within Judaism.

The members of *Hovevei Zion* tried to establish the organization as a political party in order to expound their views of Zionism, but the attempt did not succeed. With the creation of the

Ahad Ha'am (back, center) with Einstein (seated, right) in Tel Aviv (1923)

First Zionist Congress in Basel in 1897, it was clear that Ahad Ha'am's position on Zionism differed from that of Theodor Herzl and the two leaders became philosophical adversaries.

Ahad Ha'am did not believe that Herzl's political diplomacy methods would succeed. While a strong proponent of Zionism, he insisted that there had to be a Jewish "cultural" foundation for a Jewish state to be worth anything. He vociferously opposed Herzl's Uganda Plan.

Ahad Ha'am's views on Zionism were rooted in the changing nature of Jewish communal life in Eastern Europe. He realized that a new meaning of Jewish life would have to be found for the younger generation of Eastern European Jews who were rebelling against traditional Jewish practice. While Jews in the West could participate in, and benefit from, a secular culture—Jews in the East were oppressed. Whereas Herzl focused on the plight of Jews, Ahad Ha'am was interested in the plight of Judaism, which he felt could no longer be contained within the limits of traditional religion.

Ahad Ha'am became the central figure in the movement for cultural or spiritual Zionism. His visits to Palestine in 1891 and 1892 convinced him that the Zionist movement faced an uphill struggle in its attempt to create a Jewish national homeland. In particular, he warned of the difficulties associated with land purchase and cultivation, the problems with the Turkish authorities, and the impending conflict with the Arabs. Creating a Jewish cultural center in *Eretz Yisrael*, Ahad Ha'am believed, would reinforce Jewish life in the Diaspora. His hope was that a new Jewish national identity based on Jewish ethics and values might resolve the crisis in Judaism.

In the cultural Zionist vision, a small number of Jewish groups well-grounded in Jewish culture and speaking Hebrew would settle in Palestine. Ahad Ha'am believed that by settling in that ancient land, religious Jews would replace their metaphysical attachment to the Holy Land with a new Hebrew cultural

Ahad Ha'am (seated left of center) at conference of Hebrew writers (1926)

renaissance. Palestine and the Hebrew language were important not because of their religious significance, but because they had been an integral part of the Jewish people's history and cultural heritage.

His theories of Zionism were based on the needs of Judaism, not the needs of the Jews. This distinction is best illustrated in his own writing, as for example in a speech he gave in Minsk in 1902 before a conference of the Russian Zionist Organization:

> *There are 'political' Zionists for whom the spiritual aspect of the movement is of no importance; at the other extreme, there are 'spiritual' Zionists, who are dissatisfied with political work in its present form.... This being so, we must establish a special organization for this purpose to embrace all those, whether professed Zionists or not, who realize the importance of Jewish culture and desire its free growth and development. This organization should concentrate exclusively on its own specific problems, and should neither sub-serve nor be dependent on the companion political organization.*

Although Ahad Ha'am's vision of the return to the Jews' ancestral homeland was not filled with messianic yearning, his idealization of the spiritual, religious and cultural dimensions of Judaism was rooted in Jewish "messianism." For him, it would not be a divinely appointed Messiah who would bring about the realization of "God's kingdom on earth." Rather this would be the task of the Jewish people themselves. Through the creation of a Jewish state, the spiritual values of the faith would materialize in the Holy Land.

Ahad Ha'am with philosophers/writers Revinsky, Ben-Ami and Bialek (1900)

Ahad Ha'am, nee Arthur Hirsch Ginsberg, was a persistent pioneer of Israel. He spent the last five years of his life in Palestine where he continued to write about commitment to Zionism in the form he supported. His own self-questioning helped the Jewish world better to analyze its various paths. He prompted vigorous and essential debate during an historic period that prefaced the creation of the Jewish homeland. In his own words:

> *I live for the sake of the perpetuation and the well being of the community to which I belong.... When the individual loves the community as himself and identifies himself completely with its well-being, he has something to live for; he feels his personal hardships less keenly, because he knows the purpose for which he lives and suffers.*

Shai Agnon
1888 - 1970

Israel is the first flowering of our redemption.

— Shai Agnon

Shai Agnon is considered the greatest Israeli author of the twentieth century. He was the first Israeli honored to win the Nobel Prize. Agnon delighted the country in 1966 when he received this award—the highest international recognition for literature.

Shmuel Yosef Agnon ["Shai" is a Hebrew acronym] was born as Shmuel Czackes in 1888 in Buczacz, Galicia, Austro-Hungarian Empire (Ukraine). His father, an erudite follower of the Hasidic Rebbe of Chortov, was in the fur trade. Agnon, a self-educated man that never went to university later said, "All I know I have learned from my father."

The traditional Jewish education Agnon received as a child in the *heder* [schoolroom], as well as the influence of his parents' diverse Jewish backgrounds, are evident in his work. His father's family was connected to famous Hasidim, while his mother came from a family of Mitnagdim, whose rationalism contrasted with the emotional mysticism of the Hasidim. Agnon's writing reflects a unique synthesis of these two disparate world views.

Tutored by his father and a local rabbi, Agnon studied the Talmud. From this Eastern European background that viewed study of scripture as central to communal life, he acquired a deep knowledge of the rabbinic texts that would greatly impact his writing. He was also strongly influenced by his mother who introduced him to popular German literature.

By the age of eight Agnon already was writing in Hebrew and Yiddish. In 1903, when he

Shai Agnon (center) at ceremony receiving accolades (1950)

Shai Agnon ponders the moment (1954)

was fifteen, he published his first work, a Yiddish poem with a Hebrew preface. Four years later he moved to Jaffa in Palestine where he served as the first secretary of the city's Jewish Court. He legally changed his name from Czaczkes to Agnon and published the short novel *Agunot* (1908) in Hebrew.

The name "Agnon" is a literary construction intended to connect his fate to that of the Jewish people. The surname came from the title of his first story, *Agunot*. The name is derived from the status of abandoned women in Jewish law who have been left by their husbands without a writ of divorce. Without this document, these *agunot* exist in a state of limbo, belonging neither to the world of the married nor of the single. They cannot marry again, and are seen as "incomplete and impure; a woman with one foot in and one foot out" of the intricately structured patriarchal universe of Orthodox Judaism. Agnon understood this state of ambivalence and anxiety, of standing between different worlds but belonging to neither—and his literature reflects this duality.

In 1912 Agnon left Palestine and went to Berlin, where he continued his study of literature. He remained in Germany throughout World War I and worked as a research assistant to scholars. During this time he met Salman Schocken, a businessman, who became his lifelong patron and publisher. In Germany he also met and married his wife, Esther Marx.

During his days in Germany he lived quite comfortably, as did other Hebrew scholars, many of whom resided in Hamburg and Weisbaden. He joined forces with Martin Buber and began to collect Hasidic stories and folklore. In Berlin and Leipzig, Agnon established his presence and expanded his knowledge of Judaica, acquiring and collecting rare Hebrew books. Unfortunately, a fire in his home destroyed much of his collection.

Agnon returned to Jerusalem in 1924, where he lived for the rest of his life. His first major novel, *The Bridal Canopy* (1931), was an allegory about the decline of Jewish religious life in Poland. The plot chronicles the travels of a "Jewish Don Quixote," Reb Yudel, a Hasidic seeking a dowry for his daughters in early nineteenth-century Europe.

During the 1930s Agnon's works were widely published in German. When the Nazis closed the Schocken publishing house, the company moved to Tel Aviv, and later opened a branch in New York City, a move that introduced Agnon's writing to new readers. His book, *A Guest For The Night* (1939), is a story about Agnon's hometown in Poland following World War I. It describes the spiritual decline that he witnessed, his desire to restore the past, and his memories of a comforting life in the *shtetl* [village].

The Day Before Yesterday (1945) generally is considered Agnon's greatest novel. The story is set in the period of the Second Aliyah, the wave of Jewish emigration to Palestine

Agnon with Nelly Zaksh prior to Nobel Prize ceremony (1966)

between 1907 and 1913, and anticipates the emergence of Israel from the ashes of the Holocaust. The novel contrasts old and new ways in Jewish life.

The image of Agnon as a pious and parochial Jew was central to the identity he created for himself as a modern Jewish writer. He claimed that his inspirations were "first and fore-most the sacred scriptures, and after that, the teachings of the medieval Jewish sages, and the spectacles of nature and the animals of the earth." Aspects of his own biography are integrated with the history of the Jewish people in his fiction. His "craving to belong" inspired Agnon's writing.

Agnon at 78 receives congratulations on the telephone for receiving the Nobel Prize for Literature

Agnon, who died in 1970, has become an Israeli icon. His life and work developed into symbols of the hopes and longing of the Jewish state, a state that is at once ancient and modern. As expressed so eloquently in his writing, it is a state caught between different worlds and fighting for its own identity. He spoke passionately about this in his acceptance speech at the Nobel Prize ceremony in 1966:

> *I belong to the Tribe of Levi; my forbearers and I are of the minstrels that were in the Temple, and there is a tradition in my father's family that we are of the lineage of the Prophet Samuel, whose name I bear.*

Chaim Nachman Bialik
1873 - 1934

I love Tel Aviv...because all of it...was established by our own hands.

— Chaim Nachman Bialik

Chaim Nachman Bialik, the celebrated "National Poet of Israel" is considered the greatest Hebrew poet of modern times. He left a legacy that symbolizes the love of his people— his writing speaks passionately of his commitment and dedication to Jewish culture.

Bialik was born in 1873 in the small village of Radi near what has been called a "spiritual" town of Volhynia in Eastern Europe. His environment and upbringing strongly influenced his writing and thinking. Jews in this region were especially sensitive to the customs and traditions of Hasidic folklore, and Bialik immersed himself in the study of this mystical element in Judaism.

When Bialik was a child, his family suffered dire economic difficulties resulting from his father's lack of success with the family timber business. Despite the hardships resulting from poverty, Bialik had happy memories of his first six years in Radi, and those feelings were expressed in his poetry.

In 1880, after moving the family to a nearby village, Chaim's father died. Destitute, his mother sent Bialik, who was only seven, to live with his paternal grandfather, a scholarly, stern Orthodox rabbi, Reb Ya'akov Moishe Bialik. The loss of his father at an early age and life in new surroundings dramatically impacted Bialik's thoughts. His later poems about exile seem to include his feelings concerning the disruption of his childhood.

For the next ten years Chaim's grandfather raised him in a pious, austere world. He was

Bialik (far left) next to Ahad Ha'am in Odessa (1905)

121

Bialik as a delegate to the Seventeenth Zionist Congress

a lonely figure in an almost deserted house of learning. But the passionate and solitary commitment to study inherent in his early schooling, Bialik later would cherish. He dreamed of a rabbinical seminary in Berlin, and had conflicting thoughts of participating in the modern world springing up around him.

Bialik received a traditional Hebrew education, but also was influenced by his mother's interest in Russian and European literature. When he was only eleven he read the kabbalistic literature of the Middle Ages. A few years later he began to study the Talmud.

In 1890, Bialik convinced his grandfather to send him to the famous Talmudic Academy in Lithuania where he felt he could continue his religious studies and at the same time receive an introduction to the humanities. Unfortunately, the school did not meet his expectations, and the following year he went to Odessa and studied Russian and German. Absorbed with his poetry, he composed poems that reflected themes of the Jewish Enlightenment. Among his friends and mentors was the early Zionist ideologist Ahad Ha'am, whose thinking influenced Bialik's writing. Bialik wrote his first published poem, *To The Bird*, during this time. In 1891, Bialik's first complete work was released, which expounded the virtues of society and reflected the teaching of Ahad Ha'am's spiritual Zionism.

When his grandfather died in 1893, Bialik moved to Zhitomir and married Manya Averbuch. His business venture in the lumber trade with his father-in-law was unsuccessful and in 1897 he moved to Sosnowice, a small town near the Prussian border. Here Bialik worked as a teacher, and for the next three years he spent much of his time out in the forest in solitude, which afforded him the opportunity to expand his reading. It was here that he wrote *On the Threshold of the House of Study*, which championed the ultimate triumph of Israel's

Bialik (center) with Sephardi Chief Rabbi at a horse race along the Tel-Aviv shore (1931)

spirit. Bialik questioned leaders of the early Zionist Congresses, concerned that they were too secular and that their focus was being diverted away from Judaism.

By this time, Bialik's fame as a poet began to broaden and he returned to Odessa, a center of Hebrew literature. At this time most Jews were forbidden to live in Moscow or St. Petersburg, and Odessa had more Jews than any other city in Russia. Bialik worked in Odessa as a teacher from 1900 to 1921, continuing his activities in Zionist and literary circles. Many young writers visited Odessa simply for the opportunity to meet him.

Bialik's first volume of poetry appeared in 1901 in Warsaw. He visited Palestine in 1904 and 1908 and also spent time in Warsaw editing the magazine *Ha-Shiloah*, which had been founded by Ahad Ha'am. In the early 1900s, Bialik and Y.H. Ravnitzky opened a Hebrew publishing house, Moriah, which released Hebrew classics and school literature. Bialik translated various European classics, such as Shakespeare's *Julius Caesar*, Schiller's *Wilhelm Tell*, and Cervantes' *Don Quixote* into Hebrew.

Bialik's first long poem, *Ha-Matmid*, published in *Ha-Shiloah*, established his eminence as one of the most important Hebrew poets of his time. It presented the Talmudic student as a "heroic force of Judaism" and depicted the rapidly vanishing life of the traditional Orthodox Jewish past. Bialik's early poems often dealt with the gap between modern life and religious faith, and the bitterness of exile.

Having immersed himself from a young age in a traditional religious foundation, he was irresistibly attracted to the new ways of the culture—modern ideas appeared to triumph over conventional views. Bialik struggled with this apparent dichotomy all his life and his writing reflected this inner conflict. Bialik's dominant theme in much of his writing is the "crisis of faith" which confronted his generation. As the new generation separated itself from the sheltered and confined "medieval" Jewish religious culture of their adolescence, they simultaneously sought to hold onto a Jewish way of

Bialik with Dov Sadan

Bialik stamp with the poets autograph, issued the Israel Post Office (1958)

life and thought in the modern secularized world. Although Bialik's best-known poems are about the challenges of the Jewish people and national and individual redemption, he also wrote passionate love poems.

Living in czarist Russia, he witnessed first hand the brutal treatment of the Jews. In particular, he visited the city of Kishinev (modern day Chisinau, Moldova) after the 1903 pogrom in which fifty Jews were murdered, hundreds were injured and nearly two thousand were made homeless. Fueled by anger both at what had been done and at the inadequacy of Jewish response, that year he wrote his greatest poem, *City of the Killings.*

Bialik wrote this poem in what has been called "a barely controlled rage—earthy, profane, impassioned, accusatory, and even apocalyptic." It is clear even today why this poem had such an effect on world Jewry. It does not merely recount a tragedy; it challenges Jews to respond to the crimes perpetrated against them. The message in this poem marked a turning point; young Jews throughout Russia were stimulated by what they heard as a "call to arms." They participated in radical acts intending to bring down the treacherous czarist regime, which ultimately led to the Russian Revolution.

Bialik's words stimulated another revolution during this time. The massacre in Kishinev also inspired Theodor Herzl to find a safe haven for his people. It was now clear to many Jews in Russia that there was no future there and they began their trek to *Eretz Yisrael* in a wave of immigration that came to be known as the Second Aliyah. Driven by the horror of Kishinev and their rage at not fighting back, these Jews, who were immigrating to their homeland, created settlements and armed guard units that became the foundation of the Zionist Revolution.

After the Bolshevik Revolution the communist authorities, suspicious of Bialik's work, forced the closing of the Moriah publishing house. With the help of Maxim Gorky, Bialik received permission to emigrate. He moved to Berlin in 1921, where he established Dvir Publishing. A group of young writers had converged in Berlin, and it was here that he further developed his ideals, continuing to write, publish, and edit.

In 1924 he moved to Tel Aviv—at that time Palestine was administered by Britain under a League of Nations' mandate. During the last decade of his life, Bialik participated in a number of cultural and national pursuits. He delivered the address for the opening of Hebrew University in Jerusalem, and was a member of its board of governors. He visited the United States on behalf of the Palestine Foundation Fund and toured in Poland. Bialik established weekly philosophical and literary discussions in Tel Aviv, which he called *Oneg Shabbat* [enjoyment of the Sabbath]. This rich tradition continues today in synagogues all over the world.

Following surgery, Bialik died in Vienna, Austria, in 1934, and was buried in Tel Aviv. His poems have been translated into thirty languages. His home at 22 Bialik Street in Tel Aviv, a sanctuary for intellectuals in the 1920s, is now open to the public as a museum. Bialik's poems—and songs based on them—have become a fundamental part of the education and culture of modern Israel. They are read at schools, and frequently recited in festivals and public events.

Chaim Nachman Bialik had a profound effect on all those who have read his works. Prior to Bialik's entry into the world

Bialik meets new friends during first visit to Eretz Yisrael (1909)

of poetry, Hebrew poetry was provincial and largely imitative. It could not free itself from the biblical influence that had dominated it for centuries. Bialik, more than any other poet, had a thorough command of Hebrew and the ability to use the many resources of the language, which enabled Hebrew poetry to free itself from the biblical influence and yet stay true to the "language of the Jewish people." His development of the Hebrew language through literature, as well as his ability to connect the worlds of the traditional and modern, exemplify the enormous impact he has had on the Jewish world. In the poem *After My Death*, he wrote:

After my death mourn me this way:
'There was a man — and see: he is no more;
before his time this man died
and his life's song in mid-bar stopped;
and oh, it is sad! One more song he had....'

Thousands line the streets of Tel Aviv for the funeral procession of Bialik (1934)

125

Itamar Ben-Avi
1882 - 1943

> *This firstborn I will call Itamar ...{who} From the day of his entering the covenant (brit-milah) until his death will have a covenant, with Hebrew...*
> — Eliezer Ben-Yehuda (Itamar's father)

Itamar Ben-Avi fulfilled the honored tradition of *la-dor v'dor*, "generation to generation." He was the son of the great Modern Hebrew language pioneer, Eliezer Ben-Yehuda; his Hebrew name was derived from his father's initials. He was raised from infancy to hear and speak only Hebrew, making him one of the first modern Jews whose mother tongue was Hebrew.

In the introduction to his Hebrew dictionary, Eliezer Ben-Yehuda wrote: "If a language which has stopped being spoken, with nothing remaining of it save what remains of our language—[if such a language] can return and be the spoken tongue of an individual for all necessities of his life, there is no room for doubt that it can become the spoken language of a community."

In his autobiography, Itamar Ben-Avi describes some of the dramatic actions taken by Ben-Yehuda to be certain that his son would speak only Hebrew. He recollects that when visitors were in the house that did not speak Hebrew, he would be sent to bed to prevent him from hearing "foreign" languages. Inhibited by these restrictions, he did not begin to speak until he was four years old. Itamar recounted that his mother sometimes forgot her promise to speak only Hebrew. One day without thinking, she began to sing lullabies in her native Russian. When Itamar's father returned and heard the Russian singing he became irritated. Itamar wrote about the scene that followed:

> *It caused a great shock to pass over me when I saw my father in his anger and my mother in her grief and tears, and the muteness was removed from my lips, and speech came to my mouth.*

Ben-Avi strolls with Chaim Weizmann and entourage

Ben-Avi poses with his co-workers

As a young man, Itamar began publishing articles in his father's periodicals. He studied overseas in Paris and Berlin at various universities; afterward, working as a journalist, he joined his father's staff in Palestine. In 1910, Ben-Yehuda founded the first daily newspaper in Palestine, *Ha'or* [*The Light*]. He designated his son as editor.

During World War I, Ben-Avi and his family lived the United States. They returned to *Eretz Yisrael* following the war, and began publishing the Hebrew daily *Do'ar Ha-Yom*. In the 1920s, he was also an editor for the English language *Palestine Weekly* and served as correspondent for the *London Times* and *Daily Mail*.

Incorporating ideas that he observed in the French press and culture, to which he was closely aligned, Ben-Avi further modernized the Hebrew language. An eloquent speaker, he visited different countries and lectured on behalf of the Jewish National Fund and the settlement projects, several of which he co-founded. The young pioneer urged that water be supplied to Jerusalem from

Ben-Avi (seated far right) with fellow journalists

the Jordan River no matter how costly. In the 1930s he campaigned for the partitioning of Palestine into a Jewish state and Arab region, inspired by the Swiss system of cantons.

Known for not mincing words, Ben-Avi seemed nearly always to be in a fighting mood. He constantly stepped into controversy. For example, in 1931 he published a message to the rabbis of Israel urging them to find a way in which all Jews could enjoy the *Shabbat* day of rest "according to their own wishes." He took his lead from his father, Ben-Yehuda, who was often criticized for his "sensationalist" editing. However, this criticism of Ben-Yehuda paled compared to that to which Ben-Avi was subjected—such as when his reporting was called "improper" and "irresponsible" journalism.

But Ben-Avi did not alter his style; on the contrary, he appeared to enjoy the notoriety knowing it to be good for the newspaper business. Often he regretted his impetuosity, but that was his manner and his charm. He also introduced technical improvements to his newspaper, giving it an external appearance similar to modern papers abroad.

Itamar Ben-Avi visualized the transformation of the Jewish people into an independent "western" nation of Israel. Following in the footsteps of his father, one of the Hebrew words he invented was *atzma'ut*—"independence." Certainly this aptly described this "maverick" of the early 1900s, the man who was an important journalist and also the first speaker of Modern Hebrew.

Newspaper staff joins Ben-Avi for photograph

Saul Tchernichowsky
1875 - 1943

"We must return to our one language, Hebrew."
— Saul Tchernichowsky

Saul Tchernichowsky was one of the illustrious group of famous Hebrew poets that had a significant influence on the advancement of Modern Hebrew poetry. Hebrew as a living, spoken language was just being developed in the late nineteenth century, and most of Tchernichowsky's contemporaries relied on archaic biblical vocabulary in their literary work. But Tchernichowsky used modern poetic forms to describe familiar subjects, often reminiscent of the style of the Romantic poets. It is clear from his writing that his early life had a strong impact on his work.

Born in 1875 in the village of Mikhailovka, Russia, Tchernichowsky grew up in the home of pious Jewish parents. As with nearly all of the other pioneers of Israel who were writers, traditional and Zionist influences shaped his early years. He attended a Hebrew school and a Russian school, and was educated in both Jewish thinking and secular subjects.

At the age of fourteen, he went to Odessa to prepare for university. Adept in the study of languages, he mastered German, French, English, Greek and Latin. Later in his life he used this gift for languages to translate classical works by Shakespeare, Homer, Longfellow and others into Hebrew.

As a young poet, Tchernichowsky responded to Zionist themes. Captivated by Chaim Nachman Bialik and other contemporary poets and writers, he was inspired by their connection to the Jewish culture. While his style was infused with biblical form, his poetic language was modern. He added a new dimension to Hebrew poetry through his liberating concepts of

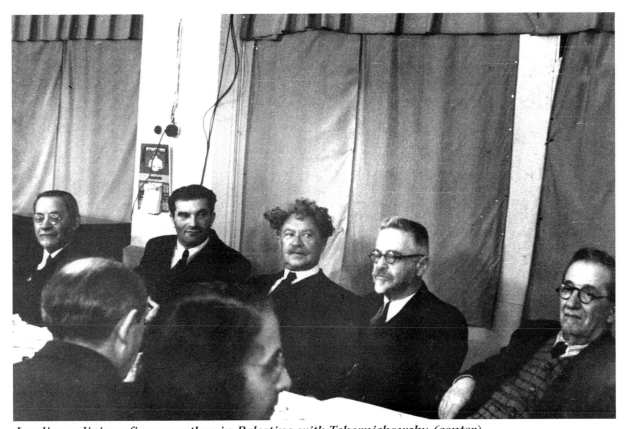

Leading religious figures gather in Palestine with Tchernichowsky (center)

Postcard of one of his Hebrew poems which reads: "Even if our redemption day comes late, we should walk step by step. Do not despair, keep hope. The sun will rise high again."

love and nature. His Zionist background is reflected in several of Tchernichowsky's early poems, which call for a "revolution" by the Jews in the Diaspora.

The eclectic nature of his education—attending both Hebrew and Russian schools—left a distinctive mark on his poetry in which the village, its life, and its landscape are intrinsic components. His education affected his developing attitude towards Diaspora Jewish culture and broadened his interest in other cultures. It stimulated his dedication to the Hebrew language, Jewish nationalism and Zionism, and influenced his thinking about traditional Jewish life.

Restricted from admission to a Russian university, he studied medicine in Heidelberg and received his medical degree in Lausanne in 1905. His poetry during this period focused on his own childhood and reflections on growing up in a *shtetl* [small village]. After completing his studies in Switzerland he returned to Russia, but found it difficult to obtain a position as a doctor because he was Jewish. Tchernichowsky served as an army surgeon during World War I and later as a medical inspector of schools in *Eretz Yisrael*.

From 1922 to 1931, unable to find work in Palestine, he returned to Berlin where he joined the Hebrew literary circle active in Germany, wrote Hebrew children's works, traveled in the United States, and wrote Zionist poems. Most of Tchernichowsky's poems about the land were inspired by German landscapes. Despite being unhappy about not moving to Palestine, he remained a prolific writer, spending much of his time working on translations and compilations. His frustration over not being able to settle in Palestine, however, was evident in his writings.

Tchernichowsky was commissioned to edit *The Book of Medical and Scientific Terms* and with the income from this project he was finally able to move to *Eretz Yisrael*. In 1936, he signed a contract with the Schocken publishing house and moved to Jerusalem, where he lived for the rest of his life. Through his work on the medical texts, he added considerably to Hebrew terminology in both botany and anatomy. During World War II, as preliminary reports of the devastation of the Holocaust became available, he actively called for the rescue of the Jewish people and the need to preserve their freedom in an independent nation of Israel.

Saul Tchernichowsky was an inspiration to the new generation of poets in Israel, and impacted the Hebrew reading society of his time. Through his writing of lyric poetry, dramatic epics, ballads and allegories, he tried to remedy the world of the Jew by injecting a spirit of personal pride and dignity, as well as a heightened awareness of nature and beauty. Tchernichowsky is one of the select circle of eminent Hebrew poets who represents the transition from ancient Jewish poetry to the modern genre.

Tchernichowsky portrait (1943)

Fellow pioneers with Tchernichowsky and Arab family

Yosef Haim Brenner
1881 - 1921

> ### *It's impossible to exist in Palestine without some backing from abroad.*
>
> — Yosef Haim Brenner

Essayist, critic, commentator, translator, novelist and poet, Yosef Haim Brenner was one of the most prominent literary figures in *Eretz Yisrael* in his day. He was one of the writers responsible for shifting the center of Hebrew literary activities away from Europe.

Brenner expounded views that seemingly were paradoxical. An enthusiastic Zionist who passionately encouraged immigration, he was an equally fierce critic of both Zionism and Jews. Although an honest pessimist by nature, his prose professes a belief in "artistic truth" where all other faith has failed. He had little patience with the rabbinic world, feeling that it had inhibited Jewish creativity in the Diaspora.

Yosef Brenner was born in the Ukraine in 1881 to a traditional Jewish family. After studying in a *yeshiva*, he went to Gomel where he joined the Bund, a Jewish left-wing labor organization. In the early 1900s, while living in Bialystok and Warsaw, he made a living teaching Hebrew. Later he served three years in the

Brenner in 1911

Russian army, but at the outbreak of the Russo-Japanese war, he was smuggled out of the country and escaped to London. There he worked in a printing shop, founded a Hebrew language periodical and became active in the *Po'alei Zion*, a socialist Zionist movement.

Four writers of the Second Aliyah (left to right) Shai Agnon, Alexander Siskind Rabinovitz, Yosef Haim Brenner and David Shimoni (1911)

Portrait of Yosef Haim Brenner (1881)

Throughout this time he continued his writing, and when he immigrated to *Eretz Yisrael* in 1909, his stories and essays were published in a number of periodicals.

In his many short stories and novels, Brenner described the life of the Jews in Russia, the plight of the Jewish workers in England, and the state of the Jewish community in Jerusalem. He was concerned about social conditions and wrote negatively about his subjects, no doubt hoping to stimulate his readers to change things. He was perhaps the most vehement among a number of the intellectuals of the Second Aliyah in his demand for an open-ended secular Hebrew identity. His personal philosophy inspired his writing.

Yosef Haim Brenner's last great novel is set in a Jewish settlement in Palestine, in the years leading up to World War I, when the future tragic pattern of Arab-Jewish relations was taking shape. Far more than an absorbing period piece, *Breakdown and Bereavement* is the "universal story of individual loneliness" integral to the human condition. Brenner's "Hefetz,"

Yosef Haim Brenner and his wife

Brenner (seated right) and pioneers including Ben-Gurion (center) and Ha'Achdut staff (1910)

the lead character, is a wanderer in search of a spiritual homeland. His desperate attempt to build a new life in Palestine has been interpreted to symbolize the entire Zionist enterprise.

Central to Brenner's works is his identification with both the physical struggle of the pioneers for a toehold in an arid, harsh land—so very different from the European countries where they were born—and their struggle, no less difficult, to shape the identity of the Jew in the Land of Israel.

During the Third Aliyah in the early 1920s, Brenner joined the *Gedud Ha'avodah* [labor battalions] and worked in road construction in the Galilee. He also assisted in founding the *Histadrut* [Labor Federation].

Brenner translated some of the world's classic books into Hebrew and both wrote and translated in Yiddish. Through his writing, he clearly made an important contribution to the development of Modern Hebrew. He was killed during the Arab riots in Jaffa, in May 1921.

Yosef Brenner was among the Jewish writers in *Eretz Yisrael* who faced the daunting challenge of creating a new body of work from a language that had been restricted for centuries to prayer and religious study. Modern Hebrew, the revived language, is in many ways an art form in itself. Because of their mastery of this language, many call Yosef Haim Brenner and Shai Agnon the "fathers" of Modern Hebrew literature.

Israel Zangwill
1864 - 1926

> *If there were no Jews they would have to be invented for the use of the politicians—they {the Jews} are indispensable.*
> — Israel Zangwill

Israel Zangwill was a playwright, poet, author and, most importantly, a spokesperson for the "magnificence" of the future State of Israel. He was acknowledged as the father of modern English-Jewish literature, and was considered the wittiest of all the early Zionist writers.

Born in London in 1864 to poor Jewish Russian immigrants, Zangwill was educated at the Jewish Free School in the East End of the city. He had degrees in French, English, and science. His early literary career started with humorous short stories that ignore the fact that he grew up in squalor and hardship. But he took notes about those difficult days knowing that someday he would write about them. These notebooks formed the basis for his eventual "ghetto" novels.

As a young man Zangwill taught at the Jewish Free School, but left in 1888 because of his opposition to corporal punishment. Zangwill worked as a journalist for the *Jewish Standard*, writing a humorous column. In this early period of his life, he was curious and intrigued by the challenges of Jews living in the Diaspora.

In 1889, he wrote an essay on Anglo-Jewry that appeared in the first volume of the *Jewish Quarterly Review* that expressed a dichotomy in his beliefs that was reflected throughout his

Israel Zangwell with his wife in Basel at the Seventh Zionist Congress (1905)

Zangwell standing to the right of center with the early Maccabees

writing career. Though he was passionately devoted to Jewish values, he wanted to escape from the "ghetto mentality." His first major novel, *Children of the Ghetto* (1892), depicted an ironic and humorous look at Jewish life, much of it based on his own history. A few years later, he published another "ghetto" study, *The King of the Schnorrers*. This was an imaginary and hilarious account of London Jewry in the eighteenth century. Though his works delved into social and religious issues, they also provided a wonderful insight into the history of the time.

Zangwill's interests and productivity were not limited exclusively to literature. He was active in important social issues including women's suffrage, pacifism, and Zionism. Zangwill was a prominent member of the Order of Ancient Maccabeans, an early Zionist society established in London in 1891. He spoke with pride about being Jewish:

> *I am a Jew, of course, and proud of it. The advantage of being of Jewish birth brought me into relationship with a good deal of suffering all over the world, and I appreciate more than Englishmen possibly do, the great advantage the English enjoy with the possession of liberty in their constitution.*

When Theodor Herzl visited London in 1896, he met with Zangwill and requested the writer and activist's help to "rebuild the Jewish state." In response, Zangwill arranged for Herzl to address his first London audience. Zangwill attended the First Zionist Congress in Basel, supported Herzl, and began his friendship with Max Nordau. He continued to attend subsequent congresses of the World Zionist Organization.

Following the rejection of Herzl's Uganda Plan, Zangwill, who had endorsed the plan, led the "territorialists" out of the Zionist organization. He established the Jewish Territorialists

Organization (ITO) in 1905, whose stated objective was to acquire a Jewish homeland "wherever possible." With the help of Lord Rothschild and American philanthropist Jacob Schiff, the ITO looked for other alternatives. One was Galveston, Texas, where several thousand Jews settled as a result of Zangwill's encouragement. Following the issuance of the Balfour Declaration, the ITO decreased its activities and by 1925 it officially was dissolved.

Zangwill was one of Zionism's most eloquent and inspirational speakers. Supporters of Zionism congregated to hear him passionately present the case for a modern Jewish state. "The literature of Israel," Zangwill wrote, "in its widest sense comprises the contribution made by Jews to the thesaurus of the world. All alphabets and all vocabularies are drawn into its service."

Near the end of his life, Israel Zangwill, in his humorous way commented: "A chosen people is really a choosing people."

Theodor Herzl with Zangwell in Basel (1897)

Zangwell , Herzl, Nordau and Wolffsohn join Russian Zionists (1903)

Martin Buber
1878 - 1965

> *This land {Eretz Yisrael} recognizes us, for it is fruitful through us: and precisely because it bears fruit for us, it recognizes us.*
>
> — Martin Buber

Martin Buber is considered the pre-eminent Jewish thinker of the twentieth century. He is described as a philosopher, theologian, storyteller, Zionist thinker and leader; he had a pervasive effect on Christian as well as Jewish thinkers.

Unlike many of his contemporaries who were born into Hasidism, Martin Buber developed his spiritual connection to the movement when he was twenty-six. Deeply stirred by its message, he felt it was his duty to convey Hasidism to the world. This religious movement emerged around 1750 in Poland and the Ukraine. It represents deep religious sentiment and a "longing for God," emphasizing emotional values, joy and love, and direct communication with the "Divine." Much of Buber's writing had its roots in this spiritual base.

Martin Buber was born in Vienna in 1878 and lived with his grandfather, Solomon Buber, the noted Midrash scholar. He grew up in a multi-lingual home, speaking Yiddish and German from birth, Hebrew and French, which he learned in his early childhood, and Polish, which he studied in school. He attended university in Berlin, Vienna, Leipzig, and Zurich where he was educated by some of the leading philosophers of the time.

Buber became a Zionist when he was twenty, and attended the Third Zionist Congress in 1899. He addressed the Congress about the importance of Zionist education and the need for new cultural creativity. Buber enthusiastically supported Ahad Ha'am, and for a short time he was the editor of the weekly Zionist house journal, *Die Welt* [*The World*].

Martin Buber testifying in Palestine following World War II (1946)

His early writings dealt with Hasidism and the tales of Rabbi Nachman of Bratslav. His books include *The Tales of Rabbi Nachman*, *The Legend of Baal-Shem*, *Hasidism and Modern Man*, and *For the Sake of Heaven*. It was through writing his stories that he presented the significance of Hasidism to others. Historians write that virtually single-handedly, Buber transformed Hasidism into one of the most mystical movements of the modern era.

Beginning in 1909 Buber toured Europe, inspiring young people to become involved in Jewish causes. With the start of World War I, he established the Jewish National Committee in Berlin, which worked to assist Jews in Eastern Europe who were being persecuted by the German authorities. The Committee also promoted *aliyah* to Palestine. In 1916 he founded the monthly periodical *Der Jude* [*The Jew*], which for some years was the most important publication for the new Jewish cultural renaissance moving across Central Europe.

Buber articulated what he called "Hebrew humanism," Zionism based on "utopian" socialism. It stressed the "divine role" of the Jewish people among nations. Buber believed that Zionism is based on the fundamental moral and spiritual values of Judaism. This belief is closely tied to the intrinsic spiritual, divine nature of Hasidism. He felt that cultural or utopian Zionism was more meaningful than the political Zionism of Theodor Herzl.

Buber took on as his lifelong work translating the Bible into German, which he started in 1925 and completed in 1961. A professor of Jewish religion and ethics from 1923 until 1930, he then was appointed an honorary professor at the University of Frankfurt. He resigned this position in protest immediately after Hitler came to power in 1933. In October 1933, Buber was forbidden by Nazi authorities to give lectures. In an effort to circumvent this action and to continue teaching, he founded the Central Office for Jewish Adult Education, which became increasingly important as Jews were banned from attending public schools in Germany.

In 1938 he moved to Palestine and settled in Jerusalem as a professor of Social Philosophy at the Hebrew University. Two of Buber's most insightful books were written in Hebrew, *The Prophetic Faith* and *Moses*, both of which delved into the connection of Israel to biblical faith. Someone once asked him, "How good is your Hebrew?" He answered, "Good enough to lec-

Portrait of Martin Buber

Buber seated (far right) listens to dissertation

ture in, but not sufficiently good to be obscure." His most widely known works include *I and Thou*, a poetic expression of his religious philosophy, and *On Judaism*, both of which contributed to his intellectual leadership of the German-Jewish community.

Martin Buber had a direct effect on immigration to the new State of Israel, as one of the founders of the Israeli Institute for Adult Education and the Israel Academy of Sciences and Humanities. He lectured overseas, especially in the United States, and inspired thinkers of every faith.

Buber was universally recognized as one of the great spiritual leaders of his generation. David Ben-Gurion called him "a metaphysical entity in his own class, a true man of the spirit." Some say his greatest gift to mankind was his concept of "dialogue." On the occasion of Buber's eighty-fifth birthday, Ben-Gurion said: "Buber deserves praise and glory in the history of our people and our time."

His wife Paula died in 1958 and, ironically, that same year he was awarded the Israel Prize. Buber received many prestigious awards in his lifetime, including the Erasmus Award in Amsterdam in 1963. He died in his home in Talbiyeh, Jerusalem in 1965 at the age of eighty-seven.

In *Tales of the Hasidim*, Buber wrote: "they asked Rabbi Levi Yitzhak, 'Why is the first page number missing in all the tractates of the Babylonian Talmud? Why does each begin with the second [the number *bet*]?' He replied, 'However much a man may learn, he should always remember that he has not even gotten to the first page.'"

Yigal Yadin
1917 - 1984

> *Nowhere else on earth are archeologists probing a richer historical dust.*
>
> — Yigal Yadin

Yigal Yadin might be described as a "man for all seasons." He was widely respected as a great military commander for Israel, serving with both the Haganah and the Israel Defense Forces (IDF), and he was equally successful and acclaimed as a renowned Israeli archeologist.

In the 1950s, the famous Hebrew University archaeologist Professor Yigal Yadin postulated that a series of monumental structures—and particularly the city gates of Hatzor, Megiddo, and Gezer, as well as certain palaces at Megiddo—were founded by Solomon, corroborating the text in I Kings 9:15. His extensive research into these famous biblical landmarks stimulated considerable interpretation and continuing additional study.

Born in Jerusalem in 1917, Yadin was a native born Israeli, a *sabra*. He was the son of famous archeologist Eliezer Lipa Sukenik. In 1933, Yadin joined the Haganah and in 1944 he became director of their officers' school. As the War of Independence approached, Yadin, only thirty-one, was appointed operations and planning officer of the Haganah, responsible for drawing up and instituting the operations of the new Israel Defense Forces (IDF). In 1949, he was appointed chief of staff, received the rank of major general, and continued in this post until 1952, when he left the army to study archeology.

Yadin studied in Jerusalem at the Hebrew University beginning in 1952, later joining the staff of the university. He received his doctorate in 1955 for his work on the Dead Sea Scrolls, for which, in 1956, he received the Israel Prize in Jewish Studies. Yadin continued his research in archeology and antiquities, teaching and publishing prolifically over the years that followed. Among his best-known works are *Masada* and *Tefilin From Qumran*. In 1970, he

Yigal Yadin chats with Ben-Gurion and Eliezer Kaplan under wing of one of Israel's first airplanes

Yadin points to map at a strategy conference (1949)

became head of the Institute of Archeology at the Hebrew University, publishing hundreds of articles in a number of languages on the topics of archeology and history.

As a result of his breakthrough research and fieldwork, Yadin came to the forefront in the international archeology world. His discoveries at Masada, Megiddo and Hatzor continue to receive acclaim for their impact and value in acquiring a deeper understanding of the intricacies of ancient history. He became world famous for his historical and philological decoding and interpretations of the Dead Sea and Judean Desert scrolls. Through his dedication, the Shrine of the Book was built as part of the Israel Museum to house the Dead Sea Scrolls.

Yadin also opened up the field of archeology to larger, more mainstream audiences. While his writing is scholarly, it is also accessible to lay people. He places his archeological findings within a cultural context, using this information as a way to interpret history.

Later in his life, Yadin was involved in yet another career—he became interested in politics and held several public positions. He served as military advisor to Prime Minister Levi Eshkol, and following the Yom Kippur War served on the Agranat Commission. For the elections in 1977 he formed a new party, *Dash*, which surprisingly received fifteen seats in the Knesset. The party eventually joined the *Likud* government of Menachem Begin and Yadin was appointed deputy prime minister, a post that he held from 1977 to 1981. He retired from political life in 1981, returning to his research until he died in 1984.

There is a wonderful anecdote told in Israel that highlights Yadin's personal commitment to Israel, as well as his compassion as a human being. The story is about a priceless religious discovery made by Professor Yadin. He discovered a pair of *tefilin* [phylactery, religious object], about two thousand years old, dating from the time of the Second Temple. Returning on the train from Tel Aviv where he had lectured on the discovery, he noticed several

Lubavitcher Hasidim [Orthodox Jews], preparing to put on *tefilin* for prayers.

One of the Hasidim invited Yadin to join in, but Yadin declined saying he was not religious. In the conversation, Yadin learned that the Hasid had escaped from Russia only two years prior. Yadin inquired, "did you put on *tefilin* in Russia?" to which the man replied that he had worn it every day since his *bar mitzvah* (he was now about 40 years old). Yadin asked himself, "How can I refuse this man, raised under communist rule, yet never missed putting on *tefilin*?"

Yigal put on the *tefilin*, recited the *Shema* and thanked the man for offering him the opportunity, recalling "the Hasid's face shone." An elderly woman, who had been watching the encounter, afterward approached Yadin, said that she recognized him and told him a story. She said that her son had also been a Hasid of Lubavitch, and was the only religious parachutist in his army unit. Her son put on *tefilin* every day. He was mortally

Yadin shows Francesco Dead Sea Scrolls (1956)

wounded during the Six Day War, and as he lay on the desert sand, critically injured, his comrades asked him what his last wish was.

Yadin surveys terrain in Eilat

"Put on *tefilin*," her son whispered, just as he died. Right then, all his fellow paratroopers put on her son's *tefilin*. She showed Yadin a photo of her son and Yadin remembered he had pictures of the ancient *tefilin* with him, which had not yet been viewed by the public. "I was overwhelmed by this chance meeting with the Lubavitcher and the bereaved mother on the train. It was unbelievable and very moving. I felt that I would break down. I took out my pictures and showed them to the mother. So she was the first to see my discovery. The elderly woman looked at the pictures and we both began to cry."

Yigal Yadin served the new State of Israel as a prolific pioneer, a man of many diverse talents, specializing in politics, archeology, and defense of the Jewish homeland.

Albert Einstein
1879 - 1955

> *We Jews should once more become conscious of our existence as a nationality and regain the self-respect that is necessary to a healthy existence.*
> — Albert Einstein

Albert Einstein was honored by *Time* magazine by being named their "Person of the Century" in January 2000. He is an icon of the modern era, adored by all generations, described universally as a scientific genius and named on virtually everyone's list of twentieth century heroes.

Time magazine introduced him in this way:

> *He was the embodiment of pure intellect, the bumbling professor with the German accent, a comic cliché in a thousand films. Instantly recognizable, like Charlie Chaplin's Little Tramp, Albert Einstein's shaggy-haired visage was as familiar to ordinary people as to the matrons who fluttered about him in salons from Berlin to Hollywood. Yet he was unfathomably profound — the genius among geniuses who discovered, merely by thinking about it, that the universe was not as it seemed.*

Einstein's scientific achievements, coupled with his unpretentious attitude and concern for humanity, made him a beloved, world-renowned figure. Wherever he traveled he was mobbed by people hoping to catch a glimpse of the genius who had changed their perception of the universe. Einstein himself never understood the public's fascination with his every word and deed, saying once: "Why is it that nobody understands me and everybody likes me?"

Mayor Dizengoff (to the right of Einstein) hosts the world-renown scientist with his wife in Tel Aviv (1923)

Albert Einstein was an extraordinary scientist and mathematician, a brilliant philosopher, moralist and teacher, and most of all, a unique and amazing human being. As one of the world's most influential scientists, his celebrity and status contributed a compelling impetus to the establishment of the State of Israel.

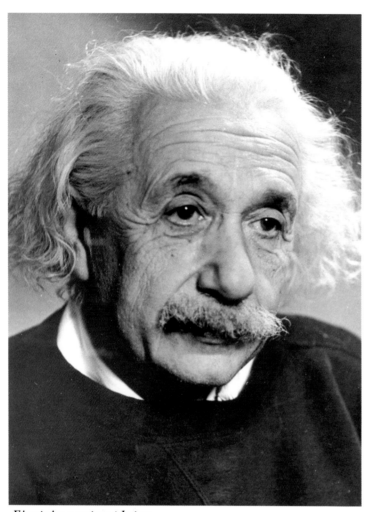

Einstein contemplates

Einstein was born on March 14, 1879 in Ulm, Germany, the first child of a Jewish couple, Hermann and Pauline Einstein. He was strongly influenced by his musically inclined mother, who encouraged his passion for the violin and classical composers such as Bach, Mozart and Schubert.

His easygoing engineer father was a struggling entrepreneur in the emerging electrochemical industry. He gave Einstein the celebrated toy compass that inspired his first "thought experiment" when the five year old asked, "What makes the needle always point north?"

The family moved to Munich in 1880, where Einstein had a normal childhood, despite the fact that he learned to speak at a late age. Even as a small boy Albert Einstein was self-sufficient and thoughtful. According to family legend he talked slowly, pausing to consider what he would say. He loved solitude and often was caught humming songs he made up while walking and hiding in his father's garden. As a boy he was fascinated by algebra and geometry, though he detested the militaristic discipline of the German schools he attended. He graduated from the Swiss Federal Polytechnic School in Zurich in 1900, and received his doctorate from Zurich in 1905.

Unable to obtain an academic position, he took a post with the patent office in Bern while continuing to pursue his fundamental interest in physics. Einstein found German nationalism repulsive; he renounced his German citizenship and formally applied for Swiss citizenship, which was granted in February 1901. While he was working in the patent office, it is said that his fellow workers marveled at the fact that he could accomplish a full day's work in an hour or so. This freedom on the job allowed him time to pursue his research in mathematics and science.

In 1905 he published three brilliant papers in the *Annalen der Physik* that transformed twentieth century scientific thought. He wrote a *Special Theory of Relativity*, proposing that physical laws do not change when observers move in relation to one another. His view of relativity of motion proved that space and time are not absolute—they are affected by the relationships of movement and mass. His first paper on "relativity" did not contain his famous equation "E=mc2." This was almost an afterthought, and it appeared in a supplemental paper in 1906. This early work was the foundation for his research and writing on the subject of relativity, which continued for years.

The second of the papers was his *Theory of Brownian Motion*, which affected future methods of scientific measurement. The third article described the *Photon Theory of Light* (photoelectric effect) for which he received the Nobel Prize in 1921. The principle of the photoelectric effect laid the cornerstone for the invention of television.

Einstein was married in January 1903 to Mileva Maric, and they had two sons, Hans Albert and Eduard. Impressed by his scientific achieve-

Bicycling on the campus of the California Institute of Technology in the early 1930s

ments, Max Planck and the physical chemist Walther Nernst lured him to Berlin to become a member of the Prussian Academy of Sciences. He was offered a teaching position at Berlin University, and the opportunity to become head of the Kaiser Wilhelm Institute of Physics. Einstein accepted this offer and moved his family to Berlin in 1914. When he was appointed director of the Wilhelm Institute and professor at the University, he once again assumed German citizenship.

As a way to relax from his work, Einstein found time to play music. He learned to play the violin when he was young, and continued to play as an adult—he was frequently seen on the street carrying his violin case. Apart from his love for music, he was also a dedicated sailor and found his time on the water a quiet time to think about the problems of physics. He had one other hobby, reciting Jewish jokes and folklore.

Einstein published another paper, *Relativity, the Special and the General Theory: A Popular Exposition, 1920,* which profoundly modified the simple concepts of space and time on which Newtonian mechanics had been based. His prediction of the deflection of light by the gravitational field of the sun was borne out by a British team of scientists at the time of the solar eclipse in 1919, making Einstein a household name.

Time magazine said this about the impact of his theories, his philosophy and especially his persona:

Much to his surprise, his ideas, like Darwin's, reverberated beyond science, influencing modern culture from painting to poetry. At first even many scientists didn't really grasp relativity, prompting Arthur Edenton's celebrated wisecrack. When asked if it was true that only three people understood relativity, the witty British astrophysicist paused, and then said, 'I am trying to think who the third person is.'

Joseph John Thompson, president of the Royal Society, stated solemnly, "this is the most important result related to the theory of gravitation since the days of Newton… this result is among the greatest achievements of human thinking." This confirmation of the predictions made Einstein world-famous, and not only among scientists. He received invitations and honors from all over the world. His achievements were reported with the highest praise.

Einstein testifying in Palestine (1946)

The world was shocked when Einstein became the subject of vigorous anti-Semitic attacks especially in Germany. Despite praise from around the world, in Germany not only his work but also his pacifist politics aroused violent animosity. Anti-Semites tried to brand his relativity theory as "un-German" and during the Third Reich they partially achieved their objective: Einstein's name could no longer be mentioned in lectures or scholarly papers, though his relativity theory was still taught.

Einstein's political views as a pacifist and a Zionist made him a target for conservatives in Germany who branded him a traitor and a defeatist. The public success accorded his theories of relativity evoked savage attacks by anti-Semitic physicists. Just how controversial the theories of relativity remained is revealed in the circumstances surrounding Einstein's receiving the Nobel Prize in 1921—it was awarded, not for relativity, but for his 1905 work on the photoelectric effect.

During the 1920s Einstein traveled extensively in the United States, Britain, France, Japan and Palestine. At that time he began to comment on political issues more frequently, based on his pacifist point of view. He also began to identity himself with Zionism. In 1922 Einstein became a member of the League of Nations International Committee on Intellectual Cooperation. Working to fight harsh immigration quotas imposed against Jews, Einstein wrote affidavits and enlisted the help of friends in assisting as many refugees as possible.

Einstein with High Commissioner Herbert Samuel and associates

When Hitler came to power in 1933, Einstein resigned his teaching position and accepted an invitation from the Institute for Advanced Study in Princeton, New Jersey. Einstein became an American citizen and he never again returned to Germany. His property in Germany was seized and a price was put on his head by Nazi fanatics. His books were among those burned in May 1933, branded as proof of his "un-German spirit."

Einstein found a warm welcome in the United States. He was a well-known figure in Princeton, due in no small part to his shock of white hair, his refusal to wear socks, and his total absorption in scientific problems. Many Princeton residents have fond memories of spotting the famous physicist, lost in thought, walking to and from his office at the Institute for Advanced Study.

With the start of World War II in 1939, Einstein grew alarmed at the prospect of Germany acquiring the atomic bomb after two German physicists discovered the fusion of uranium. Einstein signed a letter to President Roosevelt in August 1939, alerting him to the danger of atomic weapons. Motivated by a host of factors including Einstein's letter, President Roosevelt soon initiated programs that led to the Manhattan Project and the eventual development of the atomic bomb. It is ironic that the deeply pacifistic Einstein inadvertently brought attention to nuclear weapons, which he vigorously opposed.

Einstein became more active in Jewish causes, especially those associated with Zionism. In a letter written to Israeli Prime Minister David Ben-Gurion in November 1952, Einstein wrote: "my relationship to the Jewish people has become my strongest human bond, ever since I became fully aware of our precarious situation among the nations of the world."

Einstein and wife at Paramont Pictures premiere of Israeli film "New Life"

Einstein was active in raising funds for organizations such as the United Jewish Appeal and working toward securing a Jewish homeland in Palestine. When Chaim Weizmann, the first president of Israel and an old friend of Einstein's, died in 1952, Einstein was offered the presidency. The day after Weizmann's death, an Israeli newspaper wrote that Einstein's acceptance of the post would bring great prestige to the Jewish state. Einstein, then seventy-three, graciously declined the offer for two reasons: he felt he was too old, and also that he lacked the experience to deal with people as a statesman. He regretfully wrote: "I am deeply moved by the offer from our State of Israel, and at once saddened and ashamed that I cannot accept it."

Though not religious, Einstein was a believer. "I want to know how God created this world... I want to know his thoughts; the rest are details." And he had a good idea of what those thoughts were. His love for the Jewish people and Israel was evident in his writings. His faith in Jewish nationalism was strong: "We Jews should once more become conscious of our existence as a nationality and regain the self-respect that is necessary to a healthy existence." Einstein was a rare German commodity. Very few German Jews endorsed Zionism at that time. But his vision was global, as he noted: "Palestine is not primarily a place of refuge for the Jews of Eastern Europe, but the embodiment of the reawakening corporate spirit of the whole Jewish nation."

He wrote passionately on the subject of anti-Semitism:

> *Before we can effectively combat anti-Semitism, we must first of all educate ourselves out of it, and out of the slave mentality which it betokens. Only when we respect ourselves can we win the respect of others; or rather, the respect of others will then come of itself.*

In discussing Jewish individuality and the connection to the Jewish homeland, Einstein wrote:

The 'Jewish problem' cannot be solved by the assimilation of the individual Jew to his environment. Jewish individuality is too strong to be effaced by such assimilation and too conscious to be ready for such self-effacement.... The establishment of a national home for the Jewish people in Palestine would raise the status and dignity of those who would remain in their native countries and would thereby materially assist in improving the relations between Jew and non-Jew.

By 1949, Einstein's health was failing. Some time in a hospital helped him recover but in 1950 he began to prepare for death by drawing up his will. He left his scientific papers to the Hebrew University in Jerusalem, an institution for which he had served as a governor from 1925 to 1928 and for which he had raised funds on his first visit to the United States.

One week before his death in 1955, Einstein signed his last letter. It was a letter to Bertrand Russell in which he agreed to place his name on a manifesto urging all nations to give up nuclear weapons. It is fitting that one of his last acts was to argue, as he had all his life, for international peace.

Einstein died in April 1955 in Princeton Hospital, yet the world-wide fascination with this "kind and gentle genius" continues today. Einstein captured the world's imagination with his blend of brilliant scientific theories and humanitarian concern. To Einstein, individual freedom was the ultimate morality; he said it simply in 1933:

Planting a tree in the Migdal, Palestine (1921)

As long as I have any choice, I will stay only in a country where political liberty, toleration and equality of all citizens before the law are the rule.

Fortunately, he found that precious freedom and opportunity for individualism and free-thinking in the United States, and Israel and the world continue to reap the benefits from this brilliant and humble citizen, a Zionist in his soul and in his heart.

CHAPTER SIX

Religious Influences

Rav Abraham Isaac Kook
1865 - 1935

> *Those who rebuild the land are as favored in the sight of God as the ritually observant.*
>
> — Rav Abraham Isaac Kook

It is said of Rabbi Kook, the first Chief Rabbi of what was then Palestine, that he was perhaps the most misunderstood figure of his time.

Born in Latvia of staunch Hasidic stock, throughout his life he retained a unique blend of the mystical and the rational. He was a thorough master of *halachic*, *midrashic*, philosophic, ethical, and kabbalistic literature, and he brought this tradition into contemporary times. He envisioned the return to *Eretz Yisrael* as not merely a political phenomenon to save Jews from persecution, but an event of extraordinary historical and theological significance.

Kook was a truly pious man—one felt a sense of the divine inherent in him, and his deep commitment reached out to those who had deviated from the spiritual path. His devout aura was evident from a very young age; he displayed an individualism and curiosity that reflected a maturity quite different from his schoolmates.

Recognized early in his life as a child prodigy, Kook began his career as a rabbi at twenty-three. A devoutly Orthodox Jew, Kook simultaneously was an eclectic thinker, and his studies ranged from Jewish mysticism to secular studies. He developed a love for all forms of Jewish learning, including the Bible, Hebrew language, and the mysticism of Kabbalah.

Abraham Isaac Kook was born, raised and educated in the heart of traditional Eastern European Orthodox Judaism; his parents brought both Hasidic and Mitnagdim [Orthodox non-Hasidic philosophy based on religious experience] principles to the family. From this tra-

Rav Kook at religious ceremony in Jerusalem

Rav Kook explains his religious philosophy to Hadassah Hospital staff (1934)

ditional background Kook began a career as a religious Jew embracing a powerful new secular movement—Jewish nationalism. The Jewish nationalist movement that emerged in nineteenth-century Europe introduced Zionism, and Kook became a passionate advocate.

Rabbi Kook settled in *Eretz Yisrael* in 1904, as the rabbi of Jaffa, which included responsibility for the new secular Zionist agricultural settlements nearby. His influence on pioneers from different backgrounds already was evident, as he attempted to introduce Torah and *Halacha* [collective body of Jewish law] into the life of the city and the settlements.

In 1914 he participated in the Agudat Israel Conference of Religious Jews in Europe to present his philosophy of religious Zionism. Unable to return to Palestine because of World War I, Kook accepted a temporary position as rabbi for a synagogue in London, where he zealously lobbied British Jews to take part in the Zionist movement. While in Europe he was involved in activities that led to the issuance of the Balfour Declaration.

When the office of Chief Rabbinate of Palestine was established in 1921, Kook was chosen to become the first Ashkenazi Chief Rabbi, and he held this position until he died in 1935. He believed that the establishment of the Chief Rabbinate was the first step towards the reconstitution of the Sanhedrin [ancient Jewish religious court system]. Convinced that the return of Jews to *Eretz Yisrael* marked the beginning of the messianic era, Kook involved himself in many Zionist activities. In his opinion, the Zionist movement emphasized the material needs of the Jews, while the spiritual aspects of the nationalist movement were being neglected.

Kook viewed Jewish settlement in *Eretz Yisrael* not only as a modern secular movement, but also as the return to traditional Judaism as expressed in the Torah. Through the centuries, the connection of the Jews to the Land of Israel gradually had become symbolic. History transformed Judaism into a Diaspora religion and though traditional Jews "longed in their prayers" to return to *Eretz Yisrael*, the reality was that they had learned to adapt and prosper away from their biblical homeland. Judaism itself had evolved to survive in exile. Kook's thinking reversed this reality, arguing that Jews only could reach religious fulfillment by returning to the Land of Israel.

The Jews who were leading the new nationalist movement were not religious. They had abandoned strict religious ritual and consequently were subjected to the scorn of their Orthodox colleagues. Kook regarded these secular Zionists with admiration, not disapproval, and he saw their endeavors as part of a divine plan. He commended the Zionist pioneers for giving up their livelihoods in the Diaspora, instead choosing a different form of holy work, one comparable to traditional ritual observance. In this way, Kook was able to create a common ground between traditional Orthodox Judaism and modern secular Zionism.

Portrait of Rav Kook

A reporter once asked Kook why he did not protest the opening of cinemas and theaters in Israel, since it clearly states in the Talmud: "he who frequents circuses and theaters has no share in the world to come." Kook responded, "there is another passage in the Talmud that says that in the messianic era, all theaters will be converted into synagogues. Well, then, the more theaters now, the more synagogues when the Messiah comes." His position was that mankind had made tremendous cultural and scientific strides forward but had passed over religion. He optimistically commented in his writings that this was a passing fad and he predicted a rebirth of religious observance.

Kook's philosophy was based on the quest for unity and harmony in the world. The two fundamental principles he stressed most were *emunah* and *ahavah*, "belief" and "love." Kook's tolerance and acceptance of secular Jews made him unpopular with more radical Orthodox rabbis. He refused to reject Jews as long as they identified themselves as Jews. He once quoted the rabbinic dictum that "one should embrace with the right hand and rebuff with the left" and commented that he was "fully capable of rejecting, but since there were enough rejecters, he was fulfilling the role of embracer."

The founding ceremony of Kibbutz Gezar included Rav Kook and Sir Samuel (1924)

Both the non-religious and the religious extremists often misunderstood Kook. He sincerely projected his belief that the secular community needed to redirect its materialistic obsession and turn to more spiritual paths in the new national revival. He was continually at odds with rabbis and often clarified that the *Mizrahi* religious party did not speak for all the religious Jews of Palestine or abroad. He spoke of the early twentieth century as a period of clashing opposites:

> *Ours is a wonderful generation. In all of Jewish history it is difficult to find its equal. It consists of opposites; darkness and light exist in confusion. On one hand, mischievous and wild, on the other hand, exalted and refined; on the one hand, arrogant and shameless and, on the other hand, overwhelmed with a passion for justice and mercy. Its preoccupation with both facts and ideals bursts forth and ascends to Heaven.*

In a noteworthy exchange with his great friend, admirer, and philosophic opponent Rabbi Yaacov David Willowski, Rabbi Kook explained the two components of a Jew: his essential nature—the "*pintele yid*," and the path he had chosen in exercising free will. Even if the second element was weak, Kook explained, as long as the first was not renounced, there was still hope. He called for and envisioned a "spiritual renaissance where the ancient would be renewed and the new would be sanctified."

Rabbi Kook's life was filled with dichotomies of ideas, but always was based on a strong spiritual and religious foundation. He tried to broaden the outlook of the *yeshivot* [religious schools] to cope with modern ideas and to train spiritual leaders. That he was able to successfully blend both the religious and the secular made him respected and revered as a great leader and a great man.

Rav Kook and his son-in-law

In the opening ceremony in 1925 for the Hebrew University, Kook publicly advocated the merging of religious and secular studies. He maintained that the study of secular science was complimentary to the Torah. He considered evolution to be in tandem with Jewish mysticism and thought that the "overwhelming longing of man to cleave to God" could only be attained through the progressive determination of generations moving closer to the goal of "holiness."

According to Kook, God imposed a divine task upon the Jewish nation, but it was up to the Jews to accept and carry out this divine duty. Kook purported that it was the divine plan that led the people of Israel to make *Eretz Yisrael* its country and create its history there. The relationship and connection of the Jews to Israel is essential to the divine scheme in Kook's philosophy.

Though keenly aware of the large numbers of non-observant Jews, Kook had a vision of the repentance of the nation. He envisioned the repentance of the individual, as well as a repentance of the nation as a whole, a "repentance that would be joyous and healing." He looked forward to "the poet of *teshuva* [repentance], who would be the poet of life, the poet of renewal and the poet of the national soul waiting to be redeemed." Rav Kook might have been that poet.

Rabbi Abraham Kook reveled in his love for the whole of the Jewish people, and all those who are aware of his contribution to the pioneer spirit and birth of Israel have loved him in return. One of his more memorable quotes reflects his eternal spirit:

> *I still hope that the day will come when the Jews who are great will become great Jews.*

Rabbi Arthur Cohn
1862 - 1926

> ***For us the land of the Jews is not a land like any other but a Divine inheritance.***
>
> — Rabbi Arthur Cohn

Rabbi Arthur Cohn was only twenty-three years old in 1885, when he was invited to become the first rabbi of Basel, Switzerland. He was honored to be the first Orthodox rabbi in all of Switzerland.

Rabbi Cohn's uncanny insight and dynamic energy touched the hearts and souls of Jews in Switzerland, as well as those who visited him from other countries. He established the Jewish Orphanage in Basel and the Jewish Sanatorium in Davos. He played an extremely influential role in the history of the Zionist pioneers, a role that resulted from his gracious and generous invitation to Theodor Herzl.

Herzl had planned for Munich to be the location of the First Zionist Congress, but he was forced to abandon this plan in the face of vigorous and vehement protests made by German Jews. Germany's Jewish community, comprised mainly of assimilated Jews, was led by Reform rabbis who strongly opposed Jewish nationalism. This community was not responsive to Herzl's dream to hold his Congress in Germany.

Traveling to Basel to meet with Rabbi Cohn, Herzl asked if they could hold the First Zionist Congress there. Basel's rabbi was receptive to the idea and enthusiastically invited Herzl and the Zionists, delighted with the honor of having the historic meeting in his city. The president of the Jewish community in Basel also replied positively.

Over the years, Rabbi Cohn had developed an excellent rapport with the Basel city officials. This allowed him to receive courtesies and consideration for the arrangements needed to assist Herzl in establishing not only the First Zionist Congress in 1897, but also for Congresses that followed, many of which Basel hosted.

Herzl greeted on Shabbat in front of Rabbi Cohn's synagogue in Basel (1903)

Rabbi Arthur Cohn's namesake and grandson

Basel's rabbi invited Herzl to *Shabbat* services and honored him with an *aliyah* before the Torah reading. In a rare moment of humor, Herzl confided that he was more nervous about having to read the blessing in Hebrew than fulfilling his organizational responsibilities for the Congress.

Jews from around the world, including many from the United States, traveled difficult political and geographical paths to attend this conference. Many from czarist Russia were forced to furtively leave their homes and towns and surreptitiously cross borders in order to reach this Jewish historic event, which the Basel rabbi had made possible.

Standing on the platform at the First Congress, Rabbi Cohn challenged the powerful Zionist leader: "What is the attitude of Zionism to the genuine Judaism of Torah and *Mitzvot*?" Theodor

HÔTEL DES TROIS ROIS À BÂLE

A.H.J. WALD Proprietaire.

Basel's Three Kings Hotel on the Rhine River where Herzl stayed during Congresses

Herzl addresses Second Zionist Congress in Basel, drawing by M. Okin (1898)

Herzl answered simply, "Zionism is the return to Judaism before the return to the Jewish Land."

Rabbi Arthur Cohn was one of the founders of *Agudat Yisrael*, a religious political movement. His friendship and support for Herzl and the delegates to the First and subsequent Congresses in Basel greatly assisted Herzl and the Zionist movement, facilitating their efforts in creating the State of Israel.

Cohn's namesake and grandson, the Academy award winning producer Arthur Cohn, paid tribute to his grandfather when he received the prestigious Guardian of Zion award in Israel in June 2004:

> *As a child growing up in Basel, I witnessed many Zionist Congresses, planning the return to Zion and Jerusalem. It was due to the Chief Rabbi of Basel, my grandfather Arthur (Asher Michael) Cohn, that the first Zionist Congresses could take place in Basel, as other respected rabbis in Germany and Austria had refused to support the Zionistic Vision. My grandfather, who also personally addressed the First Zionist Congress, was very pleased that Theodor Herzl declared that 'the return to Judaism preceded the return to a Jewish land.'*

Haim Moshe Shapira
1902 - 1970

> *The Land of Israel for the People of Israel according to the Torah of Israel.*
>
> — Haim Moshe Shapira

Haim Moshe Shapira is considered the "uncrowned leader" of world Jewry. Deeply steeped in Jewish culture and tradition, he was universally respected for his integrity, judgment and wisdom. He was known as a "religious statesman," and one of the organizers of the *Mafdal* [National Religious Party-NRP] political party in Israel.

Shapira was born in Grodno, Belorussia in 1902, and received Orthodox Jewish instruction while attending the *yeshiva*. At seventeen he moved to Kovno, working in the field of education. He joined the *Mizrahi* movement at this young age and supported it throughout his life. This group formed the nucleus of the religious Zionist youth movement that began in Lithuania. During the early 1920s, he continued his teaching career in Vilna, also working in Warsaw and Berlin.

In 1925, Shapira settled in Palestine, and participated as a delegate to the Thirteenth and Fourteenth Zionist Congresses. A member of the Jewish Agency Executive Council in 1935, he was appointed head of the Aliyah Department, remaining in that position until the establishment of the State of Israel in 1948. He traveled to Austria in the late 1930s, organizing the rescue of Jews for immigration to Palestine.

Public service was extremely important to Shapira, and he proudly served his new country in several positions. In 1948, he was appointed as Israel's first minister of immigration and health in the Provisional Government. The next year, with the formation of the first elected cabinet, he served as the first minister of the interior. He held another ministerial portfolio during his productive career, religious affairs and social welfare.

Shapira was a traditionalist who respected all Jewish institutions. He was one of the founders of *Mafdal*, an Israeli political party representing the religious Zionist movement.

Prime Minister Moshe Sharett's government in 1954, which included Haim Moshe Shapira (standing to the right of center)

Shapira (standing third from left) welcomes immigrants from Europe at Haifa's port (1945)

The party was created in 1956, as the result of a merger between two earlier religious organizations. Their philosophy focused primarily on building a religious Jewish society rather than a secular one. *Mafdal*'s extended goals were to encourage immigration to Israel, develop the settlements, and educate children according to Jewish tradition.

Mafdal also emphasized national unity and vowed to employ unity as a bridge among the different factions of Israeli society. The group stated in its platform:

> *Religious and secular, Sephardim and Ashkenazim, right and left, old-timers and new immigrants—we are all one people. The NRP works toward national unity, absorption of immigration, and bringing people together from all sectors of the population. Without hatred and without coercion. Gently, pleasantly, and with a smile.*

Shapira was adept at synthesizing both aspects—the religious and the nationalist.

Minister Shapira speaking at B'nai Akiva Convention (1955)

He is credited as the architect of the National Unity government that was formed during one of Israel's most challenging times. He also served as chairman of Bar Ilan University and Mizrahi Bank.

In 1957, a significant incident occurred that transformed his life and inspired him to change his name. During one of the meetings of the Israeli Knesset [parliament], a hand grenade was thrown into the austere chambers causing pandemonium. Shapira was wounded severely and it was uncertain whether he would live. When he was graced with a "miraculous" recovery, in gratitude to the Divine intervention that he was certain had saved him he changed his name to "Haim," a derivation of the Hebrew word "chayim" which means "life."

Another of Shapira's celebrated moments occurred when he was minister of the interior, following the Six Day War. He was honored to be one of the signers of the historic document that unified the city of Jerusalem. Haim

Haim Moshe Shapira reading the news (1953)

Shapira possessed an innate talent in his ability to bring together the two extreme wings of the political base in Israel—the religious and the secular—and to merge the two in a way that strengthened the foundation of the new country.

Interior Minster Shapira addresses his supporters (1954)

CHAPTER SEVEN

Military Beginnings and Self Defense

Joseph Trumpeldor
1880 - 1920

A Pioneer is everything. A worker and a fighter, a builder and a soldier... one who sacrifices everything for his country and expects no reward for his efforts.

— Joseph Trumpeldor

Known as "the Lion of *Tel Hai*," Joseph Trumpeldor was a decorated soldier and a visionary pioneer in *Eretz Yisrael*. He took on the enormous responsibility of organizing the military defense of the Jewish settlements. His heroic stand at the battle of *Tel Hai* became an inspiration for pioneer youth all over the world.

Joseph Trumpeldor was born in Russia in 1880, in a small town in the northern Caucasus. His father, like many Jewish men, was conscripted into the czarist army for twenty-five years in a failed attempt to extinguish his Jewish identity. In spite of being persecuted by anti-Semitism, his father remained a Jew and instilled a love for all things Jewish in his son. Joseph attended a "gymnasium," a European high school for exceptional students.

When he was young, Trumpeldor was strongly influenced by the model of the "collective," which he observed at a nearby farming commune founded by the followers of the Russian writer, Leo Tolstoy. Trumpeldor connected the idea of "collective" life with the Zionistic ideal of settling in *Eretz Yisrael*. He dreamed about establishing this type of agricul-

A group of Jewish immigrants in 1912 with Trumpeldor (top left)

Trumpeldor poses in garden in Palestine

tural community there, which when necessary, could be defended by organized armed forces.

Although he was educated as a dentist, in 1902 he enlisted in the Russian army. He aimed to prove that widespread European bigotry about "Jewish cowardice" was a lie. He volunteered to join an extremely dangerous unit, the "shock troops." Their mission was to defend Port Arthur in Southern Manchuria against Japanese attack during the Russo-Japanese War. He was wounded severely in this action and lost his left arm.

After the fall of Port Arthur, Japanese forces took Trumpeldor prisoner. He spent many months in a prisoner of war camp in the South Pacific in deplorable conditions, but he managed to keep his spirits up. During this time, he focused on what he believed to be his most important challenge: to transform the Jewish people from a state of oppression into a strong nation.

While incarcerated in the Japanese POW camp, he organized the five hundred Jewish prisoners into a Zionist society. When he was released in 1906, he remained in the Russian army. He was the first Jew to receive an officer's commission despite ruthless anti-Semitic prejudice in Russia. He received four medals of distinguished service for his bravery, making him the most decorated Jewish soldier in Russia.

After leaving the army, Trumpeldor studied law at the University of St. Petersburg. He organized a Zionist youth group that met in Romni, Ukraine, where the young people shared their dreams of starting up agricultural settlements in Palestine. Trumpeldor's goal was to prepare a group of *chalutzim* [pioneers] to travel to the Land of Israel. He proudly defined a *chalutz*:

> *What is a* chalutz*? Is he a worker only? No! The definition includes much more. The* chalutzim *should be workers, but that is not all. We shall need people who will be 'everything'—everything that* Eretz Yisrael *needs. A worker has his labor interests, a soldier his 'esprit de corps,' a doctor and an engineer, their special inclinations. A generation of iron-men; iron from which you can forge everything the national machinery needs. You need a wheel? Here I am. A nail, a screw, a block? —here take me. You need a man to till the soil? —I'm ready.*

A soldier? I am here. Policeman, doctor, lawyer, artist, teacher, water-carrier?
Here I am. I have no form, I have no psychology. I have no personal feeling, no
name. I am a servant of Zion. Ready to do everything, not bound to do anything.
I have only one aim—Creation.

Armed with an enthusiasm that was contagious and the dreams of his youth, he immigrated to Palestine in 1912 with a group of pioneers. For a short time he worked at *Kibbutz Deganyah* and participated in the defense of the Jewish settlements in the lower Galilee.

When World War I started in 1914, Trumpeldor attempted to return to his Russian unit but was stopped by the Turkish army, now allied with Germany. He refused to become an Ottoman citizen and was exiled to Egypt. It was there, in Alexandria, that he met Ze'ev Jabotinsky. Diligently, they worked together to acquire authorization for a Jewish battalion. Trumpeldor organized the formation of a legion of volunteers drawn from Palestine Jewish deportees to assist the British in liberating Palestine from the Turks.

Trumpeldor joined the British army and officially formed the Jewish Mule Corps (also known as the Zion Mule Corps), the first Jewish fighting unit in existence in over two thousand years. The Corps was assigned by the British to the battle of Gallipoli, which was a disaster for British, Australian and New Zealand troops. Commanded by the Jewish-Australian General John Monash, the allies were slaughtered by the Turkish guns. Despite the futility of the battle, Trumpeldor fought with great courage and was recognized for his military prowess.

Ultimately Trumpeldor took over complete command of the unit. Among the soldiers it was well known that he was always the first to face danger. Calmly, and with a deep sense of his vast responsibility, he led the Jewish soldiers into the thick of the battle at Gallipoli.

Tel Hai courtyard, sight of the battle of March 1, 1920

Soldiers of the Jewish battalion (1919)

Colonel Patterson recalled:

> *During all the time of that terrible war, this gentle captain showed an unparalleled valor and unflinching determination. By his devotion to duty he set an example to all. When bullets were showering upon us, I warned him to take heed, but Trumpeldor, with his charming, simple smile, answered: 'Never mind. I am all right.'*

After the war, Trumpeldor traveled widely, spending much time in England and Russia and promoting the organization of Jewish regiments. These regiments were needed not only to fight the Turks, but also to create Jewish self-defense units to protect the settlements in *Eretz Yisrael*. To motivate young people, he established *Ha-Halutz*, a youth organization that prepared immigrants for *aliyah*. In 1919 Trumpeldor returned to Palestine, summoned to the northern Galilee to organize the defense of the settlements that were being subjected to increasingly more violent Arab attacks.

In the meantime, Ze'ev Jabotinsky founded the revisionist Zionism movement, whose philosophy was to fight for the establishment of an independent Jewish state, despite ongoing British duplicity. In an effort to gain Jewish support for their cause, the British had promised that they would support a Jewish state as affirmed in the famous Balfour Declaration in 1917. But when the war was over, the British sided openly with the Arabs, even encouraging attacks on the Jews. The Arabs, provided with arms by the British government, raided Jewish towns and villages, terrorizing and victimizing the settlers. In response to these unprovoked assaults by the Arabs, the Palestinian Jews formed a self-defense army known as the Haganah.

In 1919, the border between Jewish Palestine and Syria was the subject of a dispute between British and French authorities. The four Jewish settlements of *Metulla, Hamrah,*

Kfar Giladi and *Tel Hai* were situated in this area. Arab groups loyal to King Feisal in Syria attacked these settlements. An evacuation of *Metulla* and *Hamrah* quickly was accomplished, but the Jewish forces led by Joseph Trumpeldor attempted to hold their ground at *Tel Hai* [Hill of Life].

On March 1, 1920 a gang of Arab killers viciously stormed the Jewish town of *Tel Hai* and a fierce battle erupted as the Jews valiantly attempted to defend their homes and families. In the midst of the combat Trumpeldor was caught out in the open while attempting to close the gates of the colony. He was mortally wounded though still alive when his comrades found him. He looked up at them, attempted a smile and whispered, "Ein davar [never mind], I only want a bandage." Defying death, he calmly directed the bandaging of his wound. "These are my last moments. Tell our comrades to defend the honor of our people until the last," Trumpeldor said. Drawing on all of his strength he somehow persisted in directing the battle. When he could no longer continue, Trumpeldor died speaking these words: *"Ein davar, tov lamut be-ad artsenu"* [Never mind, it is good to die for our land].

Monument at Tel Hai in honor of Trumpeldor

Trumpeldor was buried near *Tel Hai*, and a memorial was erected at his gravesite. Shortly after his death, a new settlement at the foot of Mount Gilboa was named *Tel Yosef* in his honor, and songs, poems and stories were written about this hero of the Jewish resettlement of *Eretz Yisrael*. The story of his life has served as an inspiration to pioneering youth movements in Israel and throughout the Diaspora. One of the largest and most successful was named in his honor: Betar, an abbreviation of Berit Trumpeldor.

Tel Hai was resettled in 1921, and in 1926 was absorbed into the *Kibbutz Kefar Gil'adi*. Six of its defenders (including two killed earlier in 1919 and 1920) were buried on an adjoining hill overlooking the Hullah Valley. The site is marked by a memorial statue of the "Lion of Judah," the inscription on its base paraphrasing Trumpeldor's final words: "It is good to die for our country."

Israel continues to commemorate the brave young men who gave their lives as the ultimate sacrifice for Jewish independence. When the town of Kiryat Shemonah [Town of the Eight] was established in 1949, its name was chosen in honor of the eight fighters that lost their lives in defense of *Tel Hai*. The Hebrew date of the 11th of Adar, the anniversary of the fall of *Tel Hai*, is celebrated as "*Tel Hai* Day" in Israel and pilgrimages are made to the site, particularly by Israeli youth groups. The cemetery there has become a national shrine.

Ze'ev Jabotinsky
1880 - 1940

The duty and aim of Betar is ...to create that type of Jew which the nation needs in order to better and quicker build a Jewish state.

— Ze'ev Jabotinsky

Ze'ev Jabotinsky was one of the most renowned Jewish statesmen of the twentieth century. His life is a portrait of an extraordinary personality, a man of impeccable character—truthful and wise, modest and magnanimous, fearless and compassionate, and wholly dedicated to the welfare of the Jewish people.

Founder of the Jewish battalion, Jabotinsky (center) joins his volunteers (1919)

Jabotinsky is considered the most representative right-wing Revisionist Movement Party member. He provided the ideological map for the future policies of the Revisionist Party (post-1948 it became the *Herut* party, and later the *Likud* party). He was a philosophic statesman. To read this unsurpassed orator — who could address and rouse audiences in seven different languages — is an experience that would inspire any sensitive soul, Jewish or non-Jewish.

Born in 1880 in Odessa, Russia, as Vladimir Jabotinsky, he was a language prodigy, a journalist writing for Russian newspapers in Italy and Switzerland when he was only seventeen. In 1898 he studied law in Berne, Switzerland and Rome, while he worked as a reporter for the two major daily newspapers in Odessa. In his writing he used the pen name *Altalena*. He graduated from the university in Rome and completed his master's degree in Austria in 1908.

Returning to Odessa, he joined the editorial staff of *Odesskiya Novosti,* where his

Jabotinsky joins fellow Revisionists (1920)

daily commentaries became a popular treat for the city's intellectuals. The pogrom against the Jews of Kishinev in 1903 spurred Jabotinsky to become an active Zionist. He sensed the imminent danger of the "pogrom," an organized (usually government sanctioned) attack on helpless Jewish communities. His response was to help form a Jewish self-defense group to fight for Jewish minority rights in Russia. Meanwhile he became deeply involved in Zionism. He continued to work as a journalist while traveling in Europe, crystallizing his Zionist views, which tended to be uncompromising and political, rather than cultural.

In 1914 at the beginning of World War I, Jabotinsky was the leading Zionist lecturer in Russia, crusading throughout the country against anti-Semitism and assimilation. He was elected as a delegate to the Sixth Zionist Congress, the last in which Theodor Herzl participated. Jabotinsky actively spread the Hebrew language and culture throughout Russia, and he was instrumental in the establishment of the Hebrew University in Jerusalem.

He went to the front as a newspaper correspondent during the war. While in Alexandria he met and formed a close friendship with Joseph Trumpeldor. Together, they worked for the establishment of the Jewish Legion, achieving this goal in August 1917. Jabotinsky served as a lieutenant in the Legion and was decorated in the conquest of Esalt during the campaign to free Palestine from Turkish rule.

When the war ended, Jabotinsky focused on establishing a permanent Jewish defense force, which eventually became the Haganah. In Palestine, Arab gangs were beginning to attack Jewish villagers. When Jabotinsky went to aid the defenseless settlers, he and other members of the Haganah were arrested by the British and charged with fighting in reaction to the Arab riots. In 1920, during the Passover holiday, Jabotinsky was condemned by the pro-Arab British Mandatory government and sentenced to fifteen years hard labor. Following a public outcry against the unjust verdict, he received amnesty and was released from Acre prison after serving three months.

In 1923, Betar was created, a youth movement aimed at educating and instilling its young members with a military and nationalistic spirit. Jabotinsky, leader of the group, wrote about the philosophy of Betar:

> *The basis of the Betarian viewpoint consists of one idea: the Jewish State. In this simple idea however, lies a deep meaning indeed. What do the nations of the world symbolize? They symbolize that every nation must contribute its own share to the common culture of mankind, a share which is distinguished by its own specific spirit. This contribution should not and cannot consist merely of the ideas and good advice to other nations; it must serve as a living example of ideas and ideals, tangibly realized, expressed not only in books but in the collective life of the people as well. For this purpose, every nation must possess its own 'laboratory', a country wherein the nation alone is master and can freely suit the common life in accordance with its own conception of good and evil. A people's own state is such a laboratory.*

Jabotinsky continued to organize his ideas about how the Jewish state should be created. Much of his writing expanded and developed these ideas in his eagerness to communicate his thoughts about Zionism in the new homeland. His based his program on clearly defining the aim of Zionism as "the establishment of a Jewish state."

A member of the Zionist Executive in 1921, Jabotinsky also was one of the founders of *Keren Hayesod* [Jewish Agency]. His restlessness and impatience with British rule in Palestine soon forced him into conflict with other Zionist factions. After the Jewish Executive rejected his political program, Jabotinsky resigned from the World Zionist Organization (WZO). When he founded the revisionist group in 1925, he was headquartered in Paris, forbidden by the British from re-entering Palestine.

To some Jabotinsky became an outcast, while to others he was still a strong fighter for Herzl's dream of a Jewish homeland. Jabotinsky's follow-

Jabotinsky poses with attache

ers were accused of "revising" the basic tenets of Zionism as set down by its founder, Theodor Herzl. The group also sought to "revise" the terms of the British Mandate, specifically to provide for the re-inclusion of Transjordan into Palestine. Jabotinsky and his followers adopted the term and called themselves "revisionists." By 1931 Jabotinsky had totally split from the traditional Zionist movement and the Union of Zionist Revisionists [*Hatzohar*] became an independent force.

The main thrust of Jabotinsky's Zionist platform was to encourage European countries to solve their Jewish minority issue through the emigration of the Jewish population to a Jewish state—Palestine. Testifying before the British Royal Commission on Palestine, Jabotinsky gave an impassioned expression of his revisionist views. He stated that the source of Jewish suffering was not merely anti-Semitism, but the Diaspora [dispersion] itself; the Jews were a "stateless" people. Assigning cultural Zionism a relatively low priority, he advocated the creation of a "Palestinian Jewish state on both sides of the Jordan, with continued Jewish immigration to achieve a Jewish majority there, and employment of Jewish troops for self-defense as part of the permanent garrison."

In order to support his group and their ideas of freedom for the Jews, he once again developed the idea of a Jewish self-defense force, this one operating underground, which became known as the Irgun [*Irgun Zvai Leumi* – IZL]. In 1937, the Irgun became the military arm of the Jabotinsky movement and he became its commander.

The three bodies headed by Jabotinsky—the New Zionist Organization (NZO), founded to advance free immigration and the establishment of a Jewish state; the Betar youth movement; and the Irgun (IZL) were three extensions of the same movement. The NZO was the political arm, Betar educated the youth of the Diaspora for the liberating and building of *Eretz Yisrael*, and the IZL was the military arm that fought against the enemies of the Zionist endeavor. Additionally, these bodies cooperated in the organization

Jabotinsky and family (1920)

Jabotinsky and his editorial board in Petrograd (1912)

of "illegal" immigration. Within this framework, more than sixty ships sailed from European ports bringing to *Eretz Yisrael* tens of thousands of "illegal" immigrants—Holocaust survivors.

Throughout this period of intense political activity, Jabotinsky continued to write poetry, novels, short stories and articles on political, social and economic problems. From among his literary compendium, *The Jewish Legion, Prelude To Delilah* and *The Five* served as inspiration for Jews of the Diaspora. Being fluent in many languages, Jabotinsky also translated some of the best-known classics of world literature into Hebrew.

With the terrifying rise of Hitler and Nazism in Germany, Jabotinsky again lobbied aggressively for the creation of a Jewish army and the re-establishment of the Jewish Legion. During 1939-1940, he traveled in Britain and the United States in active pursuit of supporters for the Jewish Legion to fight alongside the Allies against the Nazis.

On August 4, 1940, while visiting the Betar camp in New York, Jabotinsky suffered a heart attack and died. In his will he requested that his remains be interred in *Eretz Yisrael* at the express order of the "Hebrew Government of the Jewish State that shall arise." His vision of the future Jewish state was resolute and unwavering.

As his will requested, Jabotinsky was reburied in Israel in 1964, the ceremony arranged by Levi Eshkol, Israel's third prime minister. A simple but impressive dark black marble tombstone covers the graves of Ze'ev Jabotinsky and his wife, reinterred to the soil of Mount Herzl, Jerusalem. This monument sits as a reminder to those who visit the site to remember this great statesman whose life was dedicated to protect and defend the Jewish homeland—his dream of the future—the State of Israel.

Yitzhak Sadeh
1890 - 1952

No Jewish settlement was evacuated and none was wiped out.
— Yitzhak Sadeh

Sadeh (with beard, center right) looks on at military ceremony with Chaim Weizmann

The founder and first commander of the Palmach was Yitzhak Sadeh. A casual meeting with Joseph Trumpeldor in 1917 had a lasting influence on his life and led to a distinguished career as a military strategist, tactician, and decorated general in the Israel Defense Forces (IDF).

Born in Lublin, Poland, Sadeh served in the Russian army during World War I. He was highly decorated for bravery while in command of the first company of the first battalion. He was educated at the University of Simferopol in the Crimea, where he studied philology and philosophy. Sadeh was also an accomplished athlete, mastering the sports of wrestling and weightlifting.

In the years between 1917 and 1919 he assisted Joseph Trumpeldor in the foundation of *Ha-Halutz* [the pioneer] movement. When Sadeh received word that Trumpeldor had died in action at *Tel Hai* in 1920, he emigrated to *Eretz Yisrael* and founded and commanded the "Joseph Trumpeldor Labor Battalion."

Sadeh began his career as a Haganah commander in Jerusalem in 1921, and during the

Moshe Dayan (left), Sadeh (center) and Yigal Allon at the founding of Kibbutz Hanita (1938)

1929 riots he participated in the battle to defend Haifa. At the beginning of the 1936 Arab riots he was the first to propose to the Haganah the strategy of "breaking out the perimeter." Sadeh's plan for defending the settlements was for his troops to go outside the fences to attack the Arab bands. The old approach was to stay behind the barbed wired enclosures of the settlements and wait for the raiders to attack. His new strategy led to the formation of Haganah field companies and special commando units that confronted the enemy in their villages and army bases.

In 1941, Sadeh helped to establish the commando fighting unit, the Palmach and

After taking a series of tests, members of the first Commanders Course of the Haganah pose for photograph in 1920 with Sadeh (seated second row, second from the right)

Haganah leadership (left to right) Dori, Galili, Yitzhak Sadeh, Moshe Sneh and Golomb (1942)

became its commanding officer. He continued in this post until 1945 when he was promoted to acting chief of the Haganah general staff. Sadeh was responsible for the joint cooperation that existed between the Haganah and the Irgun forces, coordinating their resistance operations against the British.

During the 1948 War of Independence, Sadeh took part in several important missions, which included the battle for Jerusalem. His energy and military expertise were critically important to the tank force that he led while freeing the airport at Lydda. His command of Israeli forces fighting at the Sinai border with Egypt also earned him the respect of the military. Sadeh's proficiency won him a promotion to the rank of brigadier general [*aluf*] during this campaign.

At the conclusion of the war in 1948, the Palmach was dismantled. The following year, Sadeh retired from the Israel Defense Forces. He left a valuable legacy, greatly influencing the Haganah and IDF in the areas of tactics, training and strategy. Field engineering, reconnaissance, naval and air operations were significant innovations that Sadeh also introduced into Israel's new military organization.

After Sadeh retired from the military, he embarked on a new career as a writer and educator. He wrote essays, stories and plays. The book *Around the Bonfire* includes a collection of articles he wrote under the pen name "Y. Noded" (Y. Wanderer).

Yitzhak Sadeh was often described as a "charismatic and colorful" figure. His nickname in the Palmach was *Ha-Zaken* (the Old Man). *Kibbutzim Nir Itzhak* and *Mashabey Sadeh* in the Negev are both named after him. Yitzhak Sadeh died in Tel Aviv in August 1952.

Charles Orde Wingate
1903 - 1944

Judged by ordinary standards, {Wingate} would not be regarded as normal. But his own standards were far from ordinary. He was a military genius and a wonderful man.

— Moshe Dayan

Charles Orde Wingate was a British army officer and dedicated advocate of the Jewish cause in Palestine, although he himself was not Jewish. Wingate was a devout Christian believer who saw the return of the Jews to their homeland as a realization of biblical prophecies. Stationed in Palestine in 1936, he was known as *"Ha-Yedid"* [The Friend] in appreciation for his help training Haganah fighters and opposing the Arab terror campaign.

Wingate stands out as comrade and defender of the Palestinian Jews, despite being a British officer. The British army and government in charge of Palestine in the 1930s were notorious for their pro-Arab policies and strict limitations on Jewish immigration. This was a time when Jewish people from many countries needed a safe and secure homeland. Wingate proved to be an important friend of Zionism and supporter of the future of Israel.

Born to a military family in India in 1903, he received a thorough religious education. He grew up in a non-conformist missionary family—his grandfather helped operate a Scottish mission in Budapest that tried to attract impoverished Jews. Wingate was raised with the Bible and carried one with him throughout his life. He passionately embraced the prophetic vision of Jewish redemption and the Jews' ultimate return to *Eretz Yisrael*. His many contributions to the Jewish people played an important part in realizing that ideal.

Receiving his military commission in 1923, Wingate served in India and then in the Sudan, where he studied Arabic and Semitics, becoming familiar with the cultures of the Middle East. He earned the rank of captain, and was transferred to Palestine in 1936 where he served for the next three years.

In Palestine, Wingate was assigned to a staff position as an intelligence officer. At the time, Arab guerrillas had begun a campaign of attacks against both British mandate officials and Jewish settlers. Wingate became acquainted with and befriended a number of Zionist leaders. These Jewish pioneers at first were suspicious of Wingate's enthusiastic support, but they soon demonstrated their grateful respect. His wife Lorna also was intensely active in Zionist affairs as an organizer of Youth Aliyah in Britain.

Wingate was an unconventional

Wingate poses in Burma (1944)

Charles Orde Wingate instructs his Allied troops in Burma (1943)

officer who excelled at developing unconventional tactics. In the late 1930s, the Jews of Palestine were in a poor position to defend themselves. Possessing only a few small arms and lacking formal military training, their settlements were vulnerable to attack and they could not depend on the British army for protection. Wingate believed, however, that with proper military training the beleaguered Jewish communities could develop the ability to defend themselves.

He formulated the idea of armed groups that combined both British and Jewish members and he personally took his idea to Archibald Wavell, who was then commander of British forces in Palestine. After Wavell approved the plan, Wingate convinced the Zionist Jewish Agency and leadership of the Haganah to accept it.

In June 1938, General Haining, the new British commander, authorized the creation of the "Special Night Squads," armed groups comprised of both British and Haganah volunteers. Wingate trained and commanded them, and accompanied them on their patrols. Their successful tactics were based on strategic principles of surprise, mobility, and night attacks. They were effective both as offensive and defensive units. "Hit and run" missions allowed the outgunned Jewish defenders effectively to counterattack Arab raiders. They ambushed Arab saboteurs who attacked oil pipelines of the Iraqi Petroleum Company, and they raided border villages used as bases by the Arab attackers.

The British command in Palestine, however, was not pleased by Wingate's contribution to the Jewish defense forces. Official policy was for the British Mandatory government to remain neutral. This "neutral" stance tended to serve the Arabs rather than the Jews, whose plight was of little concern to most British officials. Wingate's position as an advisor was barely tolerated by his superiors. Yet Wingate was more than an advisor; he often served as combatant, jumping into the fighting as well.

Wingate spoke out publicly in favor of the formation of a Jewish state while on leave in Britain. He provoked many of the British commanders, and they removed him from Palestine believing that he was serving Jewish interests over those of the British. In May 1939, he was transferred back to London. His passport contained a unique and disquieting advisory: "The bearer…should not be allowed to enter Palestine."

During World War II, Wingate led the British-Ethiopian Gideon Force to free Ethiopia in one of the few bright moments for the Allies during the early years of the war. When he was sent to battle against the Italians in Ethiopia in 1941, his request to bring several Jewish fighters from his Palestinian unit of the Special Night Squads to fight with him was accepted. He played a decisive role in the liberation of Ethiopia and accompanied Haile Selassie as Selassie re-entered Addis Abba and returned to his throne as emperor.

The head of the Egyptian Zionist Organization in Cairo in 1941 told Wingate: "I am prepared to give up all this idea of a mission in the world; let us just become a free nation in our own country, just like any other nation." Wingate admonished him saying: "Are you prepared to give up your mission so easily? Did your people suffer in exile for 2,000 years just to become like any other nation?"

From 1942 until his untimely death in March 1944, Wingate organized and led the famed British-Indian "Chindits" or "Wingate's raiders," in Burma against the Japanese. For seven months, he courageously assisted the Unite States Army Air Corps' 1st Air Commando Group. Commissioned as a major general, he was placed in command of a larger army that flew into Burma. Two weeks into the operation he was killed in an airplane accident and buried in Arlington National Cemetery. This honor was bestowed on the British officer since he died while flying in a United States military plane.

Wingate's personality and military genius profoundly impacted Jewish defense in the 1930s, contributing to the blue print for the modern day Israel Defense Forces (IDF). He demonstrated the effectiveness and practicality of jungle "guerrilla" warfare implemented by Western troops. His knowledge was invaluable in assisting the Jews to provide appropriate security for Israel.

Winston Churchill hailed Charles Orde Wingate as "a man of genius who might well have become also a man of destiny." Several places in Israel are named in his honor, including the Wingate Institute for Physical Education; *Yemin Orde*, a children's village in Israel; Wingate Square in Jerusalem; and a forest on Mount Gilboa.

Wingate in Palestine

Moshe Dayan
1915 - 1981

> ## *The people of Israel were exiled from their land, but their land was never exiled from their hearts.*
>
> — Moshe Dayan

He resembled a pirate with a black patch over his left eye; he was a complicated man of diverse and varied talents. Imprisoned by the British, then recruited by them to assist in fighting the Germans, he ultimately was decorated with Britain's highest military medal. The world called him a military genius and the Israelis honored him as a hero. He served his country in both the military and political arenas—Moshe Dayan is a man who will long be remembered as a legend in the history of the State of Israel. Moshe Dayan—an enigma, a hero, a political rebel, a controversial figure—a gallant son of Israel.

Moshe Dayan was a *kibbutznik* who became one of the twentieth-century's most recognized and admired military leaders. He was born on *Kibbutz Deganya* in 1915 and grew up in *Moshav Nahalal*. When he was fourteen he joined the Haganah, which was in its earliest stages of development. The Haganah was a Zionist military organization in Palestine during the British Mandate from 1920 to 1948. It later became the Israel Defense

Photograph of Dayan entering into Old Jerusalem (1967)

Forces (IDF)—Israel's army—and Dayan played a key role in its formation. In the Haganah, Dayan learned guerrilla warfare from British Captain Charles Orde Wingate, who was a leader of night patrols organized to fight bands of Arab rebels.

Wingate was British military, well respected and possessing an affinity for the Palestinian Jews—quite unique at the time. Although Dayan gained experience in tactical skills under Wingate, he had a stormy relationship with the British government. He was imprisoned by the British authorities for his involvement in the Haganah. Sentenced to ten years in prison, Dayan was released after just two years as part of the Haganah's renewed cooperation with the British during World War II.

While attached to the Australian 7th Infantry Division fighting Vichy French forces in Syria, Dayan lost his left eye and began wearing the eyepatch that became his trademark. On the recommendation of an Australian officer Dayan received the Distinguished Service Order, one of the British Empire's highest military honors.

During the 1948 Arab-Israeli War, Dayan occupied various positions of importance, first as commander of the defensive effort in the Jordan valley, then in command of units on the central front. He honed his skills as a negotiator and diplomat while mediating cease fire agreements with Jordan, and he rapidly rose through the ranks.

Dayan served as IDF Chief of Staff from 1955 to 1958, commanding the Israeli forces during the Suez crisis. He advocated an aggressive response to Arab belligerence and was a proponent of the 1956 Sinai campaign.

In 1958 Dayan left the military and entered the political arena, joining the *Mapai*, the leftist Labor-affiliated party in Israeli politics. With tensions developing in the region, Dayan was appointed by Levi Eshkol as minister of defense in 1967. When he assumed command, war frenzy was sweeping the Arab world. The leaders of the surrounding Arab countries calling for Israel's destruction, mobilized their armies, ejected United Nations peace keeping forces, and challenged one another to "throw the Jews into the sea." Only twenty-two years after the decimation of European Jewry, the mood in Israel and for Jews around the world was grim.

Dayan's reputation as an effective leader intensified during the Six Day War against Egypt, Jordan, and Syria. With the Syrians systematically shelling Israeli villages in Upper Galilee, Dayan made the decision to launch a full-scale attack against them. It was also Dayan who brought an end to the fighting by arranging a cease-fire with Syria through the United Nations. Dayan was viewed as "a solo performer, partly admired, partly feared for his political stunts."

Dayan lays out his stratgey to troops

After the war, as military commander Dayan took responsibility for the conduct of the Israeli occupation of the newly acquired territories. He opened the borders for Arab residents of those areas enabling them to travel to Arab countries, while at the same time maintaining order and security in Israeli-held regions. He repaired Jordan River bridges and facilitated the flow of people and goods between the West Bank (Judea and Samaria) and Jordan in an effort to create some level of normalization between Israel and the occupied population.

A well-known anecdote about the tactical skills of Moshe Dayan recalls how Dayan called his senior officers together on the eve of the Six Day War for a "pep" talk. When he proceeded to read to them from 1 Samuel: 17 the soldiers were amazed: "We're about to be attacked and he's reading to us from the Bible?" Dayan used the allegory about King David to illustrate how the smaller, weaker side could gain the upper hand by identifying and attacking an opponent's vulnerable points.

Goliath, Dayan explained, was weighed down by heavy weapons and moved slowly; David, unburdened, was agile and light on his feet. A heavy suit of armor protected Goliath's body, but his face remained exposed, and David aimed his sling at the one place he knew would do the most damage. Israel's ultimate decision in 1967 to pre-empt an Egyptian attack by flying under their radar and destroying the air force on the ground bore all the marks of David's strategy in the biblical story. It was Dayan's brilliance as a tactician that made the difference.

When Golda Meir became prime minister in 1969, Dayan served as minister of defense in her government. He was in that position when the Yom Kippur War erupted on October 6,

Moshe Dayan listens to David Ben-Gurion as Shimon Peres looks on (1965)

1973. Although the country was caught by surprise and basically unprepared, Dayan and the Israeli forces were able to direct the fighting and control the uprising.

Despite the fact that Dayan had warned the country's leaders about the impending danger of war with Egypt and Syria as early as May 1973, the October 1973 Arab offensive surprised Israel. Though Israel prevailed, the country was wounded and traumatized and the public took its anger out on Dayan. The Labor Party did not bring him back into the government in the next election.

Disillusioned from the war, Dayan left the *Mapai* political party and joined the right wing, *Likud*, becoming foreign minister in Menachem Begin's government in 1977. He represented Israel in secret meetings with Egyptian officials that brought Egyptian President Anwar Sadat to Jerusalem. Those meetings led to the Camp David Accords, a peace agreement signed with Egypt in 1979.

In 1981 Dayan formed a new party—*Telem*—which advocated unilateral separation from

Judea, Samaria (West Bank) and the Gaza Strip. The party received two seats in the Tenth Knesset, but Dayan died shortly thereafter in Tel Aviv. He is buried in *Nahalal* in the *kibbutz* where he was raised.

Dayan undoubtedly was a very complicated and controversial individual; his opinions were "never strictly black and white." He had few close friends; his mental brilliance and charismatic manner often were combined with cynicism and a lack of restraint. When he died in October 1981 he had the astonishing distinction of having actively participated in all of Israel's military encounters since 1936. Ariel Sharon commented about Dayan: "He would wake up with a hundred ideas. Of them ninety-five were dangerous; three more were bad; the remaining two, however, were brilliant."

Rabin sleeps as Dayan relaxes during flight back to Israeli airbase

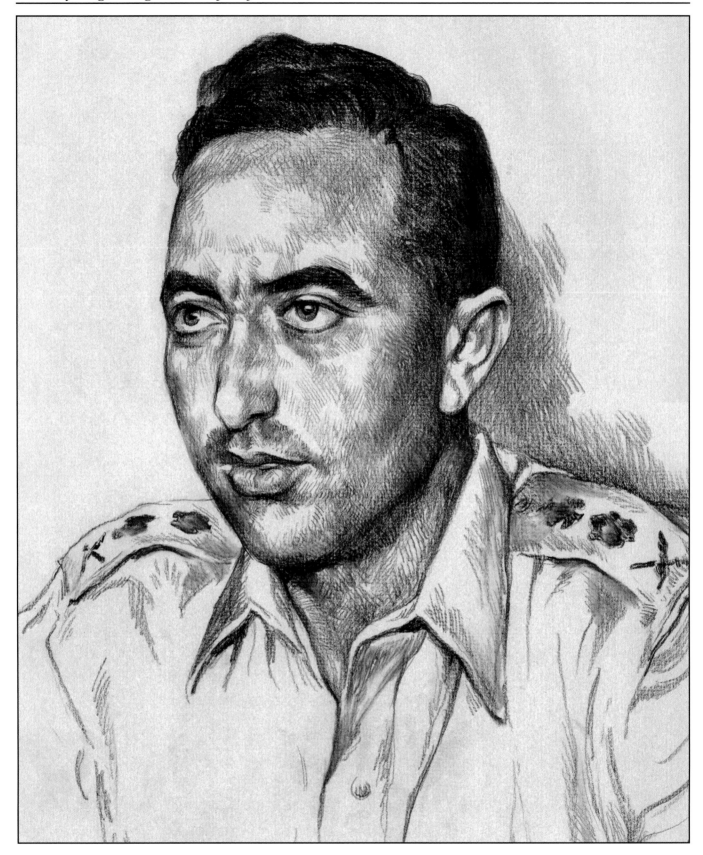

Mordechai Makleff
1920 - 1978

No aggressive action by the armed forces – land, sea or air– of either Party shall be undertaken, planned, or threatened against the people or the armed forces of the other.

— Israel-Lebanon Armistice Agreement, 1949

Makleff at ceremony with British officials at Ramat Gan (1955)

People throughout the world are all too familiar with news reports of hostilities in the Middle East and the terrible casualties that result. It is difficult to imagine, however, the horror of someone forced to view this devastation and witness one's own family members murdered. When Mordechai Makleff was only nine years old, his mother and father were killed in their home in Motza, a suburb of Jerusalem during the Arab riots of 1929. His brother and two sisters also were killed in the raid. Makleff survived the attack by taking shelter in a neighbor's home. Without question, this childhood loss and subsequent trauma left an indelible impression on him.

In 1938 he graduated from the Reali School in Haifa and joined the "Special Night Squads" organized by British officer Charles Orde Wingate. These forces were activated in

Begin lays cornerstone at Dead Sea factory in honor of Makleff (1980)

Makleff hands Moshe Dayan the flag of the Brigade at a ceremony with Ben-Gurion in background (1955)

order to defend the settlements from Arab terrorists. In 1940, Makleff joined the British army and received officer's training. He was involved in combat in World War II, serving with the Jewish Brigade in Italy.

During Israel's War of Independence in 1949, Makleff was an officer with the Haganah and served with the unit that captured Haifa. As an experienced mediator, he helped negotiate the truce with the city's Arab population. He made a significant contribution in a critical campaign to liberate the eastern area of the Galilee. Makleff also was a strategic member of the Israeli delegation to the armistice talks with Lebanon and Syria. Lieutenant Colonel Makleff played a key role in the negotiations and was the primary signer of the Armistice Agreement between Israel and Lebanon, completed on March 23, 1949.

Having just been declared a state, Israel was working intensively to come to peaceful

Evaporation pools at Dead Sea (1944)

Workers driving to evaporation pools at Sodom, Dead Sea (1944)

terms with its Arab neighbors. The Israel-Lebanon Armistice Agreement represented the new nation's yearning for peace. The document begins:

> *With a view to promoting the return of permanent peace in Palestine and in recognition of the importance in this regard of mutual assurances concerning the future military operations of the Parties, the following principles, which shall be fully observed by both Parties during the armistice, are hereby affirmed:*
>
> > *1. The injunction of the Security Council against resort to military force in settlement of the Palestine question shall henceforth be scrupulously respected by both Parties.*
> >
> > *2. No aggressive action by the armed forces—land, sea, or air—of either Party shall be undertaken, planned, or threatened against the people or the armed forces of the other; it being understood that the use of the term "planned" in this context has no bearing on normal staff planning as generally practiced in military organizations.*

The document was signed on behalf of Israel by Lieutenant Colonel Mordechai Makleff, a man who had lived with war all of his life, but carried the hope of Israelis and Jews worldwide to establish peace.

Makleff continued in his distinguished military career, serving as assistant chief of staff to Yigal Yadin in 1949 and three years later as chief of staff of the Israel Defense Forces (IDF). After retiring from his career with the Israeli military, Mordechai Makleff became involved in commerce first, as the director of the Dead Sea Works and then, as director of the Citrus Marketing Board of Israel.

David "Mickey" Marcus
1902 - 1948

> ## *Life isn't a spectator sport; you've just got to get involved.*
> — Mickey Marcus

"Mickey" Marcus was a hero who fought valiantly for the two countries he loved, the United States and Israel. He was recognized and honored for military achievements by both countries.

David Daniel Marcus was born to immigrant parents in 1902 on New York's Lower East Side. He grew up in the Brownsville section of Brooklyn where he learned to box in order to defend himself from neighborhood bullies. He entered West Point Military Academy at age eighteen and graduated in 1924.

Marcus studied law while in the army, and in 1927 he joined the United States Attorney General's Office. New York Mayor Fiorello LaGuardia admired Marcus and persuaded him to join the city's Department of Corrections in 1934. Six years later he was appointed commissioner.

Marcus keeping fit (1948)

When World War II began, Marcus returned to the army as a lieutenant colonel. Following the Japanese attack on Pearl Harbor, he served as executive officer to the military governor of Hawaii and in 1942 was named commander of the army's new Ranger School.

Appointed as a divisional judge advocate and later as a division commander, Marcus attended the meetings of the "Big Five" in 1943. When the Allies decided to invade Normandy, Marcus volunteered to join the D-Day airborne assault. Despite having had no previous training, he hooked up with the paratroopers and voluntarily parachuted into Normandy with the 101st Airborne Division. But Marcus was more than brave. Admiring colleagues described him as one of the War Department's best brains. He had a bright future ahead of him as a member of the army's senior cadre.

In 1944, Marcus' awareness of his Jewish identity took a dramatic turn. He was given the responsibility of planning how to sustain millions of starving people in the regions liberated by the Allied invasions in Europe. A major part of this assignment involved clearing out the Nazi death camps. It was here that Marcus came face to face with the survivors of Nazi atrocities. This war-toughened soldier wept when he saw the piles of

Marcus going over logistics (1948)

uncounted Jewish corpses in Europe's death camps.

Named chief of the War Crimes Division, Marcus began planning legal and security procedures preliminary to the Nuremberg trials. Through these grueling and heart breaking experiences, Marcus came to understand the depths of European anti-Semitism. Though not previously a Zionist, Marcus became convinced that the only hope for European Jewry depended on a Jewish homeland in Palestine.

In 1945, Marcus joined General Lucius D. Clay's staff to help oversee the military government in Germany after the defeat of the Nazis. He retired from the army as a colonel in 1947. His exemplary military record reflected an illustrious career.

Marcus was awarded the Distinguished Service Cross and Bronze Star by the United States government, and he also was decorated by the British.

Marcus could not rid his mind of the memories of the emaciated bodies of the living and dead Jews in the Dachau concentration camp. He resolved to contribute to Israel's survival and help ensure that Jews would have a homeland. In 1948, once the new state declared its independence, Prime Minister David Ben-Gurion asked Marcus to find an American officer to serve as military advisor to Israel. This job, Marcus decided, he wanted himself.

The Haganah and the

Marcus packing to go to next stop in Israel (1948)

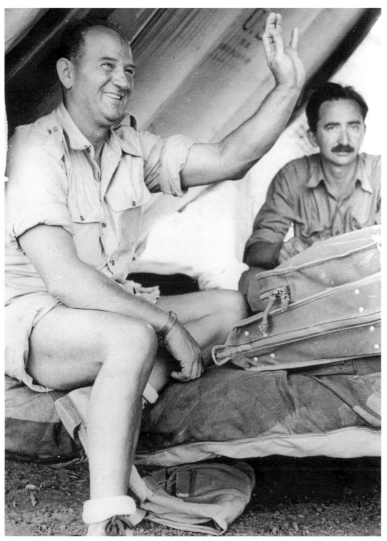

Waving to his new friends (1948)

Jewish Agency wanted Marcus' help in developing the Israeli army. Using the name "Michael Stone," he was smuggled past British soldiers in order to enter the new country. At one checkpoint, he was stopped and asked to produce his identification. The British sentry, not being very alert, accepted the forged papers with the name Michael Stone. If he had looked carefully, he would have seen Marcus' West Point ring.

"Micky Stone" arrived in Tel Aviv and immediately faced an extremely delicate situation. A sea of hostile Arabs surrounded the widely separated Jewish settlements in Palestine. Israel had no defensible borders, no air power, few tanks, ancient artillery pieces, and almost no arms or ammunition. The Haganah was an effective underground organization but it had no experience as a regular national army.

Facing the Israelis were well-supplied Arab armies determined to drive the Jews into the sea. Looming was the expectation of an imminent attack by the Transjordan Arab Legion, aimed at destroying the new state. The pro-Arab British administration in Palestine prohibited the importing of military supplies to Israel. Marcus worked day and night training the raw Israeli recruits, trying to shape them into soldiers.

Undaunted, "Stone" designed a command structure for Israel's new army and wrote training manuals, adapting his experience from Ranger School to the Haganah's special needs. He identified Israel's weakest points, specifically the scattered settlements in the Negev and the new quarter in Jerusalem. When the Arab armies attacked in May 1948, Israel was ready and extremely grateful for the meticulous planning of Mickey Marcus. His hit-and-run tactics kept the Egyptian army in the Negev off balance.

In Ted Berkman's book *Cast A Giant Shadow: The Story of Mickey Marcus Who Died To Save Jerusalem*, the situation leading up to the construction of the "Burma Road" is described with heart-stopping excitement:

> *With a cease-fire imminent, the powerful Transjordan Arab Legion sat virtually astride the main road to Jerusalem, cutting off the capital. When the Jewish section of Jerusalem was about to fall, Marcus ordered the con-*

struction of a road to bring additional men and equipment to break the Arab siege just days before the United Nations negotiated a cease-fire. Mickey gambled everything on forging a new link to the Biblical heart of Jewry.

He radioed Ben-Gurion for bulldozers, compressors, stonecutters and builders. Grizzled stonecutters and laborers came swarming into the area. The secret road Mickey was carving, across terrain that would have given pause to a mountain lion, would have to be built literally under the noses of the enemy. There were Arabs to his left at Latrun, less than five hundred yards away; and Arabs on his right. Enemy patrols were constantly poking at the Israeli positions. To make detection more difficult, work would have to be done mainly at night.

Hammers clanged; engines roared; masons grunted; foremen cursed. At strong points in the hills, sun-baked young riflemen crouched through the night. Towering over the entire turbulent scene was the sturdy figure of the brigadier from America, shaping the path hewn through rock and shellfire that was to be popularly hailed as the 'Marcus Road.'

Israel miraculously withstood the Arab assault with its borders virtually intact. In gratitude, Ben-Gurion named Mickey Marcus lieutenant general [*aluf*], the first general in the army of Israel since Judah Maccabee nearly two thousand years before. Marcus' strategy for the combined operation that eventually freed the battle-weary capital determined the outcome of the war.

During the early morning hours of June 11, 1948, six hours before the cease-fire with the Arabs was to begin, Marcus, unable to sleep, was inspecting the perimeter fence of his military headquarters in the village of *Abu Ghosh*, near Jerusalem. He walked beyond the guarded perimeter wrapped in his bed sheet. A Jewish sentry saw a white-robed figure approaching. Challenged in Hebrew, a language he did not know, Marcus was unable to respond with the proper code and was mistaken for an Arab by the

Showing his Israeli colleagues exercises (1948)

soldier. He fired a single, fatal shot and tragically killed Marcus.

Marcus' body, accompanied by Moshe Dayan and Yossi Harel, was flown back to West Point for burial. His tombstone identifies him as "A Soldier for All Humanity." He was honored by the Israeli military for his leadership and contribution to the defense of Israel. Marcus' wife, Emma, received this cable from David Ben-Gurion:

> *His name will live forever in the annals of the Jewish people. We feel confident that American Jewry will be proud of this great and gallant man who has given his life for the liberation of Israel.*

Hollywood would later immortalize Marcus in a movie based on the book, *Cast A Giant Shadow*, in which Kirk Douglas depicted the larger-than-life character of Mickey Marcus. Ben-Gurion put it simply; "He was the best man we had." *Mishmar David* is a village in Judea named for him.

The funeral of Marcus (June 1948)

Marcus continues to be remembered both in Israel and America. On June 10, 1998, the fiftieth anniversary of his death, the New York City Department of Corrections commemorated Marcus with a ceremony at the Colonel David Marcus Playground in Brooklyn. The Chief of the Department, Edward Reilly, recalled that Marcus had been commissioner of corrections under Mayor Fiorello La Guardia from 1934 to 1940.

The plaque unveiled that day reads:

Colonel David Marcus
May his Courage and the Ideals
Of Liberty and Equality for
Which he Sacrificed his Life Serve
As an Inspiration to All Children.
Died, Telshe Stone, Israel, June 10, 1948,
In the Israeli War for Independence.
Donated by
Kings County American Legion
Jewish War Veterans.

CHAPTER EIGHT

Creating the State of Israel

Menachem Ussishkin
1863 - 1941

> **When the Jewish people will have redeemed the Land of Israel, the Land of Israel will redeem the Jewish people.**
> — Menahem Ussishkin

Menachem Ussishkin was a fighter, popularly known as "the iron man." The battles he fought were to acquire land for Israel (then Palestine). He emphatically urged the continued purchase of land, convinced that this would "redeem the Jewish people." Ussishkin was best known for his development and leadership of the Jewish National Fund (JNF), which he chaired for more than eighteen years.

Born in 1863 in Dubrovno, Russia, Ussishkin moved to Moscow with his family, where he received a secular education. He attended the Moscow Technological Institute, graduating in 1889 as an engineer. While in school he was affiliated with two important organizations—*B'nai Zion* and *Hovevei Zion*—both of which produced some of the principal Zionist leaders of the time.

Ussishkin at tree planting ceremony at Kiryat Anavim (1930)

His first visit to Palestine was in 1891; he later published his diary of the trip. Ussishkin went to the First Zionist Congress in Basel in 1897 to present his concept of practical Zionism and distinguish it from Theodor Herzl's political Zionism. The basic tenet of practical Zionism was to combine political and diplomatic efforts with the practical activity of purchasing land for settlements in *Eretz Yisrael*.

When the war ended in 1919, Ussishkin immigrated to Palestine. For three years he headed the Zionist delegation to the Versailles Peace Conference in charge of Jewish Affairs. He addressed the Conference with a plea for his country:

> *The Land of Israel was forcibly taken from the Jewish people, who were exiled and dispersed throughout the world. And now, I, the descendant of the Exiles, come before you and demand that our stolen historic homeland be returned to us.*

Supporting the movement begun by Eliezer Ben-Yehuda, Ussishkin also spoke forcefully in favor of recognizing Hebrew as the official language of *Eretz Yisrael*.

Ussishkin and Albert Einstein in Palestine

In 1923, he was appointed chairman of the Jewish National Fund (JNF). Under his direction the JNF purchased land for agricultural settlements throughout Palestine. Menachem Ussishkin personally and directly is responsible for much of Israel's landscape, including the Jezreel Valley, Bet She'an Valley and Emek Hefer.

Ussishkin demonstrated his passionate spirit on one occasion just prior to his assuming leadership of the JNF. Negotiations for land in the Jezreel Valley were in progress and there were dissenting opinions concerning the viability of the purchase. Ussishkin delivered a fiery speech in which he noted that the land was "indeed costly," but in *Eretz Yisrael* time was even costlier: "If the choice is between buying dearly today or cheaply tomorrow, I choose today!" he said. "And if the land is expensive, you can say that Ussishkin and Ruppin are terrible businessmen. But had we missed the opportunity for purchase, you would have been entitled to regard us as criminals." Summing up, he concluded: "Throw me out of the leadership, but the valley will remain ours." Ultimately, all the delegates agreed with him and they approved the land purchase to thunderous applause.

When Ussishkin was appointed JNF's fourth chairman, the main office moved from London to its permanent headquarters in Jerusalem. The move from the Diaspora to the homeland took about a year, but once completed the JNF managed its work in *Eretz Yisrael* from its own soil. In the two decades that followed, Ussishkin steered the JNF towards the largest land purchases since its inception.

Following the 1929 Arab riots in Palestine, the British government commissioned the Shaw Report, which offered differing opinions as to the availability of land in Palestine for future Jewish immigration. In April 1930, shortly after publication of the report, the JNF invited local and foreign journalists to the Eden Hotel in Jerusalem to hear Menachem Ussishkin speak on the issue. After discussing the different opinions regarding future Jewish immigration, he proposed a transfer of the Arabs from Palestine:

> *We must continually proclaim our demand that our land be returned to our possession. If the land is empty of inhabitants—good! If, however there are other inhabitants there, they must be transferred to some other place, but we must receive the land! We have an ideal greater and more elevated than standing guard over hundreds of thousands of fellaheen [Arab peasants].*

Ussishkin pointed out that since the Arabs had many countries and much land at their disposal, while the Jewish people had none, it was surely "just" that Palestine be returned to the Jews. This only would be necessary in the future he said, "as for this generation, most of the land is just waiting to be reclaimed."

JNF emissaries traveled abroad to publicize the Zionist enterprise wherever Jews lived. Appearing at meetings and conferences, they described the JNF's work in *Eretz Yisrael*, and the progress being made in developing the Jewish settlements. The momentum for a Jewish homeland was building.

Many will remember growing up seeing the "blue box" designated for donations to the JNF. The coins dropped into the blue box connected the purchase of JNF stamps to the Jewish people's bond with *Eretz Yisrael*. The picture of the Jewish homeland on the stamp, journeyed along with the letter, from one coast to

Ussishkin answers question by Zionist leader in Zurich (1937)

another, reaching into the furthest cities and towns. Once received, a Jewish child could hold the letter, "touch" the land that was far away and share in its recovery. In this way, the work of the JNF was close to everyone, no matter where they lived.

Speaking at educational conferences, Ussishkin encouraged Hebrew teachers to instruct students in *Eretz Yisrael* and the Diaspora that the focus of the movement to provide a Jewish state had to be about redeeming the land. One by-product of these conferences was that a JNF corner now occupied every classroom, centered around the blue box. At a conference of the Teachers Movement in 1927, Ussishkin gave his historic address, "The Voice of the Land." He spoke about the "spiritual" connection of the children to a Jewish homeland:

> *The penny that a child gives or collects for land redemption is not important in itself, not by it will … the land of* Eretz Yisrael *be redeemed. The penny is important as an educational element: it is not the child that gives to the Fund, but rather the Fund that gives to the child. It gives him a lifelong foothold and lofty ideal.*

With his profound dedication and intense commitment, Ussishkin and the JNF added enormous tracts of land to *Eretz Yisrael*, providing a foundation and a future for the generation that would build the new state. Israel and all of its supporters worldwide are grateful to him for his relentless and unyielding pursuit of the funds needed to purchase the land, and the political battles that he fought to guarantee the Jewish homeland.

Meir Dizengoff
1861 - 1937

> *With pride and humility, I accept the honor of setting this foundation stone to mark the beginning of the city of Tel Aviv, a modern Jewish city in Palestine.*
>
> — Meir Dizengoff

Meir Dizengoff, the first mayor of Tel Aviv once was described as a "man who could reminisce about the future." With faith and vision, he saw the future in a way that made it come alive for people, and he pointed Tel Aviv in that direction.

Illustrating this visionary characteristic, one day he invited the media to the opening of the new port. Hundreds of reporters arrived. They saw nothing but water, sand and blue sky. Dizengoff took a stick and hammered it into the sand. There was nothing but water, sand, blue sky and a stick. Dizengoff stood before the crowd. He began by saying: "Ladies and gentlemen, I can still remember the day when Tel Aviv had no port."

Dizengoff was born in the town of Akimovichy (Bessarabia) in present-day Moldova. As a

Dizengoff welcomes visitors not in Tel Aviv, but Jerusalem

young man he was active in Russian revolutionary circles. In the mid-1880s he moved to Odessa, where he participated in the activities of the anti-government People's Will party. His involvement with this group prompted his arrest and eight months incarceration in 1885.

After his release from jail, he became active in the Zionist movement through *Hibbat Zion*. In the late 1880s he studied chemical engineering in Paris, specializing in glass production. He was sent to *Eretz Yisrael* in 1892 by Baron Edmond de Rothschild to establish a glass factory at Tantura (Dor) in order to supply bottles for the wines produced in the settlements. The factory was closed in 1894, however, when it was discovered that the local sand was unsuit-

Tel Aviv's Mayor at the opening ceremony of King George Street (1935)

able for making glass. During his stay in *Eretz Yisrael*, Dizengoff continued his activism, trying to form a Jewish workers' organization.

He again lived in Odessa from 1897 to 1905, working in commerce and continuing his public activities. He participated in several Zionist Congresses and was among the opponents of the Uganda Plan, a proposal to establish a temporary Jewish state in Africa. Dizengoff was a founder of the Geulah Company, formed to purchase land in Palestine; he returned to settle in Jaffa in 1905, as director of the company.

In 1909, he founded the Ahuzat Bayit Company—the association that brought Tel Aviv into existence. The company was organized to establish a modern Jewish quarter near the Arab city of Jaffa. A lottery was held for the first sixty lots. Five years later the Gymnasia Herzliya High School was established in the center of the "first Hebrew City." The city became the mecca of the Hebrew language, the Hebrew press, theater and literature. The name of the

Dizengoff (left) in Tel Aviv's Purim parade (1934)

suburb was Tel Aviv [Hill of Spring], chosen because of its association with rebirth and revitalization.

The local council of Tel Aviv elected Dizengoff as its executive leader in 1911. He was elected mayor in 1921 and served the city for sixteen dedicated years, until his death in 1937. His public service was prolific. During World War I, Dizengoff headed a committee to assist suffering victims and refugees. He was a member of the Zionist Executive from 1917 to 1919, and ran its Trade and Industry Department. In 1919 he founded *Ha-Ezrah* [*The Citizen*] to politically organize the non-labor middle class. With the outbreak of Arab riots in 1936, Dizengoff urged that the government offices be opened in Tel Aviv and succeeded in establishing a separate port.

Dizengoff's vision for the city served both the past and the future: he emphasized the modernism of the new city, yet he still was driven to represent and interpret the past. He was one of the major initiators and dedicated supporters of cultural life in Israel—Tel Aviv became its center. The main street in today's sprawling city received Dizengoff's name in 1934. It is not merely a commercial avenue, but also "an emotional space, bearing a cosmopolitan presence mingled with pioneering memories."

Interestingly, the city of Tel Aviv and the State of Israel share a birthplace. In 1909, sixty-six families gathered on a sand dune to divide up the lots of what became Tel Aviv. A civic leader at the time, Dizengoff built his home on that dune, donating and converting it into the city's art museum after his wife died.

With the announcement imminent of the new State of Israel in 1948, a location urgently was sought for the ceremonies. The stage was set and there were less than forty-eight hours left for preparations. The ceremony's location had to be secret—one well-placed explosive could wipe out the entire Jewish leadership of Palestine. The place selected was the Tel Aviv Art Museum because it was a secure location.

Destiny and history filled the former Dizengoff home as the State of Israel was declared on May 14, 1948, in the simple stucco building, now called Independence Hall. It was there that 2000 years of exile ended in wild celebration, with people weeping tears of joy.

Mayor of Tel Aviv in his office (1934)

Moshe Sneh
1909 - 1972

Thanks to the settlement of Eretz Yisrael and the Jewish people we will emerge from the world crisis with a Jewish state in the land of Israel.
— Moshe Sneh

Moshe Sneh was a statesman and political journalist, a proponent of a socialist ideology that supported the rights of struggling workers. In his nineteen years in the Israeli Knesset, he was highly respected among his colleagues and was viewed as Israel's primary parliamentarian. Known as a brilliant orator, he was an extremely sought after lecturer.

Sneh was born in Radzyn, Poland, into a traditional, well-educated Zionist family. He attended a Polish Catholic secondary school in his grandfather's village, receiving his Jewish education from his grandfather.

He was only sixteen when he published his first article—*The Concept of Nationalism*, in the journal of the Polish Freethinkers Association. From this early age he became involved in political activities, while also studying medicine at the University of Warsaw. He met Zionist leader Yitzhak Gruenbaum when he joined the radical wing of the General Zionists in Poland. When Gruenbaum left Poland to immigrate to Palestine in 1932, he recommended Sneh to lead the Zionist organization.

The following year Sneh married Hannah Weinberg, also a medical student. They had two children—Tamar and Ephraim (a leading member of the Labor Party in the twenty-first century). Moshe Sneh graduated from medical school in 1935 and took over as political editor of the Yiddish newspaper, *Heint*. His reputation as a talented political journalist was just beginning.

Moshe Sneh is joined by his young son, Ephraim, eventually a Labor Party leader

Moshe Sneh chats with Ben-Gurion

In his efforts to defend the rights of Polish Jews, Sneh called for a boycott of the elections in 1935 to protest Poland's new anti-democratic constitution. In obvious retribution, he was drafted into the Polish army and, as a doctor, went into officers' training. After his discharge, he resumed his political and Zionist activities.

Sneh argued in defense of the rights of the Jews and worked to develop close ties with the Labor movement in Palestine. He was an active participant in the World Zionist Organization (WZO), and attended Zionist Congresses with Chaim Weizmann and Gruenbaum. At the Zionist Congress in 1939, he warned of the impending disaster in Europe, and when the war broke out he joined the Polish army. With the fall of Poland, Sneh escaped to Vilna and then immigrated to Palestine in March 1940.

In *Eretz Yisrael*, David Ben-Gurion urged Sneh to join the Haganah national command. A year later, he was appointed to lead it, a position he held for five years. He was instrumental in shaping the *yishuv*'s military force and promoted the establishment and development of the Haganah's elite Palmach unit, which played a crucial role in Israel's War of Independence.

In the early 1940s he forged political ties with Ben-Gurion. In the wake of their bitter disappointment with the British Labor government of 1945, the two leaders embraced the idea of armed resistance to the British. In October 1945, Ben-Gurion gave Sneh the authority to launch armed opposition and to establish, together with the underground Irgun (IZL), the Jewish resistance. In June, the British army began arresting the leadership of the Jewish community in Palestine. Wanted by the British authorities, Sneh went into hiding.

A rift developed within the Zionist leadership led by Ben-Gurion and Sneh. The moderates, headed by Chaim Weizmann, threatened to resign if the armed opposition did not end. Instead, Sneh himself resigned in protest. In late July, he managed to flee to Paris where he attended meetings of the Jewish Agency Executive. During the meetings, the alliance between Sneh and Ben-Gurion began to unravel.

In 1947, Sneh was appointed head of the Jewish Agency's political department in Europe in charge of rescue efforts and "illegal" immigration of Jews to Palestine. He met with European leaders to enlist political support for the establishment of Israel. Through his work he was personally involved in some of the dramatic events related to "illegal" immigration to Palestine, one of which was the Exodus episode.

Sensing that there might be a possibility of Soviet support for the new state, he called for political rapprochement with the Soviet Union. In December 1947, Sneh resigned from all his Jewish Agency positions and left the Labor Party. In January 1948, he was among the founders of *Mapam*, the United Workers Party, a left-wing Zionist-socialist party with a pro-Soviet orientation. In 1949, Sneh as the representative of *Mapam* was elected to the first Knesset.

Because of the growing hostile dispute between the supporters and opponents of the Soviets, Sneh moved even more sharply to the left and established himself as the leader of *Mapam*'s left wing. The crisis in *Mapam* escalated and he left the party. In May 1953, Sneh established the Left Socialist Party of Israel, which was not successful.

Finally, Sneh joined *Maki*, the Israeli Communist Party, in October 1954, where he was actively involved in creating a bridge of friendship between Israel and the Soviet Union despite repeated disappointments. Eleven years passed from the time he joined *Maki* until a rift occurred within the party in 1965.

In the final years of his life, Sneh devoted himself to peace efforts and took vigorous action against the anti-Israeli attitudes among the world's left. During these years, he formulated a new approach to the problems of the Jewish people and Zionism, and rigorously criticized the anti-democratic regime of the Soviet Union. He emerged from his seclusion, warmly received when he appeared in public.

From the time of the establishment of the State of Israel, Sneh persisted in pursuing issues for which he had been fighting throughout his political life: the struggle for peace; equal rights for Israel's Arabs; democracy; and the separation of state and religion. He remained true to the fundamental principles of his socialist ideology, opposed the government's economic-social policies, and strongly supported the workers' rights movement.

Sneh was a gifted writer. Thousands of his articles in Yiddish, Polish, and Hebrew were published in Poland, Israel and other parts of the world. His articles appeared in many of Israel's newspapers. Tel Aviv University's Zionist Research Institute and the Sneh Memorial Committee collaborated in issuing five volumes of his selected writings, published by Am Oved.

In his will, Moshe Sneh wrote: "I devoted my entire life to the Jewish people and was guided by the principle that the future of my people was bound up with the future of human progress."

David Ben-Gurion
1886 - 1973

> *The state of Israel will prove itself not by material wealth, not by military might or technical achievement, but by its moral character and human values.*
> — David Ben-Gurion

David Ben-Gurion was named as one of *Time* magazine's 100 most important people of the century. *Time* wrote about this great statesman:

> *Part Washington, part Moses, he was the architect of a new nation state that altered the destiny of the Jewish people — and the Middle East. He became a pioneer, a farmhand, active with early Zionist-socialist groups. At age nineteen he was what he would remain all his life: a secular Jewish nationalist who combined Jewish Messianic visions with socialist ideals, a man with fierce ambition for leadership, extraordinary tactical-political skills and a sarcastic edge rather than a sense of humor.*

David Ben-Gurion was born David Green in the town of Plonsk in Poland in 1886, the sixth child in a family well-grounded in Zionism. He is considered one of the three founding figures of Zionism, standing beside Chaim Weizmann and Theodor Herzl in the pages of history.

His father, a Hebrew teacher, was a veteran member of one of the forerunners of modern Zionism—*Hibbat Zion* [Lovers of Zion]. Ben-Gurion was given a modern Jewish education in a *cheder* that taught secular as well as religious studies.

Ben-Gurion's leadership qualities and political interests manifested themselves early on. When he was just fourteen, he organized a group of youths to form Ezra—an association dedicated to Hebrew as the spoken language. At seventeen he joined *Po'alei Zion* [Workers of Zion], one of the first socialist Zionist political entities and a party that would dominate the social and political fabric of Zionism for decades, mostly under his leadership. Already an activist, during the revolution of 1905-1906 he was arrested twice, but his father used his

The three editors of the "Workers of Zion" weekly, (left to right) David Ben-Gurion, Yitzhak Ben-Zvi and Ya'akov Zerubavel (1910)

influence to have him released both times.

When Theodor Herzl died, Ben Gurion was extremely distressed. "The tragedy is so big . . . the loss is so great . . . never again will there be a man like him," he wrote to one of his friends. Ben-Gurion promised to carry through with Herzl's dream. In 1906, when he was twenty, Ben-Gurion moved to Palestine, a pioneer of the Second Aliyah. He sent a postcard home to his father: "Today at 9:00, I landed on the shores of Jaffa. I am healthy, and full of faith and courage!"

He worked on the first *moshavot* [cooperative settlements] in *Petah Tikva* and *Rishon Le Zion*. Ben-Gurion felt that if the region were to build its Jewish character, Jews would have to perform all types of jobs. Men plowed and sowed fields, women took care of the gardens and milked the cows; children herded flocks of geese. He also worked as a laborer in the orange groves and the wine cellars, and as a watchman in the Galilee. He regarded Zionism as a practical doctrine achieved by immigration to the Land of Israel, and his personal philosophy was reflected in the way he lived his life.

Ben-Gurion wrote his father poetic letters describing the beauty of the land—telling his father: "settling the land, that is the only real Zionism; everything else is only self-deception, empty verbiage and merely a pastime." He was careful to hide the hardships such as bouts of malaria and hunger. During the four years he spent on the land, Ben-Gurion already was immersed in labor politics as a member of the central committee of *Po'alei Zion*. His point of view stressed the obligation of every member to settle in *Eretz Yisrael*, and the right of immigrants and settlers to determine their own destiny.

Aligning himself with the belief of Eliezer Ben-Yehuda that Hebrew was the language of the Jewish homeland, Ben-Gurion insisted that all *Po'alei Zion* meetings be conducted in Hebrew. In 1910, he was elected to the editorial staff of the party newspaper in Jerusalem, joining with Yitzhak and Rachel Ben-Zvi to produce the new Labor Party publication *Ahdut*.

Ben-Gurion addresses provisional government ceremony at Tel Aviv Museum (1948)

Two political adversaries, Ben-Gurion and Menachem Begin, meet (1968)

Many of his articles stressed the need for Jews to gain autonomy from Ottoman-ruled Palestine.

The Ottoman authorities deported Ben-Gurion and Yitzhak Ben-Zvi (Israel's second president) from Palestine for their Zionist activism. Arriving in New York in 1915, Ben-Gurion devoted the next two years to building an "American wing" of labor Zionism. At this time, he met and married his wife Paula.

With the impact of the Balfour Declaration of 1917, Ben-Gurion responded to Ze'ev Jabotinsky's call for the formation of Jewish battalions within the British army to liberate Palestine from the Turks. Ben-Gurion volunteered, serving in Egypt in one of the three Jewish battalions, the 39th Royal Fusiliers, and returned to Israel in the uniform of the Jewish Legion.

In 1921, Ben-Gurion was elected secretary-general of the *Histadrut*, the General Federation of Labor that had been founded the previous year. He served in this position until 1935. Under Ben-Gurion's powerful leadership, the *Histadrut* created many of the social and economic institutions that dominated Israeli society for decades to come.

Long-winded meetings of the *Histadrut* were routine. When Ben-Gurion met opposition he would continue to repeat his position until the doubters were convinced or exhausted. The healthy rivalry that developed between his views and those of the right wing Ze'ev Jabotinsky focused the public on the two different political perspectives. Eventually, Israel's two leading political parties, Labor and *Likud*, would evolve from the issues argued between these two factions.

In 1930, Ben-Gurion played a key role in merging labor groups into a highly effective political machine—*Mapai*, a political party that governed Israeli society during the first critical decades of statehood, with Ben-Gurion at the helm. By 1935, labor Zionism was the most important element in the World Zionist Organization (WZO). Through the influence of *Mapai*, Ben-Gurion was appointed chairman of the Jewish Agency, the settlement arm of the Zionist movement, a post he held until 1948 when the State of Israel was established.

As chairman of the Jewish Agency Executive, Ben-Gurion joined with Chaim Weizmann in directing all Zionist affairs. They agreed to the plan of partitioning Palestine into Jewish and Arab states, believing that a state for the Jews would be a crucial advance for worldwide Zionism. At the Zionist Congress in Basel, Switzerland, in 1937, Ben-Gurion proclaimed:

> *No Jew has the right to yield the rights of the Jewish people in Israel. No Jew has the authority to do so. No Jewish body has the authority to do so. Not even the entire Jewish people alive today has the authority to yield any part of Israel. It is the right of the Jewish people over generations, a right which under no condition can be canceled. Even if Jews in a specific period proclaim they are relinquishing this right, they have neither the power nor the authority to deny this right to future generations. No concession of this type is binding or obligates the Jewish People.*

When World War II erupted, the British reversed their pledge to create a partitioned Jewish state by issuing the infamous White Paper of 1939. When a post-war change of government in Great Britain failed to bring about repeal of the White Paper, even after the tragedy of the Holocaust became known, confrontation with Britain was unavoidable.

Standing at attention, Ben-Gurion participates in military ceremony

During the war, the British did not permit Jews to enter Palestine. Ben-Gurion called on the Jews to "fight the British for the restoration of *aliya* as if there were no war with Hitler, and to fight Hitler as if the British had not closed the doors of Palestine to the Jews." At the Congress of American Zionists, which took place in New York's Biltmore Hotel, he presented a plan to establish a Jewish state. Knowing that the Arabs would never endorse a Jewish nation, Ben-Gurion told commanders of the Haganah to prepare for battle; "when we declare the establishment of a Jewish state, the Arabs will attack. If we have weapons, we will win." Emissaries were sent to buy planes, tanks and artillery.

In 1946, Ben-Gurion took over the defense portfolio of the Jewish Agency Executive and led the struggle against the British, defying the British blockade against Jewish immigration, intensifying

Israel's prime minister reading congratulation letter on UN decision (November 30, 1947)

settlement activity, and challenging British authority. He began planning for post-war Palestine and creation of the Jewish homeland.

Deterioration of the situation in Palestine induced Britain to bring the issue of Palestine before the United Nations—a step that culminated in the November 29, 1947 UN General

Ben-Gurion at Independence Day parade in Jerusalem with Weizmann and Yadin

Ben-Gurion at opening ceremony of train station (1949)

Assembly partition plan. On May 14, 1948, when the British Mandate came to an end, Ben-Gurion—as leader of the Provisional Government—declared the establishment of the State of Israel.

Ben-Gurion masterminded and carried out the transition from underground forces to regular army, dismantling pre-state politicized militias to form a united, apolitical military—the Israel Defense Forces (IDF). His military leadership was a rare mixture of pragmatism and vision. His combination of bold daring and relentless determination, dynamic organization and decisive moves, linked to a deep, almost mystical faith in Israeli youth, played an essential role in the conduct of the War of Independence and its outcome. Israel emerged from the war victorious, but paid a terrible price: 6,373 killed, almost one percent of the population.

In his first five years as prime minister, Ben-Gurion's assertive and charismatic leadership led to mass immigration that doubled the population during the first four years of statehood. His task was monumental:

- *directing absorption, investing the new nation's limited resources in integrating immigrants*

- *securing outlying areas through new settlements*

- *providing universal education in a public school system*

- *molding the character and structure of the IDF.*

Ben-Gurion remained the dominant figure in Israel's public life well into the 1960s as prime minister and minister of defense. Even during two short periods of retirement from active politics, his substantial influence remained manifest behind the scenes. In 1953, drained by years of intensive public service, Ben-Gurion resigned from the government for two years, settling in *Kibbutz Sde Boker* in the Negev to set an example for Israeli youth. As he was packing up his office, in his typical gruff fashion he rebuked teary-eyed personal staff: "Instead of crying, you would do better to come with me!" He worked in the fields and the sheep pens, living in a simple hut with his wife, Paula. He did not want the Negev to remain barren, and hoped that through his personal example people would come to live there.

Two years later, Ben-Gurion returned to active politics as minister of defense. Following the 1955 elections, he again became prime minister. Reassessing defense policy, he advocated a more resolute response to terrorism from across the borders. The 1956 Sinai campaign—despite Israeli withdrawal from Sinai under international pressure—brought a halt to sabotage and terrorist attacks on settlements in the south.

Ben-Gurion returned to *Sde Boker* in 1963, where he wrote his memoirs, leaving a testament to future generations describing how the State of Israel became a reality. He died in December 1973, and was buried beside his wife in *Sde Boker*.

Ben-Gurion at home in Tel Aviv

There are many wonderful anecdotal stories about David Ben-Gurion, one of which centered on his aversion to formal dress. On his way to a dinner event for the Jewish National Fund of America in Tel Aviv, one of his aides stopped him and insisted that he change into formal attire for the event. Ben-Gurion resisted: "Why can't I go like this? Winston Churchill told me it was all right." When the aide questioned him further about Churchill's statement, Ben-Gurion replied, "Once I was in London and I attended a formal dinner dressed as I am. Churchill said to me that this kind of dress is all right in Israel but not in England!"

On another historic occasion, one of the most important in modern Jewish history, May 14, 1948, Ben-Gurion was at the microphone at the Tel Aviv Museum (now Independence Hall). A huge portrait of Theodor Herzl was mounted on the wall behind him, draped on both sides by Zionist flags—the flag of the newly born State of Israel. At the podium Ben-Gurion raised the gavel and at 4 p.m., after 2000 years of struggle and purpose, he declared the creation of the State of Israel. He read from the new Declaration of Independence:

> Eretz Yisrael *was the birthplace of the Jewish people. Here their spiritual, religious, and political identity was shaped. Here they first attained statehood, created cultural values of national and universal significance and gave to the world the eternal Book of Books. After being forcibly expelled from their land, the people kept faith with it throughout their dispersion. They never ceased to pray and hope for their return to it and for the restoration in it of their political freedom, which would open the gates of the homeland wide to every Jew and confer upon the Jewish people the status of a full-privileged member of the comity of nations. This right is the natural right of the Jewish people to be masters of their own fate, like all other nations, in their own sovereign State.*

> *Accordingly, we, members of the People's Council, representatives of the Jewish Community of* Eretz Yisrael *and of the Zionist movement, are here assembled on the day of the termination of the British Mandate over* Eretz Yisrael *and, by virtue of our natural and historic right and on the strength of the resolution of the United Nations General Assembly, hereby declare the establishment of a Jewish State in* Eretz Yisrael, *to be known as the State of Israel.*

The Jewish Philharmonic Orchestra broke into a triumphant and rousing rendition of *Hatikvah* in a moment captured for all of time by television cameras, as the Jews danced and cried with joy—ecstatic in their newly established homeland.

Abba Eban
1915-2002

> *History teaches us that men and nations behave wisely once they have exhausted all other alternatives.*
>
> — Abba Eban

A brilliant orator and an acknowledged statesman, Abba Eban, fluent in ten languages, served as a diplomat, government minister, and member of the Israeli Knesset for nearly a half-century. One of Eban's biographers wrote: "It was not merely the wealth of his vocabulary that made listening to an Eban speech the rhetorical equivalent of attending a Mozart or Beethoven concert. It was the depth of the message that he delivered that could be so inspiring."

Born Aubrey Solomon Eban in Cape Town, South Africa in 1915, Eban moved to England with his family and was brought up in a comfortable home in London, receiving a classical education in Greek and Latin. From the end of the school day on Friday until Sunday night he went to his maternal grandfather's house, where he received an intensive private education in biblical literature, the Talmud, and Modern Hebrew. These lessons continued until after Eban's fourteenth birthday. In his autobiography, Eban notes:

> *Whatever [my grandfather's] intention, the consequence for me was formative to the ultimate degree. It was the weekend, not the weekday world that came to excite my deepest sources of feeling. The Jewish legacy was my close possession. St. Olave's [his school] belonged to its own world ... and could exist without me. On the other hand, the Jewish domain was lived on an intimate level of personal experience.*

Abba Eban watches as President Truman and Ben-Gurion meet at White House

He studied Oriental languages and the classics at Cambridge University from 1938 to 1940, where he was a research fellow and lecturer in Arabic. Eban already was establishing a reputation for his eloquence, his mastery of rhetoric and persuasive speaking, and his ease in multiple languages.

Eban's personal Zionism began in earnest when he joined *Po'alei Zion* [Workers of Zion] in 1935. He enlisted in the British army in 1940 and was trained in intelligence. He attained the rank of major at the outset of World War II, and served on the staff of the British minister of state in Cairo in 1941.

As an intelligence officer in Jerusalem, Eban trained Jewish volunteers in underground resistance to counter a Nazi invasion. This unusual assignment pointed out the

Abba Eban (1958)

appalling dichotomy that faced Jewish people living in Palestine. On the one hand, Britain was their adversary, intent on limiting the growth of the Jewish community and forbidding the Jews to carry weapons. Conversely, in their concerted effort to defeat Hitler, the British depended on the Jewish people as their allies in the war. The British secret service trained Palestinian Jewish units in resistance and espionage to prevent a Nazi conquest of the country. The irony was lost on no one. Eban wryly commented:

> *In Palestine itself, the High Commissioner and his soldiers would swoop punitively on any Jews caught in the possession of weapons. At the same time a more prestigious arm of the government in London would pour weapons and explosives into the hands of the most effectively trained and militant Jewish fighters.*

Eban acted as liaison between the British Special Operations Executive and the Jewish resistance fighters in Jerusalem who "officially" were outlawed by the British. When the war ended Eban returned to his residence in Jerusalem.

In 1946, the Jewish Agency appointed Eban political information officer in London. In this capacity, he participated in the transition of the British government prior to the declaration of the State of Israel. He represented the Jewish Agency for the United Nations Special Committee on Palestine in 1947.

Eban rose to international prominence in 1948, leading the struggle for Israel's entry into the United Nations. There was considerable heated debate in the United Nations regarding the partitioning of Palestine. Heavy lobbying and persuasive speaking by Eban and his colleagues resulted in a narrow majority in favor of partitioning Palestine into Jewish and Arab states. Eban's impressive speech to the entire General Assembly was as much intended for the American public and world opinion as for the assembled delegates. His powerful rhetoric led to Israel's admission to the United Nations.

When Israel became independent in May 1948, Eban was appointed the country's representative to the United Nations, becoming a permanent delegate in 1949 at thirty-four years old. Eban spent a decade at the United Nations from 1950 to 1959, simultaneously serving as his country's ambassador to the United States.

Following his ambassadorship, Eban returned to Israel and was appointed president of the Weizmann Institute of Science, a position he held from 1959 to 1966. Before and after the Six Day War, he led Israel in its political struggle in the United Nations, continuing to seek ways to consolidate Israel's relations with the United States and to secure a healthy rapport with the European Economic Community. From 1963 to 1966, he was deputy to Prime Minister Levi Eshkol. In May 1967, on the eve of the Six Day War, he traveled to Paris, London, and Washington in a dramatic effort to win support for Israel's position. Eban was elected to the Knesset and also served as minister of foreign affairs from 1966 to 1974.

He was reappointed foreign minister in the short-lived government formed under the premiership of Golda Meir in March 1974. In this role, Eban participated in the negotiations with Dr. Henry Kissinger leading to the agreement with Syria on the disengagement of forces. Yigal Allon replaced him as foreign minister in the cabinet formed by Yitzhak Rabin in June, and though Eban was offered the position of minister of information, he declined the post. In 1974, while retaining his seat in the Knesset, Eban accepted an invitation to serve as visiting professor in Political Science and Middle East History at Haifa University. He remained in the Knesset from 1974 to 1988, serving for many years as the chairman of the Knesset Foreign Affairs and Defense Committee.

Eban and Golda Meir arrive at airport

Eban left politics in 1988 to devote himself full time to writing, lecturing and the production of several television documentary series: *Heritage: Civilization and the Jews*, about the history of the Jewish people; *Personal Witness: A Nation is Born*, his eyewitness account of the birth of the State of Israel; and *Brink of Peace*, an overview of the history of the peace process between Israel and the Arab world.

Proclaimed as one of the finest political philosophers of the twentieth century, Eban's long-term influence may well rival his practical accomplishments in life.

Eban chats with colleague at United Nations

His oratorical skills and spontaneous wit were legendary. When Eban was seventy-five, Henry Kissinger gave a birthday party for him at the United Nations. Margaret Thatcher sent a telegram to Eban saying: "How can one not give Abba Eban his due?" Eban quipped back, "Actually, there are quite a few people in Israel who think it's possible."

Eban demonstrated how skillfully he combined his persuasive powers with his dry sense of humor when he tried to persuade a skeptical world that Israel acted properly in seizing the West Bank, Gaza Strip, Sinai Desert, Golan Heights and East Jerusalem after the 1967 War. Simultaneously, he argued that Israel should negotiate peace in exchange for the

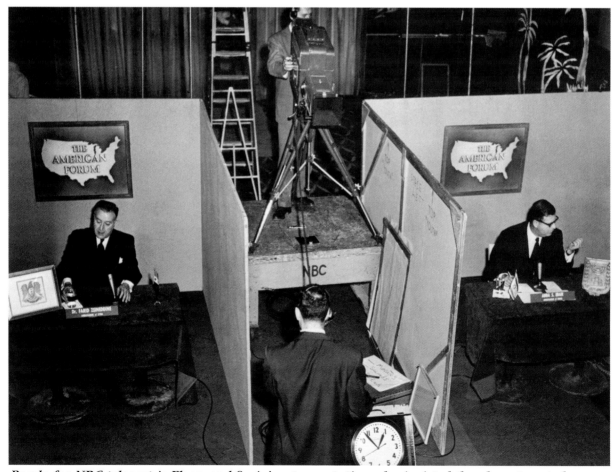

Ready for NBC telecast is Eban and Syria's representative who insisted they be separated

territories it captured. Eban, aware of the irony of his enormous popularity overseas and the mercurial ambivalence of his following at home, joked: "I could have been elected prime minister if people abroad could vote in Israeli elections!"

In 2001, Abba Eban was awarded the Israel Prize for his lifetime achievements; too ill to attend the ceremony, his wife accepted the prize on his behalf. Included in his long list of awards and accolades were twenty honorary doctorates and membership in the American Academy of Arts and Sciences. He passed away at eighty-seven, in November 2002, survived by his wife, son, and daughter.

Abba Eban, the "father of Israeli statesmanship," was buried in the *Kfar Shmaryahu* cemetery. At his funeral, Shimon Peres, who had worked with Eban for decades, praised him in his eulogy:

> *A man of peace who paved the way for peace. When Israel was attacked on all sides, he gave the message of hope for different relations with the Arab world and the Palestinians. He was Israel's voice in its most difficult hours, and explained Israel's yearning for peace. He served his people honorably, and his life will be remembered as one of the important chapters in Israel's history.*

Abba Eban was one of the quintessential diplomats of the modern era, setting the standard for defending Israel in the courts of world opinion, and in public and political circles around the globe.

Foreign Minister and Mrs. Abba Eban (l) receiving U.S. Secretary of State Dr. and Mrs. Henry Kissinger at Ben Gurion Airport (1974)

Louis Brandeis
1856 - 1941

> ## *To be good Americans, we must be better Jews, and to be better Jews, we must become Zionists.*
>
> — Louis Brandeis

Before 1914, many—if not most—major American Jewish leaders and organizations were either ambivalent or openly opposed to a Jewish state in Palestine. One man—Louis Dembitz Brandeis of Boston—did more than anyone else to change that attitude. Following Brandeis' lead, a majority of American Jews came to see a future State of Israel as essential for saving oppressed Jews abroad. They also came to understand that the creation of a nation was the key to American Jewish renewal.

When Louis Brandeis embraced Zionism, he legitimized the American call for a Jewish homeland in Palestine. On the surface, Brandeis was an unlikely candidate for a Zionist leader. Born into an affluent German-Jewish family in Louisville, Kentucky in 1865, his parents raised him with Universalist values, with little or no background in the Jewish religion. His parents both had emigrated from Prague to the United States, where his father established a grain and produce business that thrived until the 1870 depression.

Brandeis was an astute student from an early age. He especially admired his uncle, Louis Dembitz, and in his honor changed his middle name from "David" to "Dembitz." His uncle, known as "the Jewish scholar of the South," was an avid Zionist and supporter of Theodor Herzl and inspired Brandeis with his fiery Zionism.

Graduating from high school when he was only fifteen, Brandeis accompanied his parents on an extended trip to Europe. He studied in Dresden, Germany and found the repressive society distasteful. He was eager to return home. "In Kentucky," he smiled, "you could whistle."

Returning to America, he entered Harvard Law School (without having attended college) and graduated when he was only twenty years old. Brandeis achieved an academic record unsurpassed at the school; his grades were the highest in the school's history. Harvard had to make a special exception for him to receive his degree—their rules stated that a student had to be twenty-one in order to graduate.

Brandeis with friend in Boston

Brandeis, Supreme Court Justice

Brandeis formed a law practice in Boston with a former classmate and by the time he was thirty years old he had achieved considerable financial success. In appearance, he was commanding, tall and distinguished with deep-set, dark, penetrating eyes. Many compared him physically to Abraham Lincoln. President Franklin Roosevelt referred to him as "Isaiah."

Brandeis became an ardent Zionist, contributing both his time and money to Zionist causes. In Boston, he was known as "the people's attorney." He received this tribute as the result of a famous case he handled in 1911, mediating the garment workers' strike in New York. His experience with the garment workers was important because for the first time, it exposed him to a large Jewish population. The garment workers' strike made him aware of how hard life was for many Jewish immigrants—it made him think about Judaism in a different way. He began to distinguish between the Jewish religion and the Jewish people as part of a nation.

Brandeis, now exploring his role as a Zionist, was introduced to two famous Jewish Zionists, Jacob de Haas and Aaron Aaronsohn, both of whom were great proponents of Theodor Herzl. Herzl's ideas were becoming extremely popular with the masses and Zionists in America and England endeavored to enlist prominent citizens to support this cause. Both de Haas and Aaronsohn, along with their friend Rabbi Stephen Wise, influenced Brandeis' enthusiastic embrace of Zionism.

When Woodrow Wilson was elected president in 1912, he often turned to Brandeis for advice. Four years later, Wilson nominated him as a Justice to the Supreme Court. The nomination was not easily confirmed. There was an upsurge of anti-Semitism in the Senate debate over Brandeis, but Wilson would not concede. Brandeis joined the highest United States Court on June 1, 1916, the first Jewish person in history to attain this position.

During World War I, Brandeis agreed to serve as chairman of the Provisional Committee for General Zionist Affairs in the World Zionist Organization (WZO). A turning point in his Zionist activities occurred when he met Chaim Weizmann. Political differences emerged between the two men over the role of the organization. Brandeis, troubled by the lack of both budgetary controls and effectiveness of Zionist organizations—stemming from years of political jockeying for position—resigned from the leading Zionist body. This did not deter him from his commitment to forming a new Jewish state, however. Brandeis encouraged the establishment of the Palestine Economic Corporation, which worked to develop investment in important projects in *Eretz Yisrael*.

With the end of the war Brandeis sent several delegates to the Paris Peace Conference, including de Haas and Felix Frankfurter, to help urge the creation of a Jewish homeland in Palestine. Brandeis himself traveled to Paris and the Middle East during the summer of 1919. Despite his differences with the WZO, Brandeis remained a presence in the movement for the rest of his life.

A remarkable incident occurred when Brandeis went to Palestine in 1934. He was visiting with David Ben-Gurion who presented the Supreme Court Justice with a memorandum describing how economically important the small port of *Uman Rashrash*, on the Red Sea, would soon become to the Jewish people. "It is important that we establish a pioneering Jewish settlement here. But it will not bring a profit and it might cost $100,000," Ben-Gurion admitted. Brandeis read over the memorandum, took out a pen, wrote a check and handed it to the stunned Ben-Gurion saying, "Here is $100,000." Louis Dembitz Brandeis had just bought the city of Eilat for the soon to be born State of Israel.

Brandeis' life on the Supreme Court was exemplary. He formulated his brilliant legal decisions drawing from history, economics, and the social sciences. At a time when most of the Court wanted to strike down new social legislation, Brandeis stood firm for the "New Freedom." He voted to sustain minimum wage laws, price control laws and supported other significant social platforms. He retired from the Supreme Court in 1939 after serving for twenty-three years and died two years later.

Louis Brandeis believed that the first American patriots and the first settlers in *Eretz Yisrael* had much in common. Both groups risked their lives and worked hard to create a new country, and both believed in social justice. Brandeis spoke eloquently of these pioneers:

> *There is no inconsistency between loyalty to America and loyalty to Jewry. The Jewish spirit, the product of our religion and experiences is essentially modern and essentially American. Not since the destruction of the Temple have the Jews in spirit and ideals been so fully in harmony with the noblest aspirations of the country in which they lived. America's fundamental law seeks to make real the brotherhood of man. That brotherhood became the Jewish fundamental law more than 2500 years ago. America's insistent demand in the twentieth century is for social justice. That also has been the Jews' striving for ages. Their affliction as well as their religion has prepared the Jews for effective democracy. Persecution broadened their sympathies. It trained them in patient endurance, in self-control, and in sacrifice. It made them think as well as suffer. It deepened their passion for righteousness.*

Brandeis contributed both spirit and fortune to the Zionist cause; the largest bequest in his will was stipulated for the creation of a Jewish homeland. Louis Brandeis will perhaps best be remembered for his remarkable achievements as the first Jewish Justice on the United States Supreme Court. He will certainly be remembered for having purchased the land for Eilat. He will live in the hearts of Israelis and Zionists everywhere for the firm stand that he took in support of the creation of the State of Israel.

Chaim Weizmann
1874 - 1952

> *Even if all of the kings of the East and West were to give us a state, it would only be words. But if the Jewish people were to rise up and build the land of Israel, then the State of Israel would be a fait accompli.*
>
> — Chaim Weizmann

Chaim Weizmann was a scientist, leader of the Zionist movement for over thirty years, and the first president of the State of Israel. One of Chaim Weizmann's most impressive and significant achievements was to persuade the British government to issue the Balfour Declaration in 1917, the first official statement by any nation that Jews had a right to a homeland in Palestine.

Weizmann was born in 1874 in the small village of Motol, Russia (now Belarus), the son of a timber merchant. His father and mother were married when they were sixteen and fourteen, and Weizmann was one of fourteen children. He grew up in a boisterous family, immersed in Jewish tradition. His childhood was typical of the *shtetl*, living on an autonomous island surrounded by a sea of hostile Russians. In his autobiography he wrote:

> *We were strangers to their ways of thought, to each other's dreams, religions, festivals, even languages. There were times when the non-Jewish world was practically excluded from our consciousness, as on the Sabbath, and still more on the spring and autumn festivals. We were separated from the peasants by a whole inner world of memories and experiences. My father was not yet a Zionist, but the house was steeped in rich Jewish tradition; and Palestine was at the center of the ritual. The return was in the air, a vague deep-rooted Messianism, a hope which would not die.*

Weizmann (center) pictured with fellow founders of the Jewish Press in Berlin including (standing, left to right) Ephraim Mose Lilien and Leo Motzkin and sitting (left to right) Berthold Feiwel and Martin Buber (1902)

Weizmann and Warburg (center) at Haifa Port (1928)

His introduction to science was from a *cheder* teacher who surreptitiously taught him some natural science along with his Jewish studies. Weizmann left home at the age of eleven to board in Pinsk and attend high school—a rare step at the time. At this young age he wrote in a letter, "In conclusion, to Zion! Jews to Zion let us go." When Weizmann graduated from high school at eighteen, as with many of his pioneer contemporaries, he found it impossible to attend a Russian university because of the severe restrictions against Jews. By this time, his genius in the field of science was already acknowledged. He attended the Polytechnic Institute in Germany to study biochemistry, teaching Hebrew at a nearby Jewish school to supplement his income.

While at school in Berlin, he participated in several Zionist intellectual circles at a time when intense ideological divergence was evident within the movement. Weizmann was attracted to "spiritual" Zionism, which postulated that Palestine should be the spiritual center for Jewry. He became an adherent of the teachings of Ahad Ha'am, the chief proponent of this form of Zionism at the time. This same philosophy prompted Weizmann to champion the idea for a Hebrew University in Jerusalem.

Theodor Herzl's pamphlet *The Jewish State*, with his emotional and electrifying call to Jews to organize themselves as Zionists, excited Weizmann and his Russian friends. They were elated to discover that a sophisticated Western Jew like Herzl shared their vision. Because Weizmann could not leave Moscow he did not attend the First Zionist Congress in Basel, but he attended the Second Congress in 1898 as a delegate. The same year he studied at a university in Switzerland and in 1899 was awarded a doctorate with honors in chemistry. He sold his first patent in 1901, setting the foundation for his academic career.

Weizmann was a lecturer at Geneva University and simultaneously pursued his Zionist activities. He dedicated his efforts to the establishment of not only a Jewish home in Palestine, but also a Jewish university there as well. In 1904 he left Geneva for England, beginning a long research career at Manchester University that merged with his Zionist activism in England.

In 1906, he had the opportunity to meet Arthur James Balfour, the British foreign secretary. Balfour was puzzled by the Zionist leaders' rejection of the Uganda Plan—a plan for the settlement of distressed Jews from Eastern Europe to Uganda and a temporary alternative to the Holy Land as the Jewish state. When Balfour questioned Weizmann about this, the young Zionist retorted, "Would you swap London for Paris?" Balfour responded, "No, but London is the capital of my country." Weizmann's reply converted Balfour into a Zionist supporter: "Jerusalem was the capital of our country when London was still a marshland."

At the Eighth Zionist Congress in The Hague, Weizmann delivered a passionate plea. Even if all Zionists approved a common charter, he reasoned, "it would be without value unless it rested, so to say, on the very soil of Palestine, on a Jewish population rooted on that soil, on institutions established by and for that population." At the end of this Congress in 1907 he made his first journey to *Eretz Yisrael* to determine whether industry could be developed there.

Weizmann was shocked and distressed by his experience in Palestine. These were hard times for Jewish immigrants who worked to cultivate the land while draining swamps and fighting malaria. He was disappointed that the Zionist movement's impact on the landscape of the "homeland" was negligible. In the early part of twentieth century, even the powerful Jewish communities of London, Paris, and New York were extremely reluctant to speak in favor of Zionism. That first visit to Palestine reinforced Weizmann's conviction that the combination of political lobbying and settlement of the land were equally crucial to the establishment of a nation of Israel. This dual approach, the "synthesizing" of both issues, became known as "synthetic" Zionism.

With the outbreak of World War I, forty-year-old Weizmann moved to center stage as the leader of the Zionist movement. His personal link with the British government solidified his position. His friend C.P. Scott, editor of the *Manchester Guardian*, maintained close relations with cabinet ministers, including Herbert Samuel and Lloyd George. Weizmann was a striking figure of a man—a massive bald head, deep piercing eyes, set off by a tidy mustache and goatee—whose presence and eloquence left an enduring impact on others. Lord Balfour commented dryly, "Dr. Weizmann could charm a bird off a tree." Weizmann charmed Scott into supporting Zionism. Because of Scott, Weizmann was able to reach some of the most influ-

Weizmann with Zionist delegation (1918)

Weizmann (center) at Fifth Zionist Congress in Basel, Switzerland (1927)

ential British ministers of the time.

In 1916—in the midst of World War I—working as a research chemist at Manchester University, Weizmann discovered a process for synthesizing acetone, a solvent used in the manufacture of munitions. Weizmann's discovery was badly needed by the Allies for the war effort, and this gave him an ideal opportunity to champion Zionism. His contacts in Manchester society and his supervision of mass production of synthetic acetone for the Allies opened doors for him in British government circles, where he continued to serve as a passionate spokesman for Zionism.

Despite opposition from some members of the British cabinet and many British Jews, the Balfour Declaration was issued on November 2, 1917. A rare constellation of British and Jewish strategic interests, together with personal empathy for Dr. Weizmann and his cause—the fruit of eight years of negotiating—culminated in this document, approved by the British cabinet on this historic November day. The document, proclaiming the sympathy of the British government for Zionist aims in Palestine, was a pinnacle of achievement in Weizmann's life, as well as a decisive turning point in modern Jewish history. Heads of state, ministers, and high officials treated him as if he were already president of the new Jewish homeland.

During the 1920s and 1930s, he worked inside the gap between dreams and realities. Weizmann became the president of the World Zionist Organization (WZO) in 1920. When the Jewish Agency was established in 1929, he was designated as its leader. In the 1930s, Weizmann laid the foundation for the Daniel Sieff Research Institute in Rehovot. Later, as the Weizmann Institute, it became a driving force behind Israel's scientific research. In 1937 he made his home in Rehovot.

Chaim Weizmann served another term as president of WZO from 1935 to 1946. During the years leading up to World War II he invested much effort to establish the Jewish Brigade. He also tried, albeit unsuccessfully, to prevent Britain from issuing the infamous White Paper in 1939 which in effect prohibited Jewish immigration to Palestine.

When he spoke before the Twentieth Zionist Congress in Zurich in 1937

Weizmann with Arturo Toscanini in Tel Aviv (1936)

about the Report on the Palestine Commission, he made an impassioned plea:

> *I speak... as a deeply religious man, although not a strict observer of the religious ritual. I make a sharp distinction between the present realities and the Messianic hope, which is part of our very selves, a hope embedded in our traditions and sanctified by the martyrdom of thousands of years, a hope which the nation cannot forget without ceasing to be a nation.*
>
> *I told the Commission: God has promised* Eretz Yisrael *to the Jews. This is our Charter. But we are men of our time, with limited horizons, heavily laden with responsibilities toward the generations to come. I told the Royal Commission that the hopes of 6,000,000 Jews are centered on emigration.*

With the ominous approach of World War II it became more difficult to discuss Zionism with governments that were addressing gripping issues of war. There was also the daunting challenge of rescuing Jews from the Nazi grasp. By 1939 Weizmann had a vision of the future of the new state; at this time there were 450,000 Jews living in Palestine and the goal of creating an independent Jewish state became a mission of self-respect and dignity for him.

Weizmann visited New York and Washington in 1941 and 1942 in an effort to enlist American support for Zionist aims and ideals. In 1944 Churchill agreed to Weizmann's proposal for the establishment of a Jewish fighting force. He doggedly continued to press both England and America in the direction of a new Jewish state. After the war, Roosevelt died and Churchill was removed from power. Weizmann had to shift gears and redirect his energies to a new group of leaders. The United States became more fertile ground for support than the British, who were struggling to recover from the war and rebuild their own country.

When the issue of the partition of Palestine was before the United Nations General Assembly, Weizmann made a powerful appeal. He injected a humorous moment into the proceedings when he responded to the assertion from the Arab spokesman that the Jews were not descendants of the Hebrew kingdoms, but of the Khazars of southern Russia. "It is very strange," Weizmann quipped, "all my life I have been a Jew and I now learn that I am a Khazar." He went on to say, in a more serious vein, "those of us who made our homes in

Weizmann addresses Zionist Congress with Sokolow (right) and Ruppin (left)

Palestine did not do so with the object of becoming Arab citizens of the Jewish persuasion."

In the months that followed, he was able to make advances in two key areas. First, he succeeded in getting the United Nations to retain the Negev as part of the Jewish state, and, second, he took on the vast challenge of obtaining America's support and vote of confidence. On November 29, 1947, the United Nations narrowly voted in favor of the proposed partition of Palestine with America voting in favor of the proposal, thanks in large measure to Weizmann's campaign.

On May 14, 1948, Jews in Palestine proclaimed the new State of Israel. In February 1949 the first elected Knesset elevated Chaim Weizmann from the presidency of the Provisional State Council and overwhelmingly selected him as the first president of the State of Israel. After the swearing-in ceremony in Jerusalem on February 16, Weizmann's home in Rehovot became the official president's residence.

Barely two months later, President Weizmann again traveled to the United States. Met by crowds of record-breaking size, he marshaled an unprecedented twenty-three million dollars in contributions for the State of Israel and for the fledgling scientific research facility —the Weizmann Institute of Science.

By 1950 President Weizmann had to curtail his activities due to ill health, but he continued to receive foreign dignitaries and closely follow current events. Despite his poor health he was re-elected to a second term as president in November 1951. Very ill for most of his last year of life, the first president of the State of Israel, Professor Chaim Weizmann, died on November 9, 1952. He was buried according to his wishes, in the garden of his house that today is part of the campus of the Weizmann Institute of Science.

Chaim Weizmann will be inscribed in history not only as one of the great leaders in the State of Israel, but as a leader among men in the free world. His dedication and tenacity in fighting for the Jewish homeland were untiring and monumental. As he said so eloquently in his first speech addressing the Knesset:

> *It has been the lot of our generation to renew the tradition of liberty which was severed by tyrants nineteen hundred years ago. I do not know why this generation in particular has the privilege of fulfilling the desires of all the previous ones which rotted in the gloom of the Diaspora. It may be because of all the suffering and pain which have beset us the last seventy years, as one limb after another was severed from the body of our nation, until of late a third of our number was destroyed. No nation in the world has suffered as we have, but at last the vision of redemption has been fulfilled. It is our lot to bear the heavy burden of responsibility for filling the gap which has been created within the ranks of our people with the murder of the best of its sons, the bearers of its standard and the carriers of its culture.*

> *We remember all our brethren in this country and in the Zionist movement who have passed on without witnessing this day with us. We stand to attention and honor the memories of our precious and beloved children, those young heroes, who died so that the State of Israel might be established.*

Dignitaries attend Chaim Weizmann's funeral (1952)

Yitzhak Ben-Zvi
1884 - 1963

> ### *The Jews have sung the praises of their country, but they didn't actually know it {Israel} too well.*
> — Yitzhak Ben-Zvi

Yitzhak Ben-Zvi was the second president of the State of Israel, serving in that position for eleven years. He was a founder and leader of "socialist" Zionism, and initiated many programs to support labor and improve self-defense. Ben-Zvi emigrated from Russia/Ukraine, a part of Eastern Europe from which many of the pioneers fled to make their *aliyah*—their journey to the Holy Land.

The son of a Jewish scholar, Ben-Zvi studied in both a modern and traditional gymnasium (high school) in Kiev, where he later attended the university. While he was a student he visited Palestine for two months to explore the possibility of settling there. When he returned he was confronted with the terror of the pogroms in 1905 in his hometown of Poltava, Ukraine. He quickly became active in the local self-defense organization *Po'alei Zion*—the Zionist Socialist Party. Through his work with this organization he successfully motivated young people to become involved in Zionism in Germany, Austria, and Switzerland.

In 1907 he immigrated to Palestine and represented the *Po'alei Zion* as a delegate to the Eighth Zionist Congress in The Hague in Switzerland. Along with his wife Rachel, he established *HaShomer*, the Jewish organization for defense of the settlements, and the first Hebrew socialist newspaper, *Ahdut*, in 1910.

Ben-Zvi (far left) with early pioneers including Zerubavel, Ben-Gurion and Yanait

As the war erupted in Europe, Ben-Zvi and his friend David Ben-Gurion, both actively recruiting for Zionism, were imprisoned by the Ottoman authorities and deported from Palestine because of their activities. Ben-Zvi and Ben-Gurion eventually based themselves in New York, where they founded the *Ha-Halutz* [pioneer] movement in America in 1915, establishing branches in many cities. Capitalizing on the progress the British were making against the Ottoman Empire in Palestine, the two activists began this pioneer movement for American volunteers in an effort to promote immigration to Palestine. Eager to return to *Eretz Yisrael*, they enlisted in the British army, joined the King's Fusiliers and arrived in Egypt with the British in 1918. From there they traveled to Palestine as soldiers in the Jewish Legion.

Ben-Zvi was elected to the secretariat of the *Histadrut* [General Federation of Labor] when it was founded in 1920. He was fascinated by the developing culture in Jerusalem, became involved in restructuring the city, and was elected to its municipal council in 1927. He began his career as a journalist, publishing most of his articles under his own name, and others using various pseudonyms.

After the establishment of the State of Israel, Ben-Zvi was elected as a *Mapai* member to the First and Second Knesset in 1949 and 1952. When Israel's President Chaim Weizmann died in 1952, Ben-Zvi was selected as Israel's second president. He was elected to a second five-year term by the Knesset in 1957, and in 1962 to a third term. He died in office in April 1963.

It was Ben-Zvi, well-known for his warmth, openness, and simple manner who first held some of the annual events in Israel which have since become traditions—including "open

Ben-Zvi with his wife Rahkel and children (1930)

Ben-Zvi with David Ben-Gurion

house" at the president's residence during the festival of *Sukkoth* and the annual Independence Day reception.

His generosity and sense of humor are evident in this story told about the day he became president. He returned home and discovered a guard marching back and forth in front of his home. Ben-Zvi asked what he was doing there. The guard replied that he was the honor guard. "Come in and have a cup of hot tea," invited the new president. "I can't leave my post," the guard respectfully replied. Ben-Zvi thought a moment and responded, "Look I have an idea. You go into the house and have some tea and I'll borrow your gun and man your post."

The Institute for the Study of Oriental Jewish Communities in the Middle East was founded by Ben-Zvi in 1948, and later named the Ben-Zvi Institute. His scholarly works were devoted mainly to research on communities and sects and to the geography of the Land of Israel, and its ancient populations, antiquities, and traditions.

Ben-Zvi was known for his simplicity, modesty, and empathy for the different political and social groups of the Jewish people. He was a proponent of diversity, which stemmed from his exhaustive research and study of the "Tribes of Israel." He invited representatives of different ethnic groups to the president's residence each month. At the meetings, each community talked about it history, customs, and traditions. In this way, Yitzhak Ben-Zvi showcased the uniqueness of each culture, while at the same time bringing together diverse groups for greater understanding and mutual respect. Ben-Zvi, a "man of the people," was loved and esteemed by all Israelis for his many contributions as a statesman, cultural scholar, and dedicated Zionist.

Levi Eshkol
1895 - 1969

> *Put three Zionists in a room and they will form four political parties.*
> — Levi Eshkol

Levi Eshkol, a labor Zionist leader and the third prime minister of the State of Israel, was born Levi Shkolnik in the Ukraine in 1895. When he was sixteen, he attended a Hebrew high school in Vilna, Lithuania, where he joined a Zionist youth movement, *T'zeirei T'zion* [Youth of Zion]. Three years later he immigrated to Palestine, where he worked as an agricultural laborer and political activist.

Eshkol set up a wage-earning commune, *Ha'Avodah*, located in the Jewish settlement of *Petach Tikvah*. He moved from there to *Kalandia*, a commune just north of Jerusalem, and from there to *Rishon Le Zion*—one might call him a "wandering pioneer."

He volunteered for the Jewish Legion of the British army during World War I and then joined the group that founded Israel's first *kibbutz*, *Deganya Bet*. Combining manual labor with political activism, he was among the founders of the *Histadrut*, the General Federation of Labor. Working with this organization gave him valuable experience in dealing with labor issues and cooperative agricultural development.

In 1930 he participated in the creation of *Mapai*, a political party that was granted representation in the pre-statehood Knesset. During the 1930s he was sent on long dangerous missions to Nazi Germany, where he actively worked on the *Ha'avara* project to raise capital and equipment for Jewish settlements.

In those early years Eshkol confronted the problem of adequate water supply for the future of Israel. The idea for a central water supply company materialized after he observed the fail-

Eshkol at copper mines in the Negev (1952)

255

Laying a cornerstone at Be'er Tuvia (1953)

ure of local undertakings that operated in several regions. These were years of struggle in Palestine, marked with battles between the Arab and Jewish populations. Widespread immigration from Europe to Palestine increased and new settlements were established throughout the country, most of them agriculture-based. Water between Israel and the Arabs was a topic of continuing dispute. The surrounding Arab governments tried to divert water, threatened war, and shelled villages in the northern Galilee.

On his way back from the Nineteenth Zionist Congress, Eshkol's idea for a water company surfaced. To enable the rapid development of the settlements, regular and safe water supply was critical. Water supply projects were urgently needed in all parts of the country. The creation of a company for water planning, construction, and operation clearly needed to be a priority.

Eshkol founded the Mekorot Water Company in January 1937, and became the "master" of water policy and development in Israel. He was responsible for the formulation of the targets of water supply projects, the countrywide strategy, and the plan for administration and management. The proposal for a nation-wide company—Mekorot—was not well received by the British Mandatory administration, but the urgent need for water necessitated the establishment of the company, overriding the objections of the British.

In his role as the company's first director, Eshkol was instrumental in convincing the German government to allow Jews immigrating to Palestine to bring some of their assets with them—mostly in the form of German-made equipment. Serving as Mekorot's director from 1937 until 1951, he introduced a system of countrywide water management that made intensive irrigated farming possible. His endeavor culminated in the ambitious and famous National Water Carrier project. This system was an ingenious single network linking most of

the regional water projects throughout the country. This project was his most important lifetime accomplishment, an achievement that assured him immortality in the developing history of Israel.

Eshkol was asked to serve again with the Haganah from 1940 to 1948 (his previous service spanned 1921-23). Primarily he was in charge of purchases, equipment, and mobilization. In 1948, he became Israel's first director general of the Ministry of Defense, responsible for acquiring the equipment that kept the Israeli army in the field.

He was appointed director of the Settlement Department of the Jewish Agency in 1948. Eshkol remained in this post until 1963, initiating the establishment of approximately 400 new settlements in the first four years of Israel's existence. He served as minister of agriculture and development in 1951, and from 1952 to 1963 as the minister of finance. Eshkol's tenure was characterized by great economic growth, despite the need to finance the absorption of waves of immigration, development projects, Israel Defense Forces (IDF) armaments, and the expense of the Sinai operation.

When David Ben-Gurion resigned in 1963 as prime minister, Levi Eshkol was next in line as the likely designate. Eshkol became prime minister and simultaneously served as minister of defense. Included among his many significant accomplishments during this time were cementing Israel's relationship with the United States, supplying the IDF with a large quantity of American weaponry, and establishing full diplomatic relations with West Germany.

In 1964, Eshkol made the first state visit of an Israeli prime minister to Washington, laying the foundation for the close rapport that has existed between the two countries since then. A master of internal politics, Eshkol succeeded in forming the "Alignment," a merger of rival Labor factions, as well as leading his party to victory in the 1965 elections.

In a generous and conciliatory gesture, in 1964 Eshkol ordered that the remains of Labor's

Eshkol, then head of Settlement Department, speaks at Kibbutz Gesher Haziv (1949)

fiercest political rival—Ze'ev Jabotinsky, founder and ideological leader of revisionist Zionism—be brought to Israel and reinterred in a state funeral on Mount Herzl in Jerusalem. Eshkol honored Jabotinsky's will, written in 1935 requesting that his remains be transferred to Israel "only on the instruction of a future Jewish government."

In 1966 Eshkol visited six African nations on a diplomacy tour. His most significant diplomatic achievement was the establishment of relations with West Germany, a process that had been initiated by Ben-Gurion. This important international triumph resulted in his securing military assistance from Germany, underscoring Germany's moral commitment to supporting Israel. As a consequence of his efforts to mend relations with the Soviet Union consent was granted to some Soviet Jews to immigrate to Israel, and cultural ties were established between the two countries.

The highlight of his premiership was the stunning military victory of the Six Day War in June 1967. On the eve of the war, pressured by public demands, he formed a government of "National Unity" and was able to hold this government together for some time after the war. Eshkol found sources of military supplies for the Israeli armed forces, particularly in the United States after France began its military boycott of Israel just prior to the 1967 War. He relinquished the defense portfolio to Moshe Dayan out of great respect for his military skills. In 1968 Eshkol received a crucial commitment from the United States to supply Israel with sophisticated fighter planes.

The war itself was a vindication of his efforts at the Ministry of Defense to provide the IDF with the best equipment available. Israel defeated Egypt, Jordan, and Syria and occupied the Gaza Strip, the Sinai Peninsula, Judea, Samaria and the Golan Heights. Eshkol firmly believed that Israel should not return Arab territories occupied in 1967 without a solution to the entire Arab-Israel conflict.

Meeting at newly uncovered excavations

Eshkol with Moshe Dayan (1967)

Golda Meir in her book, *My Life*, wrote about Eshkol:

> *Eshkol was not, to use the fashionable word, 'charismatic'. He had no 'glam-our', but he was an unusually creative person, a man who got things done when they really needed doing, however hard the job was, and a man to whom peo-ple and their feelings meant a great deal. From the start, I liked and trusted him, though who would have dreamed when we worked together in Tel Aviv then that he would eventually be a prime minister or that I would follow him in that office.*

Eshkol's service for the thirty-five years preceding the birth of the Jewish state were bench-marks for his activity in the subsequent twenty-one years, until his death in 1969. The list of his achievements inspires awe. His water projects were monumental in scope. The draining of the Hullah swamps, the country's water system, 400 *moshavim* [settlement farms], industrial and agricultural developments—each of these projects reinforce his claim: "Water for us is blood." Knowing the right linkage between man, land, and water, Eshkol understood the tie between man's blood and the blood of the land.

Levi Eshkol died in office in February 1969 of a heart attack. He will be remembered as one of Israel's most effective and hard-working statesman and an extraordinary prime minis-ter. Eshkol was the quintessential "public servant," as Prime Minister Golda Meir explained:

> *Eshkol was typical of the practical idealists of the era: his interests were land, water and defense, though not necessarily in that order, and he was happiest dealing with such down-to-earth and crucial problems. Politics in the abstract didn't particularly attract him, and he hated bureaucratic procedures; but give him a specific challenge and he met it with an extraordinary combination of doggedness, ingenuity, and shrewdness.*

Golda Meir
1898 - 1978

> ## *We only want that which is given naturally to all peoples of the world, to be masters of our fate.*
>
> — Golda Meir

Golda Meir in the Galilee

Golde Mabovitch Meyerson, better known as Golda Meir or simply Golda, was one of the founders of the State of Israel and the most prominent woman politician of her era. Her name ranks highly in the Zionist inner sanctum with Theodor Herzl, Chaim Weizmann, and David Ben-Gurion. Distinct from the others, Golda was shaped during her formative years as an American. Golda Meir was the "Iron Lady" of Israeli politics years before the nickname was coined for Margaret Thatcher. She once was described by David Ben-Gurion as "the only man in my cabinet."

Born in 1898 near Kiev, Ukraine, Golda was named for her maternal great-grandmother, who always took salt instead of sugar in her tea to mark the bitterness of the Diaspora. Golda claimed that her memories of Ukraine were of grinding poverty, hunger, and pogroms. She describes her early childhood:

When I was a small child, we lived in Kiev, Ukraine and were poor. Often we didn't have enough food, warm clothes or even heating at home. I remember being afraid. I heard about the pogroms that had been carried out, and knew that they were planning terrible things for the Jews. My father tried to bar the entrance to our house with wooden beams. I was scared and angry; I wanted my father to do more to protect us. I felt that people who wanted to survive had to do something for themselves.

In 1903, her father, a carpenter, immigrated to America promising to return for his family when he had enough money. Her mother grew tired of waiting and, three years later took Golda and her two sisters to join him in Milwaukee. They settled into a tiny apartment in the city's poor Jewish section and Golda's mother opened a convenience store in which all the girls were expected to work.

Despite having learned English just six years earlier, Golda graduated as class valedictorian from Milwaukee's Fourth Street Elementary School. She wanted to be a teacher but her father opposed her going to high school. Showing signs of the independence that would characterize her adult life, Golda defied him and enrolled in North Division High School, work-

Golda plays with her grandchildren

ing after school to pay her expenses. When her father insisted that she quit school and find a husband, Golda ran away to Denver and moved in with her married sister. It was in Denver that Golda became impressed with Zionism. There she also met and fell in love with Morris Meyerson, a sign painter who loved poetry, music, and history, though he never shared her Zionist passion.

During her adolescence, Golda met two young Jews whom the Turks had deported from Palestine, David Ben-Gurion and Yitzhak Ben-Zvi. They had come to America to find young volunteers who would fight along with the British to free Palestine from Turkish rule. They spoke about the *kibbutz* movement and glowingly described pioneer life in *Eretz Yisrael*. Ben-Zvi introduced his friend Rachel Yanait to Golda. Golda saw this woman as a perfect example of someone who was both a pioneer and a fighter, someone on equal terms with men. As if hit by a bolt of lightening Golda decided to dedicate her life to Zionism. To support her mission—a nation for the Jewish people—she spoke at gatherings, arranged presentations, and raised money. Golda Meir dreamed of helping to create a Jewish homeland, a place, she said, "where Jews could be masters, not victims, of their fate."

She reconciled with her parents and returned to Milwaukee where she graduated from high school and enrolled in a teacher's college. She became active in the labor Zionist group, *Po'alei Zion* [Workers of Zion], and dropped out of school to work for the Zionist cause. She wrote to her close friend, Morris Myerson: "I know that you are not as interested as I am in living in *Eretz Yisrael*, but I ask that you come with me anyway." Morris agreed and they married after Golda graduated from Milwaukee Teachers College in 1917.

The couple moved to Tel Aviv in July 1921. They settled in a *kibbutz* called *Merhavya*. "Life in Merhavya was hard," she remembers. "There was very little to eat, and what there was had an awful taste: sour porridge, rancid oil, and salty fish. The pioneers lived in huts, and the washrooms and showers were outside, far from the huts. It was especially hard for people to get to the washrooms when they were sick with malaria and had a high fever." Despite everything, Golda was happy. She quickly adjusted to the harsh conditions of *kibbutz* life. Soon, however, she became involved in political and social activities that took her away from the *kibbutz*. Morris did not adapt to life there, so he and Golda left and moved to Jerusalem, where they had two children and struggled to make enough money to survive.

Golda found her calling when she met labor leader David Remez in 1928. That meeting launched her political career. Remez offered her a job as executive secretary to the Women's Labor Council, and she and her two children moved to Tel Aviv. Her husband stayed behind and the two eventually divorced.

As the executive secretary of *Mo'ezet Ha-Po'alot* [women's labor union] she was sent as an emissary to the Pioneer Women's Organization in the United States from 1932 to 1934. On her return to Palestine in 1934, she joined the executive committee of the *Histadrut*. A charismatic speaker, she rapidly became a spokesperson for the *Histadrut*, then head of its political department.

During World War II she held several important positions in the World Zionist Organization and the Jewish Agency, including serving as the Agency's director for several years leading up to the declaration of the State of Israel. These important positions in the developing nation helped to train her for her eventual role as a leading statesperson of Israel.

Golda congratulating Israeli pilot Boaz Meir after his release from the Syrians (1973)

Golda at her desk in the U.S.

With the country under threat of an attack from the Arabs in 1948, David Ben-Gurion sent Golda to the United States on an urgent fundraising campaign. The Jewish leadership in Palestine was convinced that the new nation's survival was at stake, and that only the American Jewish community had the abundant financial resources needed to help the struggling new country. She left for America on the day of her meeting with Ben-Gurion wearing the same dress and without luggage.

Meir's first appearance was in Chicago on January 21, 1948 at the General Assembly of the Council of Jewish Federations and Welfare Funds. Tired, without a chance to rehearse her speech, speaking to a group whose first priority then was not Jewish nationalism, she approached the microphone. She began telling the crowd that Jewish pioneers intended to fight to the end, with stones if necessary. Golda informed them that Israel needed between twenty-five and thirty million dollars in the next few weeks. She repeated the Israelis' decision to fight. Their dollars, she told them, would determine who would win in the battle for survival. The audience wept openly. Golda stayed in the United States for six weeks, speaking all over the country. People came and they listened. They contributed money and when they did not have the money, they took out loans. Such was the charisma of this powerful woman.

Prime Minister David Ben-Gurion sent Golda to America to raise twenty-five million dollars. She met with thousands of Jews, spoke with quick wit, charm and passion, and she collected fifty million dollars—double the amount they had set as a goal. David Ben-Gurion summed it up best: "Someday, when history will be written, it will be said that there was a Jewish woman who raised the money which made the State possible." Golda returned frequently to raise money from American Jews. As an American herself, Meir saw it as a duty of the American Jewish community to help build Israel.

In 1948, David Ben-Gurion appointed Golda Meir as a member of the Provisional Government. When the United Nations voted in favor of the partition of Palestine, Golda's responsibility was to negotiate for peace with the king of Transjordan. A few days before the declaration of Israel's independence, Ben-Gurion sent her disguised as an Arab, well aware of the danger of this hazardous mission, to persuade King Abdullah of Jordan not to attack Israel. But the king would not listen, already having decided that his army would invade the Jewish state following the British departure.

Meir served in several key posts in the new government, including ambassador to the

USSR. Traveling as the new ambassador to the Soviet Union, her courageous attendance at Rosh Hashanah services in Moscow's only synagogue in September 1948 sparked a spontaneous pro-Israeli demonstration attracting 40,000 Russian Jews.

In 1949, she became the first woman elected to the Knesset [Israeli parliament], and was appointed by Prime Minister Ben-Gurion as minister of labor. She was responsible for finding housing and jobs for the 700,000 new immigrants that arrived in Israel during the first three years of statehood.

Protecting the State of Israel was always paramount to Golda, who lived through times when survival of the Jewish state was constantly in jeopardy. "If we have to have a choice between being dead and pitied, and being alive with a bad image, we'd rather be alive and have the bad image," she said. "To be or not to be is not a question of compromise. Either you be or you don't be."

In 1956, Ben-Gurion appointed Golda Meir as Israeli foreign minister, the second-highest position in the government. In this capacity Meir built ties with the new emerging countries in Asia and Africa. Ben-Gurion also insisted that she adopt the Hebraicized version of Myerson, Meir, as her surname, which means "to illuminate." At the time she was the only woman foreign minister in the world.

Diagnosed with lymphoma in the early 1960s, Golda Meir did not disclose her condition, concerned that she would be seen as unfit for her job. Finally, in 1965, deciding that she was too old and too tired to hold political office any longer, she retired from her cabinet post. She worked for a few years as the secretary general of her political party, but resigned from that post due to failing health. Then in 1969, Prime Minister Levi Eshkol died suddenly of a heart

Golda meeting volunteers from abroad at kibbutz Ein Gedi (1971)

Golda discusses Israel's future with U.S. officials

attack. To avoid a power struggle between Moshe Dayan and Yigal Allon that would have divided the country, the Labor Party chose Golda as the candidate whom all would accept. After serving as acting prime minister for a short time, she was again chosen in the national election as Israel's prime minister—she was seventy-one years old.

Golda Meir began her premiership after Israel's stunning victory in the Six Day War of 1967. Yet, with the ink barely dry on the cease-fire agreement, Abdul Nassar began the Egyptian War of Attrition, continuously firing on Israeli troops and civilians near the negotiated cease-fire lines. Not one country pressured Nassar to stop the terrorism and violence against the Israeli state. On the contrary, the Soviet Union rushed to arm the Egyptians with a flood of military equipment, including tanks, aircraft, and missiles, along with Soviet instructors to retrain the battered Egyptian army. European countries, including France and Great Britain, announced that Israel "should refrain from retaliation."

Golda attempted to contact the Arab leaders to discuss peace negotiations, but Nassar pontificated: "There is no voice transcending the sounds of war . . . and no call holier than the call to war." To counter the growing Egyptian military threat, Meir

Golda Meir with Yosef Berg (1954)

Golda delivers address to Executive Council

turned to the United States for weapons. She was received warmly by President Nixon who agreed to her requests. Despite the difficult times, Golda kept her sense of humor. At her meeting with President Nixon he told her that he would trade any three American generals for General Moshe Dayan. "Okay," she quickly responded, "I'll take General Motors, General Electric, and General Dynamics."

Despite her lifetime of dedication, as with every prominent public figure, she also endured failures. She was widely criticized for the country's lack of preparedness for the surprise Arab attack inciting the Yom Kippur War. Although the Egyptian and Syrian forces ultimately were defeated, 2,500 Israeli soldiers died and another 3,000 were wounded. Bowing to public pressure, she left office in 1974. Golda Meir was deeply pained by the Yom Kippur War: "When peace comes, we will perhaps in time be able to forgive the Arabs for killing our sons. But it will be harder for us to forgive them for having forced us to kill their sons."

What was Golda Meir's secret for success? She possessed a rare mixture of courage and authenticity. While modern political leaders market themselves for mass media, Golda Meir achieved fame through hard work and was admired universally for her simplicity and straight talk. She stood firm for peace and expressed it poignantly: "There is nothing Israel wants so much as peace. There is nothing Israel needs so much as peace. With all the bleakness of the desert, the desert of hate around us is even more bleak." Golda was tough and stubborn and had nerves of steel, yet she retained the image of a warm and loving "global Jewish mother."

When Golda Meir died at age eighty in 1978, all of world Jewry mourned. In the eyes of the world she personified the Israeli spirit. Golda Meir is now considered one of the eminent female heads of state in modern history. Walter Cronkite, eulogizing her greatness, remarked, "She lived a life under pressure that we, in this country, would find impossible to understand. She is the strongest woman to head a government in our time and for a very long time past."

Menachem Begin
1913 - 1992

> *I believe with all my heart that Israel belongs to the whole Jewish people and not only to those Jewish people who live in it.*
> — Menachem Begin

Writer Sidney Zion wrote about Menachem Begin in 1983, "he was run out of Poland by the Nazis, imprisoned by the Soviets, hunted by the British and nearly murdered by the Jews. To have survived would have been impressive enough. To have flourished—Begin led the first (Jewish nationalist) revolution in nearly 2,000 years (and) signed the first peace treaty in Israeli history—ranks as something of a miracle."

Born in Brest-Litovsk, Poland in 1913, Menachem Begin lived his life in relentless pursuit of a Jewish nation. The son of a Jewish timber merchant in czarist Russia who became Israel's sixth prime minister, Begin was a man driven to "feats of courage and the depths of despair." His vision was forged from his personal experience of the horrors of the Holocaust and his unlimited love for the Jewish people. Combining this unconditional love with determination and strength, he created a personal formula that propelled a peace agreement between Israel and Egypt.

From the age of sixteen Begin was an avid Zionist. He welcomed the ideas of the revisionist Ze'ev Jabotinsky and joined the Betar Zionist youth movement in Poland. He eventually developed an even more rigorous form of Zionism than Jabotinsky. Awarded his law degree in 1935 from Warsaw University, he became the head of Betar Poland in 1938, an organization with 100,000 members trained to defend Polish Jewry, to assist "illegal" immigrants traveling to *Eretz Yisrael*, and to give agricultural instruction.

Forged identity card used by Begin after his release from the Polish army (1942)

Fleeing the devastation of World War II, Begin escaped from Poland and fled to Russia. The KGB (Russian secret police) arrested him in 1941, charging him with espionage. In a chilling demonstration of Begin's humor and courage, a story is told that he was playing chess with his wife when the KGB, shouting and belligerent, broke into their home and dragged him out. As the Russian police were pulling him roughly through the front door, he shouted to his wife, "I concede the match!"

The Russians sentenced him to eight years in prison, but he was released after serving one year as part of an agreement with the Polish government. He later learned that his parents and brother had perished in the carnage of the Holocaust. His father was among the five thousand Brest Jews rounded up by the Nazis at the end of June 1941, ostensibly for forced labor. In fact, they were taken outside the city limits and shot or drowned in a river. His mother died in Brest's Jewish hospital, while his brother Herzl perished without a trace in the Holocaust.

After he was freed in 1941, Begin found his sister, the only other survivor of their family. He continued the work he had started with Betar and again became active in helping "illegal" Jewish immigrants to reach Palestine.

When Germany invaded the Soviet Union, Begin joined the Polish army. He reached Palestine as a soldier in 1943 and, after demobilization from the army, joined the underground resistance organization, *Irgun Zvai Leumi* (IZL). Eventually Begin became commander of the IZL and led its members in clandestine defense missions.

Begin initiated a rebellion of Jewish resistance forces against the British in January 1944. His organization first called in a warning, and then was responsible for the bombing of the British offices at the King David Hotel. The Haganah (later the Israel Defense Forces) ceased cooperation with the Irgun (IZL) after this incident. When the State of Israel was declared in 1948 the Irgun was disbanded.

With the creation of the new nation, Begin formed a new political party *Herut*. In 1949, he was elected to the First Knesset and remained a member for thirty-five years, until 1984. Through this experience he developed an important understanding of parliamentary and legal matters. In 1965, as leader of the opposition party, *Herut*, he agreed to merge with the Liberals to form *Gahal*, which later became the foundation of the *Likud* Party.

The crisis atmosphere in 1967 necessitated the establishment of a National Unity government, which finally brought Begin and other *Gahal* leaders to the cabinet table. The National Unity government continued until

Menachem Begin (right) joins Eshkol's Unity government along with Yosef Sapir and Moshe Dayan (1967)

Begin reaches to shake hands with Sadat as Carter looks on at Camp David

1970. After years of being in "second-place," Menachem Begin's *Likud* Party won the 1977 election in a stunning upset, and Begin assumed the mantle of prime minister, a position he held for six years.

Begin was responsible for many crucial advances in Israel's progress as a developing country. Perhaps his most illustrious and memorable accomplishment was initiating the peace process with Egypt. In an unprecedented event between Israel and an Arab nation, Egypt's President Anwar Sadat accepted Begin's invitation for a meeting in Israel. Sadat, in his address to the Israeli Knesset in Jerusalem, was candid in his stand for peace:

> *The declaration of my readiness to proceed to Israel came as a great surprise that stirred many feelings and confounded many minds. Some of them even doubted its intent.*
>
> *Despite all that, the decision was inspired by all the clarity and purity of belief and with all the true passions of my people's will and intentions, and I have chosen this road, considered by many to be the most difficult road.*
>
> *I have chosen to come to you with an open heart and an open mind. I have chosen to give this great impetus to all international efforts exerted for peace. I have chosen to present to you, in your own home, the realities, devoid of any scheme or whim. Not to maneuver, or win a round, but for us to win together, the most dangerous of rounds embattled in modern history, the battle of permanent peace based on justice.*

It is not my battle alone. Nor is it the battle of the leadership in Israel alone. It is the battle of all and every citizen in all our territories, whose right it is to live in peace. It is the commitment of conscience and responsibility in the hearts of millions.

After two years of negotiations, this unparalleled call for peace by both leaders resulted in Begin and Sadat signing the Camp David Peace Accords on September 17, 1978, for which they were both awarded the Nobel Peace Prize that year. Begin, a tough negotiator, at first would not sign the United States' version because it did not recognize Israel's annexation of East Jerusalem. Begin held his ground and the Jerusalem issue was removed from the letter of agreement.

Begin in Polish uniform in Tel Aviv (1942)

Both Begin and Sadat took great risks to accomplish this visit and agreement. Sadat acted against the wishes and advice of the other Arab nations that vigorously protested his gesture of negotiation. The cautious peace entered into by Begin and Sadat signaled the beginning of Egyptian interest in seeking a diplomatic solution over another military encounter. This historic meeting between the two heads of state strategically and significantly altered the geopolitical landscape in the Middle East.

In 1978, in his acceptance speech at the Nobel Peace Prize awards ceremony, Begin's voice was raw with emotion as he gave his impassioned address for peace:

Let it, however, be declared and known, stressed, and noted that fighters for freedom hate war. My friends and I learned this precept from Ze'ev Jabotinsky. Our brothers in spirit, wherever they dwell, learned it from their masters and teachers. This is our common maxim and belief—that if through your efforts and sacrifices you win liberty and with it the prospect of peace, then work for peace because there is no mission in life more sacred.

And so reborn Israel always strove for peace, yearned for it, made endless endeavors to achieve it. My colleagues and I have gone in the footsteps of our predecessors since the very first day we were called by our people to care for their future. We went any place, we looked for any avenue, we made any effort to bring about negotiations between Israel and its neighbors, negotiations without which peace remains an abstract desire.

We have labored long and hard to turn it into a reality—because of the blessings it holds for ourselves, our neighbors, the world.

Begin deeply valued his friendship with Anwar Sadat, Egypt's president. When Muslim fundamentalists brutally assassinated the Egyptian leader in October 1981, Begin went to Cairo and walked with the funeral procession.

In 1981 the Israeli Air Force, in a surprise attack, destroyed the nuclear reactor near Baghdad in Iraq just before it became operational. Begin succinctly stated his feelings about his decision: "Better a condemnation and no reactor, than a reactor and no condemnation." The wisdom of this decision and its successful execution, which was condemned by the international community at the time, became fully apparent a decade later—in the 1991 Gulf War.

Begin's passionate pursuit of freedom and peace for the Jewish people was foremost throughout his life. When the Reagan administration threatened to withhold financial aid to Israel after the annexation of the Golan Heights, Begin wrote in a letter to the United States president:

Begin addresses Likud followers at party headquarters

Begin greets supporters at Western Wall

A week ago the Knesset adopted the Golan law, and again you declare that you are 'punishing' Israel. What kind of talk is that, 'punishing' Israel? Are we a vassal state? A banana republic? Are we fourteen-year-old boys, that if we don't behave we have our knuckles smacked? I will tell you of whom this government is composed. It is composed of men who fought, risked their lives and suffered. You cannot and will not frighten us with punishment and threats…. The people of Israel have lived for 3,700 years without a memorandum of understanding with America and will continue to live without it for another 3,700 years.

His greatest challenges involved the war in Lebanon and the economy. Deeply troubled after the war with Lebanon, Begin suffered a fur-

Sadat drives Begin for tour of Ismalia, Egypt (1977)

ther crushing blow when his cherished wife, Aliza, died in November 1982. He stepped down as prime minister, saying he could no longer remain in office. He spent the final decade of his life living with his daughter; he was nearly a total recluse, visited only by a few friends. He died in March 1992 at the age of seventy-nine and was buried on the Mount of Olives in Jerusalem.

Among his many accomplishments and contributions to Israel, Begin was also the leader most responsible for closing the gap between Ashkenazim and

New chief of staff Rafael Eitan receives new insignia from Begin and Minister of Defense Ezer Weizman (1978)

Sephardim in Israel, by giving political opportunity to the Sephardim. Begin's decision to encourage Ethiopian Jews to immigrate to Israel culminated in Operation Moses, which brought thousands en masse to Israel in the mid-1980s. His work as a bridge-builder between the communities dates from his earliest days in Israel, when he declared, as he frequently did, "Yehudim Anakhnu!" [We are Jews!].

Begin greeted by students from a Jewish day school upon arrival at Andrews airport (1977)

Yitzhak Rabin
1922 - 1995

He has been described as a soldier who became a peacemaker, the general that became a statesman. He led his country into uncharted territory and offered peace to the Palestinians with a plea to end the wars—attempting to stop the bloodshed and terrorism that had beleaguered his country since its inception.

Yitzhak Rabin was born in Jerusalem in 1922 to parents who were very active in political and social issues of the day. His father, Nehemiah, immigrated to Israel from the United States and joined the Jewish Legion in World War I. His mother, Rosa, was one of the first members of the Haganah. Rabin recalls: "Ours was a workers' home ... ours was not a religious home, but it was imbued with the pride of being Jewish ... our home was permeated with a sense of mission ... work was considered a value in itself."

Chief of Staff Yitzhak Rabin addresses audience in Jerusalem (1967)

Rabin attended the School for Workers' Children in Tel Aviv, a school established by the *Histadrut* [General Federation of Labor] in 1924. The mission of the school was to instill the city's young people with a love of the country and offer the new generation an opportunity to develop the land. Students were taught to honor responsibility, sharing and solidarity, and to be involved actively in social matters.

A student of farming and land development at the Kadoorie Agricultural College, Rabin graduated with distinction. As with many of the patriotic young people at the time, he surrendered his childhood ambition to be an agronomist and instead joined the Palmach when it was founded in 1940. The Palmach was the elite strike force of the Haganah; because of this training, Rabin evolved into a brilliant military tactician.

In 1944, as second in command of a Palmach battalion, he took part in underground actions against the British Mandatory authority and on June 29, 1946, he was arrested and imprisoned for six months in a camp in Gaza. Shortly after his release, the British turned the problem of Palestine over to the United Nations where, in 1947, they narrowly voted in favor of partitioning the country into Jewish and Arab states.

As deputy commander of the Palmach during the War of Independence in 1948 Rabin commanded the Harel Brigade, a unit renowned for its valor in the battle for Jerusalem. He also was a member of the Israel truce delegation to the Rhodes armistice talks. Rabin was chief of the northern command from 1956 to 1959, appointed as deputy chief of staff of the Israel Defense Forces (IDF) in 1961, and became its seventh chief of staff on January 1, 1964.

Rabin signs treaty with King Hussein of Jordan as President Clinton looks on (1994)

Although he was experienced and effective in combat from his early days with the Palmach through the time he became ambassador, his true genius was as a planner. This clearly was illustrated in his stunning victory over the Arabs in the Six Day War in June 1967. In this conflict, the IDF fought on three fronts and beat the armies of Egypt, Syria, and Jordan, previously considered a formidable threat.

The mood of the Israeli public was suddenly transformed from pre-war gloom into joy and disbelief emanating from total and conclusive victory. The triumphant campaign originated from Rabin's meticulous plans, especially his emphasis on manpower and training. This success, considered one of the greatest achievements in world military history, was accomplished while Rabin was serving as IDF chief of staff. Rabin wrote in his memoirs:

> *Our warriors prevailed not by their weapons but by their sense of mission, by the consciousness of the rightness of their cause, by a deep love for their country and an understanding of the difficult task laid upon them: to ensure the existence of our people in their homeland, to protect, even at the price of their lives, the right of the Jewish people to live in their own state, free, independent, and in peace.*

Rabin retired from the army in 1968 to become Israel's ambassador to the United States, a position in which he served with distinction for five years. Elected to the Israeli parliament, the Knesset, at the end of 1973, he then was appointed as a cabinet minister. In 1974 following the retirement of Prime Minister Golda Meir, he became prime minister of Israel and served until he resigned in 1977.

During his term of office, in June 1976, the Rabin government ordered the Entebbe

Operation. This mission dramatically demonstrated to the world Israel's refusal to capitulate to terrorism, when the IDF's long arm reached deep into Uganda to rescue hostages hijacked by the Palestine Liberation Organization (PLO).

Foreign Minister Shimon Peres replaced Rabin as leader of the Labor Party, which lost the following election to the right wing *Likud* Party. Rabin remained active in the Labor Party and became defense minister in the National Unity government from 1984 through 1990.

Rabin (second from right) participates in the Rhodes talks with Harkabi, Yadin and Simon (1949)

Elected prime minister for a second time, Rabin led the Labor Party to victory in the 1992 elections. He believed he understood the sacrifices and compromises needed to achieve peace in the Middle East; on September 13, 1993, a reluctant Rabin shook hands with PLO Chairman Yasser Arafat, sealing their joint Declaration of Principles (DOP).

The DOP provided for Palestinian autonomy in the Gaza Strip and Jericho region as a first step toward a comprehensive settlement. In May 1994 Rabin signed an agreement in Cairo granting self-rule to Palestinians in Gaza and Jericho as stipulated in the DOP, and in the same month, Israeli troops fully withdrew from these areas.

In that same year, Rabin signed an historic peace treaty with Jordan's King Hussein, ending the forty-six year state of war. For his extraordinary efforts to bring peace to the Middle East, Rabin was awarded the Nobel Peace Prize in 1994 (together with Arafat and Peres). In 1995, Rabin signed an agreement with Arafat at the White House in Washington, D.C., expanding Palestinian autonomy in Judea and Samaria.

That year in a cruel and shocking act of violence, Rabin was assassinated. Ironically, he had been participating in a peace rally demonstrating the Israeli citizens' support of the peace process. Israelis and people all over the world were stunned at the senseless murder of a man whose entire life had been dedicated to seeking peace and defending the rights of his people to live in freedom. Rabin was buried on Mount Herzl in Jerusalem.

As memoirs of intimates reveal the "*mensch*" behind the man, Yitzhak Rabin grows in public esteem. A handsome young Palmach officer, he epitomized the *sabra*. A shy man, he projected a remote presence while earning credibility as an honest, crusty pragmatist. His legacy is one of a brilliant political strategist. Israelis trusted his devotion to the country and his deep and righteous sense of integrity. Rabin was beautifully succinct in his memoirs: "There is no doubt whatsoever in my mind that the risks of peace are preferable by far to the grim certainties that await every nation in war."

Rabin belonged to the generation of 1948—the young men whose military prowess gave Israel a fighting start. Perhaps more than any other of his generation he will be remembered by history as "the general who waged both war and peace."

GLOSSARY*

Agudat Yisrael - religious political movement

Agunot - novel by Shai Agnon

Ahavah - love

Ahdut - first Hebrew socialist (Labor Party) newspaper founded by Ben-Zvi

Al HaMishmar - radical wing of the General Zionists in Poland, also their newspaper

Aliyah - immigration to Israel

Aliyah Bet - "illegal immigration"- the organized entry of Jewish refugees into Palestine during British Mandate restricting Jewish immigration

Altalena – pen name of Ze'ev Jabotinsky

Altneuland [*Old New Land*]; a book by Theodor Herzl

Aluf - general; brigadier general

Andak - (Arabic) "be careful"

Annalen der Physik (Ger) - publication of three scientific papers of Albert Einstein

Atzma'ut – independence

Bar mitzvah - ceremony for a young man at age thirteen confirming his manhood

Betar - youth group, abbreviation of Brit Trumpeldor

BILU – "*Beit Ya'akov Lekhu Ve-Nelekh*"- [House of Jacob, letus go up]; an acronym for the first group of Russian Jewish immigrants with political purpose of a Jewish homeland in Palestine

Bilu'im - group of Russian Jewish pioneers that were part of BILU

B'nai Zion - Jewish organization

B'noth Zion [Daughters of Zion]; counterpart to B'nai Zion

B'riha - flight

Brit-Milah - a Jewish infant boy is consecrated to God by circumcision when he is eight days old

Brit Shalom [Covenant of Peace]; a group supporting better understanding between Jews and Arabs in Palestine

Cause celebre - an important cause, mission

Chalutz/Chalutzim - pioneer/pioneers (also halutz)

Cheder [room] schoolroom, where Jewish students study Torah and Talmud (also heder)

Davar [*Word*] - Israeli newspaper

Der Jude [*The Jew*]; monthly periodical founded by Martin Buber

Der Judenstaat [*The Jewish State*]; pamphlet written by Theodor Herzl; "bible" of Zionism

Diaspora [dispersion]; dispersion or scattering of Jewish people throughout the world

Die Juden Der Gegenwart - book analyzing sociology of the Jewish people by Arthur Ruppin

Die Welt [*The World*]; Zionist "house" journal

Do'ar HaYom [*Today's Mail*]; Hebrew daily newspaper

"Ein davar—tov lamut be-ad artsenu" - ["Never mind— it is good to die for our land."] quotation from Joseph Trumpeldor

Emunah – belief

Eretz Yisrael - land making up the ancient Jewish Kingdoms of Israel and Judah; commonly refers to the land region that Jews believe God specially designated for them to live in; Hebrew: "Land of Israel"

Ezra - group dedicated to Hebrew as the spoken language

Fellaheen - Arab peasants

First Aliyah - (BILU); "going up"- period of Jewish immigration from the Diaspora to *Eretz Yisrael* from 1881-1904

Gahal - political party in Israel

Golah – exile, Diaspora

Gymnasium - European high school

Ha'Am [*The Nation*] newspaper

Ha'Avodah - Wage earning commune founded by Levi Eshkol

Ha'avara - Transfer Agreement; enabled Jews to remove assets from Nazi Germany

Hadassah - women's organization dedicated to helping Israel founded by Henrietta Szold

Ha'Ezrah [*The Citizen*]

Haganah - defense organization, became Israel Defense Forces (IDF)

Ha-Halutz - the pioneer (movement)

Halacha - collective body of Jewish law

Halutz - pioneer (also chalutz)

Ha'Matmid - long poem by Chaim Nachman Bialik

Ha'or [*The Light*]; first Hebrew daily newspaper in Palestine founded by Ben-Yehuda

Hapoel - Zionist movement

Ha-Shiloah - Hebrew periodical founded by Ahad Ha'am

HaShomer - Jewish organization established in 1909 for defense of the settlements

Hasidic - referring to Hasidic sect in Judaism

Hasidic Rebbe - leader/teacher of Hasidic sect

Hasidim - members (plural) of the Hasidic sect

Hasidism - Orthodox religious philosophy in Judaism (alternate spelling: Chassidism)

Hatikvah [*The Hope*]; Israel's national anthem

Hatzohar - Union of Zionist Revisionists

Hatzvi [*The Deer*]; newspaper published by Eliezer Ben-Yehuda

Ha-Yedid [The Friend]; nickname for Charles Orde Wingate

Ha-Zaken [the Old Man]; nickname for Yitzhak Sadeh

Ha-Zefirah [*The Counting*]; newspaper whose editor was Nahum Sokolow

Hebras Zion - Zionist organization

Heder [room] schoolroom; where Jewish students study Torah and Talmud (also cheder)

Heint - Yiddish newspaper in Poland

Herut - political party formed by Menachem Begin

Hibbat Zion [Lovers of Zion]; Zionist organization

Histadrut - The General Federation of Labor; early political party

Hovevei Zion [Lovers of Zion]; early Zionist organization founded to establish settlements in *Eretz Yisrael*

Irgun Zva'i Leumi (IZL) - Irgun; Jewish resistance organization for defense (also Irgun Tsva'i Leumi)

Kabbalah [receiving]; study of Jewish mysticism; *Zohar* - book on which practice is based

Kabbalistic - pertaining to Kabbalah

Keren Hayesod - Jewish Agency

Kibbutz - agricultural farm; collective settlement where people share equally in the work and profits

Kibbutznik - settler

Kibbutzim - several settlements (plural of kibbutz)

Kol Ha'am [*Voice of the People*]; Hebrew newspaper

Kvutzah - little community group

La-dor V'dor - from generation to generation

Land of Israel - ancient Biblical reference to Israel

Likud - Israeli political party

Lubavitcher "Chassidim" - sect of Hasidism that believes in reaching out to all Jewish people

Mafdal - National Religious Party

Maki - Israeli Communist Party

Ma'apilim - "illegal" immigrants

Mapai - Labor political party

Mapam - United Workers Party, a left-wing Zionist-socialist party with a pro-Soviet orientation

Mensch - (Yiddish); a real human being

Mitnagdim - Orthodox, non-Hasidic philosophy

Mitzvah - good deed

Mitzvot - good deeds (plural of mitzvah)

Mizel Volny - Polish Freethinkers Association

Mizrahi - religious political party

Mo'ezet Ha-Po'alot - women's labor union

Moriah - Hebrew publishing house which released Hebrew classics and school literature

Moshav - cooperative settlement, individual farms are worked separately but the produce is pooled and marketed by the settlement

Moshava - small holder's settlement, individual farms are worked as private enterprises

Moshavot/moshavim - Jewish cooperative settlements (plural)

Neue Frieie Presse [*New Free Press*]; Viennese newspaper

NILI [Nezah Yisrael Lo Yeshaker] - acronym of the Hebrew verse "The strength of Israel will not lie," Jewish espionage group working with the British against the Turks

Odesskiya Novosti - (Russian) newspaper

Oneg Shabbat [celebration of the Sabbath]; usually a meal, singing, and short   program on Friday evenings in a synagogue or in the home

Orthodox - one of the three major Jewish religious denominations; apply strict adherence to *Halakah* (code of Jewish laws)

Palmach - elite strike force of the Haganah defense organization

Pasha - leader in Ottoman Empire

Pintele Yid - (Yiddish); essential nature of a Jew

Po'alei Zion [Workers of Zion]; one of the first socialist Zionist political parties

Pogrom - an organized (usually government sanctioned) attack on unsuspecting Jewish communities

Rebbitzin - wife of a rabbi

Reform - movement in Judaism originating in Germany; least religious of the 3 forms of Judaism; established to accommodate "assimilated" Jews

Sabra - native-born Israeli

Sanhedrin - ancient Jewish religious court system

Schnorrer - pejorative Yiddish term referring to a person who borrows or asks for items

Second Aliyah - period of Jewish immigration from the Diaspora to *Eretz Yisrael* from 1904-1914

Shabbat - Jewish Sabbath or day of rest (Friday at sundown through Saturday at sundown)

SHAHU - Hebrew acronym for "return of the craftsmen and smiths;" an association of artisans in Palestine

Shema - most important of Jewish prayers that proclaims the oneness of God

Shohet - person charged with ritual slaughter of animals in accordance with Jewish law

Shtetl - small village

Tallit - prayer shawl

Tefilin - ritual object worn for Jewish prayers; phylactery; men wrap this around their arm and forehead during morning prayers

Tel Aviv [Hill of Spring]; Israel's largest and most industrialized city

Telem - political party founded by Moshe Dayan

Teshuva - repentance

Torah [a teaching]; the first five books of the Hebrew Bible; God's written law to the Jewish people

T'zeirei T'zion [Youth of Zion]; Zionist youth movement "Yehudim Anakhnu" [We are Jews]; quotation by Menachem Begin

Yeshiva/Yeshivot - school/schools for Jewish learning

Yidiot Ahronot [*The Latest News*] Israeli newspaper

Yishuv - community settlement

Yizkor - Jewish memorial prayer for the deceased

Yom Kippur - Jewish Day of Atonement; the most sacred holiday of the Jewish people

Youth Aliyah - organization founded by Reicha Freier and Henrietta Szold to bring Jewish youth to Israel to escape war in Europe

*Notes on the Glossary

The glossary is a list of foreign language terms that are found in Pioneers of Israel, *most of which are in Hebrew unless otherwise indicated. There are often alternate spellings of the same Hebrew words, e.g.: Hasidism- alternate spelling is "Chassidism." Many of these alternate spellings are included in the glossary. There are often slight differences when Hebrew words are translated into English. The translations used here are commonly accepted, but are not meant to be comprehensive or conclusive.*

REFERENCES

Abraham, M. (1982). *The Day is Short: An Autobiography.* New York: HarcourtBrace Jovanovich.

Adler, C. (1941). *I Have Considered the Days.* Philadelphia: Jewish Publication Society.

Adler, S., and Connolly, T.E. (1960), *From Ararat to Suburbia: The History of the Jewish Community of Buffalo.* Philadelphia: Jewish Publication Society.

Allon, Y. (1976). *My Father's House.* New York: W.W. Norton.

Ausubel, N. (1948). *A Treasury of Jewish Folklore.* New York: Crown.

Begin, M. (1977). *The Revolt.* New York: Nash.

Bellow, S. (1976). *To Jerusalem and Back.* New York: Viking.

Bildersee, A. (1918). *Jewish Post-Biblical History Through Great Personalities.* Cincinnati: Union of American Hebrew Congregations.

Birmingham, S. (1967). *"Our Crowd": The Great Jewish Families of New York.* New York: Harper & Row.

Borochov, B. (1984). *Class Struggle and the Jewish Nation,* ed. M. Cohen.

Braude, J.M. (1957). *Braude's Second Encyclopedia of Stories, Quotations, and Anecdotes.* Englewood Cliffs, NJ: Prentice-Hall. (1963). *The Speaker's Desk Book of Quips, Quotes, and Anecdotes.* Englewood Cliffs, NJ: Prentice-Hall. (1971). *Speaker's and Toastmaster's Handbook of Anecdotes by and about Famous Personalities.* Englewood Cliffs, NJ: Prentice-Hall.

<http://www.britannica.com.

Buber, M. (1947). *Between Man and Man.* London: Routledge and Kegan Paul.

Carmel, A. (1977). *So Strange My Path.* New York: Bloch.

Chissin, C. (1976). *A Palestine Diary: Memoirs of a Bilu Pioneer,* 1882-1887 New York: Herzl Press.

Chomsky, W. (1957). *Hebrew: The Eternal Language.* Philadelphia: Jewish Publication Society.

Cowan, P. (1982). *An Orphan in History.* Garden City, NY: Doubleday.

Cowan, P., with Rachel Cowan. (1987). *Mixed Blessings,* New York: Doubleday.

Cowen, I., and Gunther I. (1984). *A Spy For Freedom: The Story of Sarah Aaronsohn.* New York: Lodestar Books.

Dash, J. (1979). *Summoned to Jerusalem.* New York: Harper & Row.

Dayan, M (1976). *Moshe Dayan: Story of My Life.* New York: William Morrow.

<http://www.doingzionism.org.il/resources.

Eban, A. (1977). *Abba Eban: An Autobiography.* New York: Random House, 1977.

<http://en.wikipedia.org/wiki.

Elon. A. (1975). Herzl. New York: *Holt, Rinehart and Winston.*

<http://encyclopedia.thefreedictionary.com.

Encyclopedia Judaica, ©1972, Keter Publishing House Jerusalem Ltd.

Epstein, L.J. (1984). *Zion's Call.* Lanham, ND: University Press of America.

<http://www.fact-index.com.

Frankl, V. (1962). *Man's Search for Meaning.* New York: Touchstone.

Gersh, H. (1959). *These Are My People.* New York: Behrman House.

Gilbert, M. (1985) *The Holocaust.* New York: Holt, Rinehart and Winston.

Grose, P. (1983). *Israel in the Mind of America.* New York: Knopf.

Gross, D.C. (1981) *The Jewish People's Almanac.* Garden City, NY: Doubleday.

Haber, J. (1956). *The Odyssey of an American Zionist.* New York: Twayne.

Hart, K. (1982) *Return to Auschwitz.* New York: Atheneum.

Heschel, S., ed. (1983) *On Being a Jewish Feminist.* New York: Schocken.

Humes, J.C. (1978). *Speaker's Treasury of Anecdotes About the Famous.* New York: Harper & Row.

Jacobs, L. (1984). *The Book of Jewish Belief.* New York: Behrman House.

<http://www.jafi.org.il/education.

<http://www.jajz-ed.org.il/100/people/bios.

<http://www.jewishgates.com/file.

<http://www.jewishvirtuallibrary.org/.

<http://www.jnf-canada.org.

Josephus (1972). *The Jewish War.* Middlesex, England: Penguin.

<http://judaism.about.com.

Katz, S. (1968). *Days of Fire.* Jerusalem: Steimatzsky's Agency.

<http://www.knesset.gov.

Kurzman, D. (1978). *The Bravest Battle.* Los Angeles: Pinnacle Books.(1983). *Ben-Gurion: Prophet of Fire.* New York: Simon & Schuster.

Landau, R. (1984). *The Book of Jewish Lists.* New York: Stein & Day.

Levin, M. (1950). *In Search.* New York: Horizon Press.

Meir, G. (1976) *My Life.* New York: Dell.

<http://www.mfa.gov.il/mfa.

<http://www.miriamscup.com.

Mortkowicz-Olczakowa, H. (1963). *The Massacre of European Jewry.* Kibbutz Merchavia, Israel: World *Hashomer Hatzair.*

<http://news.bbc.co.uk.

<http://www.nobel.se/peace.

Nordau, A., and Nordau, M. (1943). *Max Nordau.* New York: Nordau Committee.

<http://www.ou.org/chagim/.

Rosenstein, N. (1976) *The Unbroken Chain.* New York: Shengold.

Rosenzweig, F. (1972). *The Star of Redemption.* Boston: Beacon Press.

Roth, C., and Wigoder, G., Eds. (1972) *Encyclopaedia Judaica.* Jerusalem: Israel:Keter.

Ruppin, A. (1971) *Arthur Ruppin.* New York: Herzl Press.

Rywell, M. (1960). *Laughing With Tears.* Harriman, TN: Pioneer Press.

Saint, John, R. (1952). *Tongue of the Prophets.* Garden City, NY: Dolphin.

Samuel, M. (1966) *Blood Accusation.* New York: Knopf.

Schechtman, J.B. (1986). *The Life and Times of Vladimir Jabotinsky, Rebel and Statesman: The Early Years.* Silver Spring, MD: Eshel.

Schwarz, L.W. (1945). *Memoirs of My People Through a Thousand Years.* Philadelphia: Jewish Publication Society.

Senesh, H. (1972). *Her Life and Diary.* New York: Schocken.

Siegel, R., and Rheins, C., Eds. (1980). *The Jewish Almanac.* New York: Bantam.

Silver, E. (1984) *Begin: The Haunted Prophet.* New York: Random House.

Simon, L. (1960). *Ahad Ha'am.* Philadelphia: Jewish Publication Society.

Slater, R. (1971). *Rabin of Israel.* London: Robson Books.

<http://www.time.com/time/time100.

Urofsky, M.I. (1976). *American Zionism From Herzl to the Holocaust.* Garden City, NY: Anchor Books.

<http://www.us-israel.org/jsource.

<http://womenshistory.about.com.

<http://www.wzo.org

PHOTOGRAPH CREDITS

• Central Zionist Archives of the Jewish Agency for Israel (Jerusalem). Reuven Kottler of the Zionist Archives, Reuven Milon and Sari Sapir
• The Israel Government Press Office,
• Corbis Photo Archives.

SPECIAL THANKS

George Robins and Hanan Druker (Graphic Design), Carol Belitz (Text Editing) and Sue Liberman (Photographs)
Printed by: LAMODEM.COM

INDEX

285

288